This book analyses the key factors determining current and future European competitiveness. It focuses in particular on the issues of internationalisation of firms and markets, the role of technology and innovation, and of continuing European integration, and deals with these issues on the level of firms, industries and countries. The competitiveness of the EC as a whole, relative to the USA and Japan, is also examined. Part 1 deals with internationalisation, the organisation of firms, and the activities of multinationals in Europe. Part 2 focuses on trends in technological competitiveness, and its importance in growth and trade performance. Part 3 is concerned with structural change, the integration of the European market, competition and mergers, the role of the public sector, and the role of cultural differences. The book ends by addressing the role of industrial policy in the future of the Eastern European economies.

European competitiveness

European competitiveness

EDITED BY
Kirsty S. Hughes
Policy Studies Institute

Published by the Press Syndicate of the University of Cambridge
The Pitt Building, Trumpington Street, Cambridge CB2 1RP
40 West 20th Street, New York, NY 10011–4211, USA
10 Stamford Road, Oakleigh, Victoria 3166, Australia

First published 1993

Printed in Great Britain at the University Press, Cambridge

A catalogue record for this book is available from the British Library

Library of Congress cataloguing in publication data
European competitiveness / Kirsty S. Hughes, editor.
p. cm.
Developed from two workshops held at and funded by the Wissenschaftszentrum Berlin in December 1989 and in June 1991.
ISBN 0 521 43443 2
1. Competition – European Economic Community countries – Congresses. 2. European Economic Community countries – Economic policy – Congresses. 3. Technological innovations – Economic aspects – European Economic Community countries – Congresses. 4. International business enterprises – European Economic Community countries – Congresses. 5. Europe 1992 – Congresses. I. Hughes, Kirsty. II. Wissenschaftszentrum Berlin.
HF1532.92.E885 1993
338.6′048′094 – dc20 92–19760 CIP
ISBN 0 521 43443 2 hardback

CE

Contents

Contributors

Alain Alcouffe, Professor of Economics, Université de Haute Alsace

Gianluigi Alzona, Professor of Industrial Organisation, Faculty of Economics, University of Turin

Daniele Archibugi, Researcher, Institute for Studies on Scientific Research, National Research Council, Rome and Visiting Scholar, Department of Applied Economics, University of Cambridge

David Audretsch, Research Professor, Wissenschaftszentrum, Berlin

Danielle Galliano, Senior Researcher, Institut National de la Recherche Agronomique, Laboratoire d'Economie Industrielle Agroalimentaire, Ivry

John Hagedoorn, Professorial Research Fellow, Maastricht Economic Research Institute on Innovation and Technology, Faculty of Economics, University of Limburg

Shaun Hargreaves-Heap, Lecturer in Economics, University of East Anglia

Kirsty Hughes, Senior Research Fellow, Policy Studies Institute, London

Neil Kay, Professor of Economics, University of Strathclyde

Hugh Mosley, Research Fellow, Wissenschaftszentrum, Berlin

Christine Oughton, Lecturer in Economics, University of Glasgow

Mario Pianta, Researcher, Institute for Studies on Scientific Research, National Research Council, Rome

Laura Rondi, Researcher at CERIS–CNR, Institute of Research on Firms and Development, National Research Council, Turin

Jos Schakenraad, Research Fellow, Maastricht Economic Research Institute on Innovation and Technology, Faculty of Economics, University of Limburg

Günther Schmid, Director, Labour Market Policy and Employment Research Unit, Wissenschaftszentrum, Berlin

Giampaolo Vitali, Researcher at CERIS–CNR, Institute of Research on Firms and Development, National Research Council, Turin
Hideki Yamawaki, Associate Professor of Economics, Catholic University of Louvain

Acknowledgements

This book developed from two workshops held at, and funded by, the Wissenschaftszentrum Berlin (WZB). The first was held in December 1989, one month after the Berlin Wall collapsed, and brought together researchers from East and West Europe who founded the European Competitiveness Network. A subgroup from this network agreed to work on a project on European competitiveness and met again in Berlin in June 1991 to discuss and present their work. This project resulted in the chapters included in this volume.

I am grateful to the WZB for providing the funding that enabled this project to develop. I would like to thank in particular my colleagues David Audretsch, Joachim Schwalbach and Hideki Yamawaki.

1 Introduction: internationalisation, integration and European competitiveness

KIRSTY HUGHES

1.1 Introduction

This book is concerned with some of the key factors that will determine current and future European competitiveness. Key issues in understanding current and future competitiveness are the nature of and trends in internationalisation, and the likely effects of European integration on firm and country structure and performance. In this volume we analyse the experience of firms and countries in order to throw some light on these processes.

Competitiveness is a concept that is widely but not consistently used and that can be analysed at various levels – by groups of countries, country, industry, and firm. Two broad attitudes to competitiveness can be distinguished. The first is that competitiveness is a question of relative efficiency, whether dynamic or static. This can be measured by looking at relative performance levels – productivity and productivity growth, for example. The second is that competitiveness is reflected in relative international trade performance – whether measured as shares of world export markets, the degree of import penetration or an index of revealed comparative advantage. These two broad concepts of competitiveness may coincide but need not. Thus, the country with the highest level of productivity may not have the highest trade share. If trade shares depend on strategic competition in world markets, then they will be determined by a mixture of efficiency and market power considerations.

In looking at Europe, we use both these concepts of competitiveness, recognising that a complex combination of efficiency and strategic factors determine final outcomes. Furthermore, we recognise that European competitiveness may be analysed at various levels, and that it is necessary to analyse firms, countries and groups of countries to obtain an understanding of patterns of competitiveness both within Europe and between Europe and its main competitors, particularly the USA and Japan.

1.2 Internationalisation

Competitiveness is no longer, if it ever was, a simple question of differences in country characteristics; rather it depends on a complex series of links between firms and countries that are changing over time. Both firms and countries are increasingly international in their economic structures. This is not only that firms are becoming multinationals or that countries export and import and receive and provide foreign direct investment. Firms have a variety of possible ways of becoming more internationalised whether through various forms of ownership links or through inter-firm agreements on technology, marketing, market entry or other areas. There is a large literature that documents and analyses the internationalisation of firms (see, for example, Casson, 1983; 1986; Dunning, 1981). This internationalisation means that the analysis of competitiveness must draw on a number of different areas of economic analysis – international trade, industrial organisation, theories of the firm, the analysis of technological change. Only through bringing together analytical tools and empirical approaches from these different areas is it possible to build a coherent picture of the constituents and determinants of international competitiveness.

The international links of firms break any simple relationship between the competitiveness of firms and the competitiveness of countries. Thus, in the presence of internationalisation of firms and markets, the common presumption that the competitiveness of an economy depends in a simple way on the competitiveness of the firms located within its boundaries, or even on the competitiveness of firms of its nationality, is no longer valid. If we consider the example of trade performance, the extent of international firms' exporting and importing activities will be determined by their global structures and strategies. The international firm will gain, potentially, advantages from the global distribution of its activities, that are not simply a sum of its constituent parts in each country. Thus, a firm may be highly successful globally, without necessarily being a dominant firm in either an efficiency or market-power sense in all of its constituent economies. The patterns and nature of internationalisation of firms is, therefore, one important ingredient in understanding competitiveness. Understanding of these patterns can also be furthered by looking at the variety of structural and organisational forms firms choose within countries and how this affects performance, competition and structural change.

In this volume, we focus on selected aspects of the internationalisation of firms and their organisational structure to investigate some of the key characteristics of the internationalisation process. We focus partly on the multinational activities of firms in Europe to consider both the nature of the international organisational form chosen by firms and the determinants of their location decisions, including those made by multinational enterprises (MNEs) from outside the EC, where concern has been expressed, in particular, at the investment activities of Japanese MNEs. Another striking trend that started in the 1980s is the increase in international technological agreements between firms within and between countries; the pattern of these trends is investigated in this volume. Technology is, of course, one aspect of competitiveness that has received a great amount of attention. Here, we ask how important it has been and what future trends look like in terms of patterns of specialisation and implications for future performance.

1.3 European integration and structural change

The concept of individual country competitiveness is made complex not only through the internationalisation of firms, but also due to the variety of links and relationships among countries. The creation of the EC internal market through the 1992 process and the push to political and economic union also complicates the factors determining the performance of any one country. At the same time, the process of European integration has not yet gone so far that country characteristics are no longer important or that we can simply refer to Europe as one bloc or 'country' directly comparable to the USA or Japan. Individual countries retain many differences that are important in determining their economic competitiveness. Nor is it automatic that these differences will disappear over time due to a steady and inevitable convergence. Nevertheless, the process of European integration has major implications for internationalisation and competitiveness.

One simple interpretation of the EC's internal market process would be to say that it will increase competition which will increase efficiency which will increase competitiveness. However, the processes involved are more complex. Firstly, 1992 may not result in an increase in competition. Depending on firms' reactions to the process – the effects on decisions on merger, on the recognition of oligopolistic interdependence, on the power of non-EC multinationals – the overall competition effect could vary. Furthermore, the link between efficiency and competitiveness is also not straightforward, as discussed above, and increased strategic competition may be more important for European competitiveness than increased competition in a traditional sense.

In this volume, the likely changes consequent on increased integration of the European market are discussed from various angles. Will benefits flow from increased competition or will this be distorted by misplaced emphasis on firm size or through the potentially disruptive and negative effects of structural change? Are these structural changes likely to encourage convergence among the EC countries and in that way to promote EC competitiveness or will they in fact exacerbate differences and impede any positive gains from integration? Integration is not simply a question of convergence in industrial structures. Major differences between countries remain that may directly and indirectly affect competitiveness. Thus, the public sector accounts for a large share of economic activity in the EC countries but the precise nature and organisation of the public sector varies sharply both within Europe and relative to the USA and Japan. There are many implications for economic performance here, but they require detailed analysis to disentangle. Furthermore, different countries have different underlying beliefs and views that we may term 'cultural differences' which may also have various and profound effects on the organisation and outcome of economic activity. Thus, the likely changes through the 1990s and beyond are not simply that European integration will promote convergence and improved performance, rather the changes will depend on the interaction of these varied influences, which are analysed in this volume.

The primary concern of the studies presented here is with the competitiveness of the West European economies. However, major influences on European integration and performance will develop as the East European economies proceed with their transition processes and the reindustrialisation of their economies. These transition processes will take a number of years and the resulting structures and implications for European performance are not straightforward. The nature of the pressures and the benefits that may result will depend on the nature and speed of the transition process and its effect on static and dynamic efficiency in these economies. Here, we analyse current industrial structures in Eastern Europe, their implications for performance and how they are likely to change depending on the nature of policies adopted.

1.4 An overview

The book is set out following the pattern of the argument developed above. Thus part 1 concerns the internationalisation and organisational structure of firms; part 2 analyses the role of technology in competitiveness; and part 3 considers the structural changes associated with the internal market process, and the role of key factors – the public sector, culture – that will continue to differentiate countries and to impact on their competitiveness.

The internationalisation and organisation of firms is analysed in four chapters. Yamawaki analyses the factors behind the surge in Japanese foreign direct investment (FDI) in Western Europe in the late 1980s, using a new data set on Japanese firms in Europe. While this surge is connected to the creation of the EC internal market, the pattern of location decisions still needs to be explained. Japanese FDI is unevenly spread across European countries and its distributional pattern also varies across industries in different countries. Yamawaki shows that Japanese FDI is attracted to countries where labour costs are low, where R&D capacity is large and where market size is large – reflecting the importance of the comparative advantage of each host country.

Alzona, Rondi and Vitali analyse the increase in FDI and international technological agreements by Italian firms in the late 1980s in order to throw light on the internationalisation processes of Italian firms. They focus on the type of ownership link chosen by Italian firms – joint ventures and non-controlling interests – and explain this choice through a logit analysis looking at firm, industry and country characteristics. They also differentiate intra- and inter-industry FDI and consider how the determinants vary for these two different modes of internationalisation. Non-controlling interests are found to be chosen in particular by smaller firms and by firms with less multinational experience. The characteristics of the FDI also have relevance to the merger wave within the EC and its implications for competition, a theme taken up in chapter 8. The final section of chapter 3 considers technological agreements, an issue also focused on in chapter 4.

Hagedoorn and Schakenraad address the question of internationalisation and competitiveness through focusing on strategic partnering and technological cooperation between firms. Using a detailed database on thousands of strategic technology partnerships, they investigate the patterns of, and trends in, these alliances. They focus in particular on international alliances, looking at the relationships between European, US and Japanese firms in the 1970s and 1980s. They analyse the increase in these alliances during the 1980s by technology, sector and region, to assess their contribution to the internationalisation of firms and economies. The increased importance of these alliances is also important in interpreting the industry and country evidence on technological change analysed in chapters 6 and 7.

Galliano and Alcouffe focus on the French case to assess the links between corporate control, organisational form and competitiveness. They focus on the group structure that is being increasingly chosen by French firms. They present an historical overview of the development and role of the group in the French economy and then focus on the food industry to compare the performance of firms within and outside of groups. Firms within groups perform better in most cases and across most size classes, and the groups also demonstrate more flexibility and adaptability, better coordination and financial advantages. The importance of organisational factors is addressed from the cultural angle in chapter 11, while chapter 12, on Eastern Europe, also discusses the importance of corporate control.

The relationship between technology and competitiveness at industry and country level is addressed in two chapters. Archibugi and Pianta use a detailed patent database to investigate patterns of, and trends in, technological specialisation by European countries, the USA and Japan. They investigate the extent of similarity in these countries' specialisation and whether this is increasing or decreasing over time. They analyse which patterns of specialisation may be most appropriate for fostering growth of national technological and economic activities by classifying patents according to whether they are in declining, stagnant, medium or fast growing categories. Patterns of specialisation are shown to vary across countries and there are differences within Europe as well as between Europe, the USA and Japan – however, they conclude that the outlook for European technological specialisation and its impact on competitiveness is not encouraging.

Hughes analyses the relative international competitiveness of the four largest EC economies in comparison with the USA and Japan in the 1980s. The chapter shows that while these six economies have similar patterns of manufacturing exports, their patterns of competitiveness are not similar and are diverging slightly over time. With respect to technology, the evidence indicates that the three most successful economies in terms of trade performance – Japan, Germany and Italy – had their best performance respectively in high, medium and low technology sectors. An econometric analysis shows that R&D is an important positive determinant of Japanese performance relative to the EC economies but not of US relative performance.

The effect of the completion of the internal market on European competitiveness is addressed in two chapters. Kay, chapter 8, argues that while the completion of the internal market is intended to increase competition, there could be adverse effects on competitiveness, relating, in particular, to the role of merger and acquisition. The chapter argues that the Commission has adopted a too permissive attitude towards European merger and acquisition activity, with too much emphasis placed on the benefits of size and a neglect of the empirical evidence on the anti-efficiency effects of merger. European competitiveness does not, contrary to the Commission's belief, require amalgamation and consolidation.

Oughton analyses the EC's argument that the completion of the internal market should encourage the convergence among countries that has always been an aim of European integration. She builds on classical models of economic growth to show that investment patterns, and so the prospects for convergence, are determined by the deviation of industry profitability from average profitability. In an empirical section, data are presented on member countries' growth rates and profit rates on fixed capital. The analysis shows that on current trends the prospects for convergence are poor.

Two further chapters address the question of similarity or divergence among countries and the implications for competitiveness from another angle. Mosley and Schmid undertake a systematic survey of the issues and evidence with respect to the public services and competitiveness. They argue that while the conventional view suggests the public sector is a threat to efficient markets, the actual role, functioning and contribution of the public sector is much more complex. Further, the institutions and services involved vary widely across countries. Many 'welfare' state functions can be regarded as indirectly productive, while some services may be provided not only more equitably but more efficiently through the public sector.

Hargeaves-Heap addresses the question of culture, and how the presence of shared beliefs can affect numerous aspects of decision-making. Cultural beliefs vary within Europe and not simply between Europe, the USA and Japan. The differences in culture among countries can then constitute an important part of the explanation and understanding of their performance differences. These potential effects on competitiveness are illustrated with respect to wage bargaining and the adoption of flexible specialisation.

Developments in Eastern Europe are addressed in the chapter by Audretsch. He considers the way in which industrial policy can affect international competitiveness and how Eastern European competitiveness was affected by the policies determining industrial structure in those countries. While there is no one optimal industrial structure, he argues that the Eastern European economies will have to achieve a much more variegated industrial structure if they are to develop their comparative advantage in the future.

References

Casson, M. (ed.) 1983. *The Growth of International Business*, London: Allen and Unwin.

Casson, M. 1986. *Multinationals and World Trade: Vertical Integration and the Division of Labour in World Industries*, London: Allen and Unwin.

Dunning, J. H. 1981. *International Production and the Multinational Enterprise*, London: Allen and Unwin.

Part 1

Internationalisation and corporate control

2 Location decisions of Japanese multinational firms in European manufacturing industries

HIDEKI YAMAWAKI

2.1 Introduction

One of the major economic developments that emerged in Europe during the late 1980s is the sudden growth of Japanese direct investment into the European markets. While Japanese direct investment has grown most spectacularly in the United States during the 1980s, its growth in Europe is equally notable particularly after 1987. The flow of Japanese direct investment into European manufacturing surged from $323 million in 1985 to $852 million in 1987 and further increased to $1,548 million in 1988. Indeed, the investment flow of 1987 and 1988 alone accounted for approximately half of the cumulative flow of Japanese direct investment into Europe between 1965 and 1988.

Just as the growing presence of Japanese direct investment in the United States has generated debates regarding its impact on the US economy,[1] the sudden increase in Japanese direct investment into Europe has sparked policy discussions over its influence on European trade and industry.[2] One of the fundamental questions that is raised by these policy discussions within the European Community (EC) is whether the issue of Japanese direct investment should be considered from the perspective of each member state or from the EC-wide perspective (Stopford, 1990, and Micossi and Viesti, 1991). Despite the importance of this issue that constitutes a reference point for the formulation of a common EC-wide policy towards foreign direct investment, there is a scarcity of systematic analysis of the data that guides the discussion (Dunning and Cantwell, 1989).[3] The purpose of this chapter is to fill this gap in the literature by presenting some empirical evidence on the patterns and characteristics of Japanese direct investment in European manufacturing. In particular, this chapter asks the following questions: (1) how is Japanese direct investment in Europe distributed among different manufacturing industries?; (2) how is Japanese direct investment in manufacturing distributed among European countries? and (3) what factors explain these inter-industry and inter-country variations in the extent of Japanese direct investment in European manufacturing?

The second section of the chapter provides a descriptive analysis of the data for 236 European manufacturing subsidiaries that are 50 per cent or more controlled by Japanese manufacturing firms in 1988. The data show that Japanese direct investment is distributed among different industries, while it tends to concentrate in electric and electronic equipment, machinery, plastic products, instruments and motor cars. They also show that Japanese firms choose not only the United Kingdom and West Germany but also France, Spain, Belgium and The Netherlands as major host countries in Europe. In the third section, the inter-country and inter-industry variations of Japanese direct investment into Europe are explained by using a regression model which focuses on the location decisions of Japanese firms. Finally, in the fourth section, a summary and conclusion are provided.

2.2 Patterns of Japanese direct investment in Europe

2.2.1 Data

The data source used in this study is Toyokeizai (1989), which lists 296 manufacturing subsidiaries of Japanese firms in manufacturing that are distributed across fifteen European countries in 1988. From this sample of 296 European subsidiaries 236 subsidiaries were selected that are 50 per cent or more controlled by Japanese parent firms, and for which data are available.[4] Thus, more than 70 per cent of European manufacturing subsidiaries of Japanese multinational enterprises (MNEs) listed in this data source are majority-controlled subsidiaries. The coverage of this sample is highly comparable to that of the Japan External Trade Organization (JETRO) data.[5] Where necessary information was missing, the Toyokeizai data were supplemented by the JETRO data.

2.2.2 Descriptive analysis of the data

Table 2.1 shows the distribution of the 236 European manufacturing subsidiaries of Japanese MNEs among host countries and two-digit industries in 1988. Among the host countries that are most preferred by Japanese MNEs are the United Kingdom, West Germany, France, Spain, Belgium, and The Netherlands. The United Kingdom hosted 71 Japanese affiliates, while West Germany and France hosted, respectively, 49 and 30 Japanese affiliates. Among the two-digit manufacturing industries,

Table 2.1. *The number of European manufacturing subsidiaries more than 50 per cent owned by Japanese firms, by host country and by manufacturing industry, August 1988*

	Belgium	Denmark	France	Greece	Ireland	Italy	Nether-lands	Portugal	Spain	United Kingdom	West Germany	Austria	Norway	Sweden	Switzer-land	Total
Food			3						1	2						6
Textile					2				1	1						4
Apparel			1			1										2
Wood and paper products																0
Chemicals	1		4	1	2	2	2	1	3	1	5		1			23
Rubber and plastic products	1		1				4		1	8	2	1			1	19
Stone, clay, and glass products	4				1	1										6
Primary metal	1		1													2
Fabricated metal products										1						1
Machinery, except electrical	1		7			2	3		2	15	13	1				44
Electric and electronic equipment	5		8		3		1		8	29	19	1		1		75
Transport-ation equipment	1		1					1	6	5						14
Instruments	1	1					2			2	7		1	1		15
Miscellaneous industries	1	1	4	1		3	1	1	1	7	3	1			1	25
Manufac-turing total	16	2	30	2	8	9	13	3	23	71	49	4	2	2	2	236

Source: Toyokeizai (1989); JETRO (1988).

Table 2.2. *Employment in European manufacturing subsidiaries more than 50 per cent owned by Japanese firms, by host country, August 1988*

Host country	Total employment	Average per subsidiary
Belgium	5730	358
Denmark	49	25
France	9821	327
Greece	227	114
Ireland	1176	147
Italy	696	77
Netherlands	1714	132
Portugal	1178	393
Spain	11324	492
United Kingdom	18554	261
West Germany	11076	226
Austria	397	99
Norway	43	22
Sweden	136	68
Switzerland	60	30
Total	62181	185

Source: As table 2.1.

Japanese direct investment tends to concentrate in electric and electronic equipment (74 affiliates), non-electrical machinery (47), miscellaneous industries (25), chemicals (22) and rubber and plastic products (19).

This observation on the general pattern of Japanese direct investment into Europe remains virtually unchanged when the extent of direct investment is measured by employment. As shown in table 2.2, the UK subsidiaries of Japanese MNEs employed more than 18,000 employees in 1988, which reinforces the finding that the United Kingdom is the largest host country of Japanese direct investment within Europe. The presence of Japanese direct investment is also high in Spain and West Germany where Japanese affiliates employ more than 11,000 employees. France and Belgium follow these countries as other favourite destinations for Japanese direct investment.

While the UK affiliates employ the largest number of employees, their average size is smaller than that in Spain and Portugal. In fact, the average size of Spanish affiliates is approximately 90 per cent larger than the average size of UK affiliates and 120 per cent larger than the average size of German affiliates. This difference in the average size of subsidiaries

Table 2.3. *Percentage distribution of employment of subsidiaries more than 50 per cent owned by Japanese firms among major manufacturing industries, by host country, August 1988*

	Belgium	Denmark	France	Greece	Ireland	Italy	Netherlands	Portugal	Spain	United Kingdom	West Germany	Austria	Norway	Sweden	Switzerland
Food			0.7						0.3	0.4					
Textile					21.9				0.7	0.1					
Apparel			0.2			3.4									
Wood and paper products															
Chemicals	2.8		5.4	82.4	12.1	19.3	31.4	21.9	5.6	0.5	5.4		46.5		
Rubber and plastic products	0.5		37.7				20.2		0.9	15.8	31.7	32.7			50.0
Stone, clay, and glass products	66.5				15.3	2.9									
Primary metal	0.6		0.6												
Fabricated metal products										1.7					
Machinery, except electrical	2.1		16.5			6.0	17.4		3.3	9.9	18.9	10.8			
Electric and electronic equipment	17.4		20.8		50.7		1.9		24.7	57.1	36.4	45.3		18.4	
Transportation equipment	4.9		14.8					74.7	62.5	9.2					
Instruments	4.7	51.0					26.5			0.4	4.3		53.5	81.6	
Miscellaneous industries	0.5	49.0	3.4	17.6		68.4	2.5	3.4	1.9	4.8	3.3	11.1			50.0
Manufacturing total	100.0	100.0	100.0	100.0	100.0	100.0	100.0	100.0	100.0	100.0	100.0	100.0	100.0	100.0	100.0

Note: Percentages may not sum to 100 because of rounding errors.
Source: As table 2.1.

Table 2.4. *Percentage distribution of employment of subsidiaries more than 50 per cent owned by Japanese firms among European countries, by major manufacturing industry, August 1988*

	Belgium	Denmark	France	Greece	Ireland	Italy	Netherlands	Portugal	Spain	United Kingdom	West Germany	Austria	Norway	Sweden	Switzerland	Total
Food			36.6						19.4	44.0						100
Textile					70.3				22.6	7.1						100
Apparel			38.5			61.5										100
Wood and paper products																
Chemicals	4.8		16.0	5.7	4.3	4.1	16.4	7.8	19.4	2.8	18.0		0.6			100
Rubber and plastic products	0.3		34.3				3.2		0.9	27.2	32.6	1.2			0.3	100
Stone, clay, and glass products	95.0				4.5	0.5										100
Primary metal	36.7		63.3													100
Fabricated metal products										100.0						100
Machinery, except electrical	1.8		25.2			0.7	4.6		5.9	28.6	32.5	0.7				100
Electric and electronic equipment	4.7		9.6		2.8		0.2		13.1	49.7	18.9	0.8		0.1		100
Transportation equipment	2.5		12.7					7.7	62.0	15.1						100
Instruments	18.9	1.7					31.6			5.2	33.3		1.6	7.7		100
Miscellaneous industries	1.2	0.9	13.2	1.6		18.7	1.7	1.6	8.6	35.2	14.5	1.7			1.2	100

Note: Percentages may not sum to 100 because of rounding errors.
Source: As table 2.1.

Table 2.5. *Host countries most preferred by Japanese investors by industry, August 1988*

Industry	Most preferred host country
Food	UK, France
Textile	Ireland
Apparel	Italy, France
Chemicals	Spain, West Germany, Netherlands, France
Rubber and plastics	France, West Germany, UK
Stone, clay and glass	Belgium
Primary metal	France, Belgium
Metal products	UK
Machinery	West Germany, UK, France
Electric equipment	UK, West Germany
Transportation equipment	Spain, UK
Instruments	West Germany, Netherlands
Miscellaneous	UK, Italy, West Germany, France

among European countries occurs because the sectoral composition of Japanese direct investment varies across these countries.

Table 2.3 uses the number of employees to measure the extent of Japanese direct investment and shows its percentage distribution among the two-digit industries for each host country. The pattern that emerges from this table is that some countries host Japanese MNEs from one or two predominant industries, while others host Japanese MNEs from a broader range of industries. For example, in Spain and Portugal more than 60 per cent of total affiliate employment is engaged in the transportation equipment industry. In the United Kingdom 57 per cent of total affiliate employment is engaged in the electric and electronic equipment industry. Similarly, Belgium hosts Japanese MNEs that are predominantly manufacturers of stone, clay and glass products. On the other hand, West Germany, France and The Netherlands tend to host Japanese direct investment originating from several different industries that are of equal importance.

In contrast to table 2.3 table 2.4 shows the percentage distribution of affiliate employment among European countries for each industry. Thus, this table identifies the host countries that are most preferred by Japanese MNEs for each industry. For example, in electric and electronic equipment, the United Kingdom is by far the most preferred destination of Japanese direct investment. While Spain is most preferred by Japanese motor manufacturers, West Germany is the major host country for

Japanese manufacturers of non-electrical machinery and instruments. Japanese manufacturers of stone, clay, and glass products go to Belgium, and those producing chemical products prefer equally Spain, West Germany, The Netherlands and France.

Thus, tables 2.3 and 2.4 indicate, most importantly, that the pattern of Japanese direct investment varies across European countries and across their industries. As summarised in table 2.5, while Japanese MNEs tend to choose the United Kingdom, West Germany, Spain, France, Belgium and The Netherlands as major host countries for production in Europe, their distributional patterns differ among different industries.

2.3 Locational decisions of Japanese MNEs in the EC

The descriptive analysis of the data in the last section has shown that the extent of Japanese direct investment in European manufacturing differs among industries and countries. One of the interesting questions that emerges from this observation is: What factors explain the distribution of Japanese direct investment among industries? The theoretical literature on the existence of the multinational corporation has suggested that the distribution of foreign direct investment among industries can be explained by the presence of intangible assets that create firm-specific advantages to becoming multinational and to internalise arm's-length transactions (Hymer, 1960; Kindleberger, 1969; Caves, 1971; Buckley and Casson, 1976; Dunning, 1977, among others).[6] Many empirical studies on the incidence of US MNEs have provided support for this intangible asset model (Caves, 1982, for a survey). More recent studies (Kogut and Chang, 1990, and Drake and Caves, 1990) have also found that Japanese direct investment into the United States is drawn to industries intensive in R&D and advertising expenditures. Thus, we may expect that the intangible asset model provides an explanation for the distribution of Japanese direct investment among European manufacturing industries as well.

A question that is perhaps more interesting currently is: what factors explain the distribution of Japanese foreign direct investment among European countries? As the unification process of the EC markets approaches its completion in 1992, more Japanese firms may move strategically and decide to produce within the European common market.[7] The prospective Japanese MNEs then decide where to locate their manufacturing plants within the EC. What factors determine their locational decisions? In this section we attempt to pin down these factors that determine the location decisions of Japanese MNEs in the EC. For this purpose, a statistical model is used for the industry and country panel data.

2.3.1 Hypotheses

The distribution pattern of Japanese foreign direct investment among the EC countries suggests the hypothesis that the Japanese firm in a particular industry invests in the country whose industry has a comparative advantage over its counterparts in other EC countries. To the extent that the Japanese MNE establishes manufacturing subsidiaries within the EC to respond to the emergence of the European common market and to circumvent the trade barriers against imports from the non-EC countries, it will use the local subsidiary as a base to export to the rest of the EC market as well as to serve the local market. Then, the Japanese MNE will choose the location of production by evaluating the sources of comparative advantage of prospective host countries in the EC that determine their export opportunities. Thus, just as the traditional theory suggests that the pattern of international trade depends on comparative advantage, we expect that the pattern of Japanese foreign direct investment in the EC depends also on the comparative advantages of the EC countries.[8]

The hypothesis that MNEs' location decisions depend on cost considerations and the factors underlying them has been under statistical scrutiny. Kravis and Lipsey (1982) found that the exports of foreign affiliates of US MNEs tend to become larger where access to raw and semi-finished materials is easier and the size of the host country market is larger. They also found that unit labour costs tend to have a negative effect on the exports of foreign affiliates of US MNEs, although the estimated coefficient is not significant.

While the Kravis–Lipsey study suggests that a US MNE chooses the location of foreign production based on cost-minimising decision, other studies have produced some contradictory results particularly on the effect of labour costs. Swedenborg's (1979) study of Swedish foreign direct investment found that Swedish direct investment is drawn to countries where labour costs are relatively high. Dunning's (1980) study of US MNEs also found that the share of local production in foreign markets is high where wages are relatively high. Both Swedenborg and Dunning, however, identified the positive relation between the extent of MNE activity and the size of the host country market, suggesting the presence of some scale-economy effects.

While the economic factors studied in the above mentioned studies – labour costs, material costs and market size – are expected to affect Japanese MNEs' location decisions in the EC as well, this is not an exhaustive list of the sources of comparative advantage. In particular, if the Japanese MNE chooses a host country based on its export potential within the EC market, its location decision depends not only on comparative advantage in factor costs but also on comparative advantage in technology. Since the major Japanese MNEs in the EC are the manufacturers of technologically sophisticated products such as electrical and electronic equipment, machinery, transportation equipment and instruments, it is essential for their local subsidiaries to employ skilled workers and engineers as the local workforce, and procure technologically advanced and high-quality parts and components from local suppliers. They may also demand local research and development (R&D) capacity to develop new processes and products and adapt products to local standards and tastes. Countries well endowed with skilled labour and engineers and populated with technologically capable suppliers, and countries with R&D capacity, will therefore attract Japanese foreign direct investment. Thus, the existence of educational and technological infrastructure determines the MNE's locational decision. The hypothesis that technologically advanced countries draw the MNEs that source technological capabilities has been supported with empirical evidence (Cantwell, 1989; and Kogut and Chang, 1990).

In addition to these factors that vary across industries and countries, there are country-specific factors that determine the country distribution of Japanese foreign direct investment in the EC: (1) government policy towards foreign direct investment, including investment incentives, taxes, subsidy, and procurement policy; and (2) national characteristics such as language and culture (e.g., Caves, 1982, ch. 2; Dunning, 1986, ch. 3). While Japanese MNEs' decisions whether to produce within the EC are presumably affected by the prospects on tariffs and other trade barriers that will be maintained against imports from non-EC countries after 1992, their decisions where to locate plants within the EC should be independent of the trade barriers that are eliminated among the EC member countries.[9]

2.3.2 *Statistical model*

The hypothesis that Japanese MNEs' locational decisions within the EC are dependent upon the comparative advantages of the EC countries is tested by estimating a model which focuses on three observable sources of comparative advantage: labour costs and productivity, technological capacity, and market size:

$$JSUB_{ij} = a_0 + a_1 LABC_{ij} + a_2 PROD_{ij} + a_3 PAT_{ij} + a_4 SIZE_{ij} + e_{ij} \quad (2.1)$$

where i = industry and j = country. The dependent variable, *JSUB*, indicates the distribution of Japanese MNE activity among manufacturing industries and EC countries. The extent of MNE activity is measured by

Table 2.6. *Variable definitions ('i' = industry; 'j' = country)*

Symbol	Variable
$JSUB_{ij}$	Employment in manufacturing subsidiaries more than 50 per cent controlled by Japanese multinational enterprises, divided by total employment in all EC manufacturing subsidiaries more than 50 per cent controlled by Japanese multinational enterprises, 1988
$LABC_{ij}$	Wages and salaries divided by employment, 1985
$PROD_{ij}$	Value added divided by employment, 1985
PAT_{ij}	Cumulative number of patents granted in the United States to residents of country j, 1984–6
$SIZE_{ij}$	Value of shipments (in logarithm), 1985
EXP_{ij}	Exports divided by value of shipments, 1985

Notes: All variables vary among industries and countries and are constructed for the cross-sections of fifteen industries and eight countries. Thus, the full sample covers 120 points of observation. *LABC*, *PROD*, and *SIZE* are expressed in terms of ECU.

the number of employees in majority-controlled subsidiaries of Japanese firms in 1988. *LABC* is a measure of labour costs and should have a negative sign on its coefficient. *PROD* controls for the difference in labour productivity and is expected to have a positive relation to *JSUB*. *PAT* is a proxy measure for technological capacity and is the cumulative number of patents granted in the United States to the residents of the foreign country. The US patent data were used on the assumption that the US market represents the international market for technologies developed outside the US. The coefficient for *PAT* is expected to have a positive sign when Japanese MNEs choose to produce in countries where technological capability is a source of comparative advantage. Finally, *SIZE* is a measure of the size of the host country market and captures the effect of scale economies on MNEs' locational decisions. Thus, its coefficient should have a positive sign. *LABC*, *PROD*, and *SIZE* are all expressed in terms of ECU by using current exchange rates. The definitions of these variables are provided in table 2.6.

The relationships that concern us are those varying over countries and not between industries. Since the number of EC member countries for which comparable data are available is too small (eight) to run equation (2.1) for each industry separately, equation (2.1) is estimated by pooling country and industry data and by including a set of industry dummy variables to control for the industry-specific effect.

Because the variables that represent country characteristics are available only for industry, and each of the EC subsidiaries of Japanese firms can be assigned with confidence to one of the NACE two-digit industries, all the variables are constructed at the two-digit level of industry classification. Due to missing observations, the full sample consists of fifteen manufacturing industries in eight EC-member countries (Belgium, West Germany, Spain, France, Ireland, Italy, The Netherlands, and the United Kingdom).

2.3.3 The estimation result

Table 2.7 presents the estimation result of the regression equations which include fourteen industry dummy variables to control for the industry-specific effect. All the equations in table 2.7 are estimates by the ordinary least squares (OLS) method. Equation (i) shows that the coefficient for *LABC* has a negative sign as expected and is statistically significant. When *PROD* is added to the regression in equation (ii), the significant and negative effect of *LABC* on *JSUB* remains virtually unchanged. On the other hand, the coefficient for *PROD* is not significant. Thus, this result suggests that Japanese MNEs' location decisions depend on the labour cost conditions in the EC countries, and Japanese MNEs are attracted to countries where labour costs are relatively low.

The effect of R&D capacity on Japanese MNEs' location decisions is tested by examining the coefficient for *PAT*. In equations (i) and (ii), *PAT* has a significant positive coefficient. Japanese MNEs are drawn to countries whose industries generate more patents and thus are leading in technology.

The market size variable, *SIZE*, also has a statistically significant positive relation to the country distribution of Japanese foreign direct investment. Japanese MNEs tend to locate their manufacturing plants in countries where the size of market is large enough to take advantage of scale economies.

Equation (iii) adds the variable that measures the share of output exported, *EXP*, to the specification to test if export opportunities affect the location decisions of Japanese MNEs. While the coefficient for *EXP* is not statistically significant, it has a positive sign, implying that Japanese MNEs tend to locate their manufacturing plants in countries whose industries face large export opportunities.

The industry-specific dummies indicate the industries where local production by foreign subsidiaries is most prevalent among Japanese MNEs. Among the industries whose dummies have significant and positive coefficients are electrical machinery, motor vehicles, office and computing

Table 2.7. *Determinants of Japanese MNEs' locational decisions in the EC. The dependent variable is* $JSUB_{ij}$

Variable	Equation (i)	(ii)	(iii)
$LABC_{ij}$	−0.117	−0.093	−0.101
	(1.949)[b]	(1.667)[b]	(1.801)[b]
$PROD_{ij}$		−0.003	−0.002
		(0.300)	(0.210)
PAT_{ij}	0.001	0.0004	0.0004
	(1.579)[c]	(1.433)[c]	(1.390)[c]
$SIZE_{ij}$	0.283	0.288	0.362
	(1.540)[c]	(1.617)c	(1.881)[b]
EXP_{ij}			0.174
			(1.018)
Industry Dummy			
Stone, clay and glass	0.547	0.628	0.625
	(0.509)	(0.588)	(0.586)
Chemicals	0.103	0.143	0.093
	(0.096)	(0.132)	(0.085)
Pharmaceuticals	0.538	0.603	0.689
	(0.494)	(0.529)	(0.602)
Metal products	−0.719	−0.603	−0.586
	(0.647)	(0.549)	(0.533)
Non-electrical machinery	−0.273	−0.136	−0.190
	(0.233)	(0.118)	(0.164)
Office and computing machines	1.685	1.364	1.280
	(1.377)[c]	(1.171)	(1.096)
Electrical machinery	3.719	3.814	3.807
	(3.369)[a]	(3.487)[a]	(3.481)[a]
Motor vehicles	1.875	1.932	1.904
	(1.750)[b]	(1.815)[b]	(1.789)[b]
Instruments	−0.185	0.173	−0.140
	(0.150)	(0.148)	(0.115)
Food	−0.793	−0.718	−0.930
	(0.709)	(0.647)	(0.824)
Textiles	−0.673	−0.524	−0.561
	(0.590)	(0.467)	(0.500)
Clothing	−1.017	−0.793	−0.805
	(0.797)	(0.638)	(0.647)
Rubber products	2.099	2.186	2.284
	(1.855)[b]	(1.955)[b]	(2.036)[b]
Plastic products	−0.482	−0.337	−0.254
	(0.414)	(0.294)	(0.221)
Constant	0.051	−0.439	−1.037
	(0.025)	(0.230)	(0.518)
$\bar{R}^2$	0.220	0.209	0.209
F	2.893	2.718	2.630
	(17,97)	(18,99)	(19,98)

Notes: Absolute values of *t*-statistics are in parentheses. The levels of significance for a one-tailed *t*-test are [a] 1 per cent; [b] 5 per cent; [c] 10 per cent. Constant represents the primary metal industry.

machines, and rubber products. The result reinforces the finding of the descriptive analysis in the preceding section that Japanese foreign direct investment tends to concentrate in electrical and electronic machinery, and motor vehicles.

To examine if slope coefficients vary across different industries, a set of industry dummy variables that interact with *LABC* were included in an unreported regression. The coefficient for the slope shift dummy was significant and negative for electrical machinery and motor vehicles, indicating that the location decision of the Japanese MNE in these two industries is highly sensitive to the difference in labour costs among the EC countries. A similar experiment was implemented for the slope coefficient on *PAT*. While the slope shifts were found to be statistically insignificant for all industries, the office and computing machine industry showed a relatively large slope shift, indicating that the location decision in this industry is more sensitive to the country difference in R&D activity.

2.4 Conclusions

This chapter has analysed the pattern of Japanese foreign direct investment in European manufacturing industries by using the data on 236 majority-owned manufacturing subsidiaries of Japanese firms distributed across fifteen European countries. The descriptive analysis found that while the United Kingdom, West Germany, Spain, France, Belgium, and The Netherlands tend to attract Japanese foreign direct investment in manufacturing, its distributional pattern among these countries differs across different industries.

The statistical analysis was conducted to identify the factors that determine the country distribution of Japanese foreign direct investment in EC manufacturing industries. The regression analysis found that Japanese foreign direct investment is attracted to countries where labour costs are low, where R&D capacity is large, and where market size is large. Thus, these results provide evidence supporting the hypothesis that the location decisions of Japanese MNEs are based on cost-minimising decisions and depend on the factors that determine the comparative advantages of host countries. While this finding is consistent with the previous finding on US multinationals by Kravis and Lipsey (1982), this chapter finds a much stronger effect of labour costs on the location of production by multinational firms. In particular, the Japanese manufacturers of electrical machinery and motor vehicles tend to respond more sensitively to the difference in labour costs among the EC countries when they choose the location of local production.

The findings of this chapter thus suggest that when the Japanese firm chooses the site of local production within the EC, it compares the locational advantage of each host country. This decision process seems to be motivated by the Japanese firm's strategic plan to use the local manufacturing subsidiary as a foothold to penetrate the European common market as well as the local market.

While Japanese manufacturers have been attracted to produce within the European common market, it appears that they do not see the 1992 programme leading to a complete internal market at once. Rather, they seem to take a view that the adjustment towards a complete internal market is not immediate and takes some years. The statistically significant positive effect of market size on the location decision confirms this hypothesis and implies that Japanese MNEs tend to regard the market size of individual member states as an important factor in choosing the location of their manufacturing subsidiaries. If they see '1992' leading to a complete common market, the market size of individual member states should not affect their location decisions since the emergence of the common market would guarantee scale economies regardless of where they locate their manufacturing plants.

The view that the adjustment process towards the completion of the common market is not quick is also reflected in the Japanese MNEs' decisions to invest in the EC countries where labour costs are currently low. As the statistical analysis of this chapter shows, the Japanese manufacturers of cars and electrical equipment currently implement the location strategy that chooses the host countries within the EC according to cost-minimising calculations. While this strategy is presumably based on the assumption that the equalisation of labour costs among the EC countries will not take place immediately after 1992, it will certainly not be an optimal strategy if the factor-price equalisation process advances further in the long run.

One of the important factors that should affect the Japanese MNEs' location decisions, but was not elaborated in our statistical analysis, is the existence of supporting firms and industries in the local market from which Japanese manufacturers are able to procure parts and semi-finished products necessary for the production of final products. It appears that this is a key to the question of whether Japanese firms abroad can remain as competitive as they are at home. It would not be so easy for the Japanese manufacturers of cars and electrical equipment to implement the well-known 'just-in-time' production method if there did not exist local suppliers and other supporting firms able to comply with this method and supply innovative and high-quality parts. As implied by our statistical results the Japanese MNEs may thus choose a host country that has a high concentration of suppliers and supporting industries with great technological capabilities. However, whether this location factor will continue to be as significant in the future may depend on the ability and willingness of Japanese firms to cut off existing subcontracting relationships with particular suppliers at home and switch to EC suppliers to source parts and other import materials. Otherwise, a large number of the Japanese suppliers of parts would crowd into the European markets to follow the Japanese assemblers of manufactured goods as observed in the US motor industry.

While the present study has identified some of the most important locational factors for Japanese MNEs within the EC, whether their manufacturing subsidiaries will remain competitive vis-à-vis their European rivals in the future should prove to be an important question for future research. Future research should be directed toward investigating the effects of the supplier–manufacturer relationship, the sourcing of technology, parts and other inputs, labour relations and distributional activities on the competitiveness of Japanese MNEs in the EC.

Appendix

Sources of data

JSUB was constructed from Toyokeizai (1988). The number of employees in the European manufacturing subsidiaries of Japanese manufacturing firms was aggregated to the two-digit industry level to obtain this variable. A European subsidiary is defined as a subsidiary more than 50 per cent owned by Japanese manufacturing firms. Whenever possible the missing information was supplemented from the appendix table in JETRO (1988).

LABC, *PROD*, and *SIZE* were constructed from Statistical Office of the European Communities (1989), *Eurostat: Industry 1988*, theme 4, Series 4, Luxembourg, Statistical Office of the European Communities. The data on exports to construct *EXP* were obtained from United Nations, *International Trade Statistics Yearbook, Vol. I, Trade by Country*, New York, United Nations. *PAT* was taken from US Patent and Trademark Office (1987), *Patenting Trends in the United States: 1963–1986*, Washington, DC.

Notes

I am grateful to Richard E. Caves, Kirsty Hughes, Leo Sleuwaegen and John M. Stopford for comments and suggestions. Any remaining errors are my own.

1 See Graham, and Krugman (1989) for the analytical discussion of the debates. For recent empirical studies on the determinants of Japanese direct investment in the United States, see Drake and Caves (1990), and Mann (1990).
2 For a survey of these policy issues, see Micossi and Viesti (1991).
3 Dunning (1986) and Burton and Saelens (1987) analyse Japanese direct investment in Europe before the mid-1980s.
4 This data source publishes the statistics of employment and equity capital for most of the listed affiliates. Sales are available only for a limited number of affiliates.
5 See JETRO (1988), table 4, pp. 50–82.
6 For a survey of this literature, see Caves (1982).
7 JETRO (1990) suggests this tendency among Japanese firms particularly after 1987.
8 For more detailed accounts of locational forces, see Dunning, 1980; Caves, 1982, ch. 2; Kravis and Lipsey, 1982.
9 For the theoretical discussion on the effect of tariffs on MNEs' locational decisions, see Horst (1971). For empirical evidence on the effect of the formation of the EC on US foreign direct investment, for example, see Schmitz and Bieri (1972)

References

Buckley, Peter J. and Casson, Mark C., 1976. *The Future of Multinational Enterprise*, London: Macmillan.

Burton, F. N. and Saelens, F. H., 1987. 'Trade barriers and Japanese foreign direct investment in the colour television industry', *Managerial and Decision Economics*, 8, 285–93.

Cantwell, John, 1989. *Technical Innovations in Multinational Corporations*, Oxford: Basil Blackwell.

Caves, Richard E., 1971. 'International corporations: the industrial economics of foreign investment', *Economica*, 38, 1–27.

1982. *Multinational Enterprise and Economic Analysis*, Cambridge: Cambridge University Press.

Drake, Tracey A. and Caves, Richard E., 1990. 'Changing determinants of Japan's foreign investment in the United States', Discussion Paper no 1483 (May), Harvard Institute of Economic Research, Harvard University.

Dunning, John H., 1977. 'Trade, location of economic activity and the MNE: a search for an eclectic approach', in B. Ohlin, P.-O. Hesselborn, and P. M. Wijkman (eds.), *The International Allocation of Economic Activity: Proceedings of a Nobel Symposium Held at Stockholm*, London: Macmillan.

1980. 'Toward an eclectic theory of international production: some empirical tests', *Journal of International Business Studies*, 11, 9–31.

1986. *Japanese Participation in British Industry*, London: Croom Helm.

Dunning, John H. and Cantwell, John A., 1989. 'Japanese manufacturing direct investment in the EEC, post 1992: some alternative scenarios', *Discussion Papers in International Investment and Business Studies*, Series B, Vol. II (1989/90), University of Reading, Department of Economics, September.

Graham, Edward M. and Krugman, Paul R., 1989. *Foreign Direct Investment in the United States*, Washington, DC: Institute for International Economics.

Horst, Thomas, 1971. 'The theory of the multinational firm: optimal behavior under different tariff and tax rules', *Journal of Political Economy*, 79, 1059–72.

Hymer, Stephen H., 1960. The International Operations of National Firms: A Study of Direct Foreign Investment, PhD dissertation, MIT, Cambridge, MA: MIT Press (published 1976).

JETRO (Japan External Trade Organization), 1988. *Zaiou Nikkeiseizogyo Keiei no Jittai: Dai 4 Kai Kittai Chosa Hokoku* (The 4th Report on the Management of European Manufacturing Subsidiaries of Japanese Firms), Tokyo.

1990. *Zaiou Nikkeiseizogyo Keiei no Jittai: 1990* (The 1990 Report on the Management of European Manufacturing Subsidiaries of Japanese Firms), Tokyo.

Kindleberger, Charles P., 1969. *American Business Abroad: Six Lectures on Direct Investment*, New Haven, CT: Yale University Press.

Kogut, Bruce and Chang Sea-jin, 1990. 'Technological capabilities and Japanese foreign direct investment in the United States', mimeo, Department of Management, Wharton School, May.

Kravis, Irving B. and Lipsey, Robert E., 1982. 'The location of overseas production and production for exports by US multinational firms', *Journal of International Economics*, 12, 201–23.

Mann, Catherine L., 1990. 'Determinants of Japanese direct investment in US manufacturing industries', mimeo, International Finance Division, Federal Reserve Board, July.

Micossi, Stephano and Viesti, Gianfranco, 1991. 'Japanese investment in manufacturing in Europe', in L. A. Winters and A. Venables (eds.), *European Integration: Trade and Industry*, Cambridge: Cambridge University Press.

Schmitz, Andres and Bieri, Jurg, 1972. 'EEC tariffs and US direct investment', *European Economic Review*, 3, 259–70.

Stopford, John M., 1990. 'Japanese investment in Europe: the British experience', Nomisma, *Europa e Giappone: l'Impatto del 1992 e le Scelte Italiane*, documentazione, October.

Swedenborg, Brigitta, 1979. *The Multinational Operations of Swedish Firms: An Analysis of Determinants and Effects*, Stockholm: The Industrial Institute for Economic and Social Research.

Toyokeizai, 1988 (ed.). *Kaigai Shinshutsu Kiguo Soran: 1988* (Directory of Japanese Multinational Corporations, 1988), Tokyo: Toyokeizaishinposha.

1989 (ed.). *Kaigai Shinshutsu Kigyo Soran: 1989* (Directory of Japanese Multinational Corporations: 1989) Tokyo: Toyokeizaishinposha.

3 New forms of international involvement, competition and competitiveness: the case of Italy

GIANLUIGI ALZONA, LAURA RONDI and GIAMPAOLO VITALI

3.1 Introduction

In recent years there has been mounting interest in foreign direct investments (FDI) and in cross-border agreements between firms. In view of the completion of the European market, external corporate strategies have attracted attention because of their possible effects in terms of competition and competitiveness, both intra-EC and vis-à-vis the USA and Japan. In this respect, the EC Commission has adopted a basically favourable attitude towards mergers and agreements in most industries.[1]

In this chapter an attempt is made to examine, in the case of Italy, how the main features of the process of internationalisation of production towards OECD countries are in some ways related to the issues of competition and competitiveness. The analysis focuses on possible diversity within controlling holdings and the so-called new forms of international involvement (i.e., joint ventures, minority interests and agreements), in that this diversity possibly displays different outcomes in terms of competition and competitiveness. In fact the choice of the ownership structure of the foreign investment relates in a different way to firm, industry and country characteristics which in turn are linked to various market failures and imperfections. We consider that a focus on non-controlling interests (NCI) may contribute to understanding whether the choice of these forms of ownership is unconstrained or not and therefore if they are a 'last resort' strategy for companies that, in servicing foreign markets, face hurdles of different kinds and cannot take control of foreign subsidiaries.

The chapter is organised as follows: section 2 spells out the methodological problems inherent to the assessment of the effects of FDI (and in particular NCI) in terms of competition and competitiveness. In section 3 the patterns of the international production of Italian industry are related to its trade performance. In section 4 a logit analysis of Italian FDI is presented, which focuses on the propensity to NCI (vis-à-vis controlling interests) in connection with a group of variables related to firm, industry and country effects: empirical results are presented for the whole sample of FDI, for both the intra-industry and the inter-industry investments; a logit model of the propensity to diversified vis-à-vis horizontal mergers is also estimated. Section 5 expands the analysis with an overview of technological agreements between Italian and foreign companies and section 6 puts forward some hypotheses on the possible effects on competition of Italian corporations' external strategies. Section 7 summarises the general conclusions.

3.2 Methodological issues

So far, the new forms of international involvement between companies located in industrialised partners have not received much attention within empirical literature, especially with reference to their impact on competition and competitiveness. This is not surprising if one considers the complexity of the concept of competitiveness and of its links with the issue of competition in a world of imperfect markets, of multinational enterprises and of technological and institutional change (see Hughes, 1990). Once all these aspects have been taken into account, a basic general question is: are the welfare gains associated with internationalisation of production likely to be large relative to any efficiency losses associated with imperfect market structure or, more precisely, with efficiency losses due to a change in market structure?

Cross-frontier corporate strategies – including NCI – can in fact be, in part, responsible for a change in home country competitiveness. Moreover, they also affect international competition and, accordingly, competitiveness.

In our opinion, a better understanding of the effects on competition and competitiveness of mergers and cooperative agreements requires us to learn about the motivations and the aims underlying these activities as well as the choice of control structure. And as the effects are linked to corporate goals, it would seem reasonable to spell out the implications for the choice between controlling and non-controlling interests. For this we can rely on the literature on international production, bearing in mind that the above mentioned effects were never taken explicitly into account.

The internalisation approach, based on an institutionalist view of the firm, and the 'eclectic' paradigm (Dunning, 1981) have in fact introduced important changes within the rationale of NCI. On the one hand, a twofold nature of NCI – both an intermediate institution and a cooperative form – has been emphasised by the fact that, using joint ventures and minority interests, the partners want to establish lasting forms of coordination and cooperation. On the other hand, after Dunning's approach, NCI are now viewed as a viable choice for firms when 'ownership' and 'location' advantages are more important than 'internalisation' advantages.

As for the goals underlying the use of NCI, the literature has put forward several explanations – all linked to different market failures, i.e., distortions compared with the outcomes of perfect competition – that in turn are conducive to end results which may be related to the issues of competition and competitiveness.

In some cases NCI are viewed as a device to overcome market failures (e.g., on capital or skilled-labour markets) that constrain external strategies of individual companies, thus restoring their potential efficiency and increasing the absolute level of competitiveness (Richardson, 1972; Williamson, 1975).

In other cases NCI are instrumental in patterns of behaviour which cause the breakdown of existing equilibria or previous oligopolistic patterns (Graham, 1985; Cantwell, 1989). Here the effect may be positive in terms of competition (should there be an increase in rivalry). On the other hand, in the long run, end results may vary depending on the possibility of monopolisation in that market and of collusive behaviour after the operation.

Finally NCI can be part of a corporate strategy to protect and/or increase its monopoly power: this can be achieved either by 'cooperating' with potential small competitors (but actually neutralising and thereafter acquiring them) or by using mutual hostages in order to reduce rivalry among the partners and attenuating contractual hazards (Williamson, 1983; Chesnais, 1988; Cowling and Sudgen, 1987; Kogut, 1989). In this case, a favourable result for the firm is likely to correspond to a reduction of competition and of consumer welfare.

It is therefore clear that, although mainly inspired by market failures, the motivations underlying the corporate choice of control structure when investing abroad – as well as the goals they pursue – are inherently heterogeneous. What is more important, however, is that the results of external strategies are heterogeneous as well, and, to the extent to which they are potentially conflicting and activate contrasting forces within the markets, may produce opposite effects in welfare terms. Consequently, outcomes are on the whole difficult to assess and, above all, uncertain as to their implications for competition and competitiveness.

Noticeably, in fact, whereas market failures may be crucial in determining the choice of the control form, the outcomes of this choice – and, more generally, of external activity – also affect market structures, potentially generating new kinds of imperfections. So it is, from a model-building point of view, that most of the variables (explaining the propensity to NCI and measuring the effects) are jointly endogenous, at least in the long run. Under these circumstances, the estimation of structural parameters related to the 'net effect' of NCI (and generally speaking of merger activity) on competition and competitiveness is very difficult: so in this study we have chosen to use statistical analysis to summarise data, rather than to look for causal relationships. In particular we have emphasised the problem of heterogeneity of companies' behaviour as to the choice of the foreign investment control form, and henceforth take into account the possible interrelations with various kind of market failures.

By integrating the information from the pattern of Italian FDI with that deriving from the peculiarities of the structure and the trade performance of Italian manufacturing industry, an attempt will be made to advance some hypotheses about the impact on competition of corporate external activities. In order to do this, the classification of industries for merger control purposes produced by the EC Commission (Jacquemin, Buigues and Ilzkovitz, 1989) will be used as a general reference framework.

3.3 Italian FDI and trade performance

In this section we want to explore whether the structure of Italian FDI by industry and by country is positively or negatively related to Italy's international trade position in manufacturing. All this should help us to understand if Italian companies engage in international production to exploit their competitive advantages or to take advantage of the host country endowments (e.g., skilled labour, technology opportunities, managerial skills, etc.).

Before turning to the analysis of the data, three peculiarities of Italy with respect to the leading industrialised countries must be noted, in that they provide a useful background in interpreting the results: first, with respect to industry structure, Italian companies are comparatively undersized and generally have a low monopoly power on foreign markets; second, with regard to trade pattern and performance, Italy is mainly specialised in the so-called traditional sectors, and third, with regard to cross-border corporate activity, Italy can be considered a latecomer, since the upsurge of FDI only dates back to 1986.

The pattern of internationalisation of production for the case of Italy has been studied with respect to the OECD area, due to the importance of both trade and investment flows towards non-EC countries (see table 3.1 for a comparison between the two areas). From these data we obtain a

Table 3.1. *FDI stocks and external trade of Italy in OECD and EEC countries (1987)*

	OECD/World		OECD		EEC/World		EEC	
	Out FDI[a]	Exp.	Out FDI / In FDI [a]	Exp. / Imp.	Out FDI[a]	Exp.	Out FDI / In FDI [a]	Exp. /
Energy products	0.56	0.63	1.98	1.67	0.28	0.40	1.47	1.44
Industrial products	0.59	0.80	0.40	1.11	0.37	0.56	0.41	1.01
Minerals and metals	0.16	0.76	0.61	1.10	0.07	0.52	0.51	0.92
Chemicals	0.63	0.73	0.48	0.48	0.45	0.51	0.60	0.42
Mechanical, electric eng.,	0.75	0.73[b]	0.27	1.11[b]	0.39	0.52[b]	0.29	1.13[b]
office machine and adp. equip.,	–	0.93	–	0.64	–	0.70	–	0.72
telecom. and sound record app.,	–	0.70	–	0.43	–	0.52	–	0.48
specialised machinery	–	0.63	–	1.56	–	0.42	–	1.42
Transport	0.75	0.86	0.40	0.78	0.72	0.63	0.41	0.66
Foods and drink	0.42	0.85	0.43	0.53	0.23	0.61	0.34	0.42
Textiles and clothing	0.75	0.91	0.59	3.08	0.35	0.65	0.35	2.91
Total	0.59	0.80	0.50	1.12	0.34	0.55	0.48	1.02

Notes: [a] three-year average (1986–88); [b] including metal products.
Sources: Elaborations on data from Bank of Italy, OECD, ISCO.

general picture of the relative position of Italian major industries, on the basis of the coverage ratios of both FDIs' stocks and trade (i.e., the ratio of outward to inward FDI and the ratio of exports to imports). The coverage ratios for the FDI show that, in spite of the recent wave, the comparative weakness of Italy (in effect the imbalance between the outward and inward investments' stocks) is present in all the industries at the level of aggregation.[2] This is also found in industries with a good trade performance (namely textiles and clothing and mechanical and electrical engineering). Actually, in many industries, barriers to entry are low and in several cases small and medium-sized companies with financial and managerial constraints to growth willingly agreed to merge with foreign multinationals.

In order to obtain a more detailed picture of the international production of Italy with respect to the trade pattern and competitiveness, we use a database including nearly all the outward investments in OECD until 1987, on the three-digit NACE classification and the 1987 export and import data on the same level of disaggregation (see appendix). As for the FDI, the share of each industry in the overall investments in OECD countries and the specialisation index for an individual industry in a country are calculated. Thus for the investments in an individual industry i in country j, the specialisation index is:

$$\mathrm{IS}_{ijk} = (\mathrm{FDI}_{ij}/\Sigma_k \mathrm{FDI}_{ik})/(\Sigma_i \mathrm{FDI}_{ij}/\Sigma_i \Sigma_k \mathrm{FDI}_{ik})$$

where k = all the OECD countries.

As an indication of competitiveness in a particular world market, we use the net trade balance:

$$\mathrm{NTB} = (X_{ij} - M_{ij})/(X_{ij} + M_{ij})$$

where X = exports and M = imports.

A study of the industries' shares shows that the number of outward investments is higher in chemicals, mechanical and electrical engineering, motor vehicles, food and drink, rubber and plastics. No clear relationship emerges between the rank of investment shares and net trade balances with respect to OECD overall. Therefore the specialisation indexes and the net trade balances for each industry and country were summed to obtain the data on the two-digit level of aggregation, for those sectors where the FDI share is higher (see table 3.2). Displaying the frequencies (and the corresponding number of investments) in a cross-tabulation according to the values of the index (whether greater or less than 1) and of the net trade balance (whether greater or less than 0) we see that, in many important industries, the FDI specialisation is consistent with international competitiveness (i.e., investments tend to be located in industries

Table 3.2. *FDI and trade performance in the main industries (1987)*

Industries	Number of FDIs	% of Total FDI in OECD	NTB[a] < 0	NTB[a] > 0	Spec. of NCI[b]
Manufacture of non-metallic mineral products	24	5.39	1	23	1.20
Chemical industry	55	12.36	44	11	0.92
Mechanical engineering	52	11.69	2	50	1.39
Office machinery and data processing machinery	18	4.04	13	5	1.40
Electrical Engineering	53	11.90	15	38	0.88
Motor vehicles and motor vehicle parts and accessories	36	8.09	16	20	1.01
Food industry	20	4.49	12	8	0.36
Other food products, drinks and tobacco	36	8.09	20	16	0.90
Textile industry	17	3.82	2	15	0.63
Clothing industry	9	2.02	–	9	0.40
Paper and paper products; printing and publishing	23	5.17	9	14	0.94
Processing of rubber and plastics	29	6.52	6	23	0.62

Notes: [a] Number of FDIs in industries with a negative or positive NTB.
[b] Specialisation indexes of NCI vis-à-vis controlling interests (see note 4).
Sources: Elaborations on data from REPRINT database, OECD and ISCO.

– and countries – where the trade performance is good).[3] This pattern is confirmed in mechanical and electrical engineering, in the manufacture of non-metallic mineral products, in rubber and plastics, paper products and publishing and in textile and clothing industries. On the other hand, among the most representative sectors in terms of FDI, we also find important instances of an opposite behaviour, that is high specialisation (and number of investments) in industries where the net trade balance is negative, such as chemicals, information technology and – to a lesser extent – food and drink.

In terms of companies' behaviour, this puzzling distribution of investments with respect to trade performance provides further confirmation of the heterogeneity of the motivations and goals behind external corporate strategies. In some cases FDI are 'pushed' by the previous existence of comparative advantages (and consequently strong ownership advantages of the firms). In other cases FDI are 'pulled' by the comparative abundance of another country's assets and resources that are considered fundamental in order to increase the firm's competitiveness. The opposite patterns of textiles/clothing and information technology are exemplary in this respect.

Finally, the international trade position in the above industries is considered with regard to the ownership structure of the foreign subsidiaries. On the basis of the eclectic theory of international production (Dunning, 1977) the more comparative advantages are possessed by a company, the greater the inducement to internalise them by means of a majority interest. To measure the relative shares of non-controlling interests (FDI) vis-à-vis controlling interests, the specialisation indexes[4] for each industry were constructed (see the right-hand column in table 3.2). The indexes show that controlling interests outnumber FDI in most cases, not only in export-leading sectors, but in industries with trade deficits as well. On the other hand NCI prevail in mechanical engineering and non-metallic mineral products where the net trade balance is positive, thus showing that, on the whole, Italian enterprises seem inclined to hold control whenever possible and quite independently of the trade performance.

In the next section we will go deeper into the analysis of the control structure of the Italian FDI in OECD countries, by taking into account some of the variables which may be related to the choice between controlling and non-controlling interests.

3.4 A logit analysis of ownership forms and investment strategies

In this section we focus on the problem of the diversity that underlies corporate choices with regard to the ownership form of the foreign subsidiary (non-controlling vs controlling interests) and the related policies (diversification vs horizontal integration). The aim is to obtain more information about the external corporate strategies that may be useful in commenting on the possible effects of these investments on competition.

A basic general assumption is that the patterns of behaviour are a result of the diversity within companies' goals which in turn are related to various kinds of market failures (see section 2).

The data used are those covering the foreign direct investments of Italian companies in OECD countries and a list of variables capturing firm, industry and country effects, which may be related to market failures (see appendix).

A series of logit models was estimated where the dependent variable is the likelihood of a firm taking on a specific form of ownership or setting up a specific type of strategy, with respect to the foreign subsidiary.

Let $L[NCI\ (P, S)]$ be the probability that parent company P takes on a NCI (rather than a majority interest) in subsidiary S:

$$L[NCI(P,S)] = f[X(P), Y(S), Z(OI), W(DI), T(DC)] \qquad (3.1)$$

where:

- $X(P)$ = a vector of characteristics of the parent company;
- $Y(S)$ = a vector of characteristics of the foreign subsidiary;
- $Z(OI)$ = a vector of characteristics of origin industry;
- $W(DI)$ = a vector of characteristics of destination industry;
- $T(DC)$ = a vector of characteristics of destination country.

Independent variables for our samples are the following:

- *LPSIZE* = the log of parent's sales;
- *PMULT* = the ratio of the total of subsidiaries' sales to the parent sales;
- *PINT* = *PMULT* + the share of parent exports;
- *DIV* = a dummy variable for diversification;
- *AGE* = age of the first investment abroad of the parent company;
- *LSSIZE* = the log of subsidiary sales;
- *ORD* = R&D intensity (R&D/sales) in the origin industry;
- *DCO* = concentration in destination industry (the four-firm concentration ratio, CR4, in the main areas of investment i.e., EEC and USA);
- DSB, DSS, DSC = dummy variables for science-based, specialised suppliers and scale intensity of destination industry (according to the

Table 3.3. *Logit analyses of Italian FDI to OECD: non-controlling interests and diversification patterns*[a]

Independent variables	Dependent variable *NCI*				Dependent variable *DIV*
	All sample		Intra-industry	Inter-industry	
	(1)	(2)	(3)	(4)	(5)
Firm-specific variables					
LPSIZE	−0.26	−0.22	−0.21		0.47
	(−2.33)	(−3.19)	(−2.53)		(4.54)
PMULT	0.19	−0.47	−0.42		0.73
	(0.26)	(−3.19)	(−2.29)		(5.03)
PINT	−0.60				
	(−0.83)				
LSSIZE	0.08				
	(0.61)				
DIV	0.73	0.64			
	(1.82)	(1.90)			
NCI					0.75
					(2.06)
AGE	0.006				−0.03
	(0.66)				(−3.21)
Country-specific variable					
LY	−0.63	−0.55	−0.61		
	(−2.57)	(−3.19)	(−2.47)		

Industry-specific variables					
Origin industry					
ORD	0.11	0.12	0.59		
	(1.31)	(2.57)	(3.12)		
Destination industry					
DCO	−0.14				−1.69
	(−0.13)				(−1.68)
DSB	−0.36	−3.89	1.90		−0.90
	(−0.46)	(−2.60)	(2.02)		(−1.65)
DSS	0.47	−0.61	1.54		−0.14
	(1.04)	(−1.22)	(1.95)		(−0.31)
DSC	−0.16	−0.76	0.56		−1.07
	(−0.37)	(−1.66)	(0.70)		(−2.64)
Country and industry specific variable					
ADV	0.14				−0.67
	(0.39)				(−1.87)
Constant	6.99	6.70	7.07	−1.90	−6.87
	(2.86)	(3.22)	(2.88)	(−3.06)	(−4.78)
R	0.11	0.09	0.16	0.09	0.20
Sample size	307	356	284	72	329
Non controlling/Diversified cases	75	84	65	19	68
Controlling/Horizontal cases	232	272	219	53	261

Note: [a] *t*-statistics in parentheses

taxonomy of Pavitt (1984); traditional sectors stand for 'otherwise');

ADV = the net trade balance for each industry in each country, on the 3-digit NACE classification;

LY = the log of host country per capita income.

A series of logit models have been estimated where the dependent variable is the likelihood of a firm taking on a diversified FDI vis-à-vis a horizontal one and the independent variables are those listed above (except *DIV*), plus *NCI*, the dummy variable for the control form:

$$L[DIV(P,S)] = f[X(P), Y(S), Z(OI), W(DI), T(DC)] \qquad (3.2)$$

The estimation results are given in table 3.3.

3.4.1 *The choice of ownership forms within Italian FDI*

In this subsection we examine the empirical results of the logit analysis where the dependent variable is the probability of having NCI vis-à-vis controlling interest within our full sample of FDI (model (3.1)). In the first column of table 3.3, the results for the model including all the independent variables are reported for a descriptive purpose; only the estimated coefficients for the selected model (col. 2) will be commented on.

The empirical results of the statistical analysis of Italian FDI in OECD countries show the relative importance of firm-specific variables, as far as the choice of control type is concerned. *LPSIZE* and *PMULT* are both negatively related to the probability of taking on an NCI, thus suggesting that both small firms and companies with less multinational experience prefer or are forced to prefer these forms of investments. In a world of imperfect markets, where agency costs and information asymmetries can stop small enterprises from gaining control over a foreign partner, this is not a surprise. Under these circumstances it is difficult to assess whether the decision to establish a joint-venture or to acquire a minority interest is the result of a voluntary policy or a makeshift solution, thus reducing our capacity to set up links with competitiveness and competition. Without other (possibly qualitative) firm-specific variables all we can say is that NCI may be viewed as a last resort strategy for firms that otherwise would not be able to produce abroad or at least take the first steps.

An interesting hint, however, comes from the diversification dummy *DIV*, which appears with a positive sign, thus suggesting that NCI are considered by companies as a viable form either to obtain economies of scope (possibly for small firms) or to enter new industries (conglomerate diversification is more likely to be carried out by large companies).

Among industry-specific variables only *ORD* performs well in the regression. The coefficient is positive and significant, but its magnitude does not allow us to state that R&D intensity of the origin industry is strongly related to the probability of taking on an NCI abroad. Other things being equal, however, the positive relationship between *ORD* and *NCI* suggests two different interpretations of the behaviour of firms starting from more innovative sectors: either they do not have strong ownership advantages to protect with control or they are impeded by structural constraints (either firm- or destination industry-specific). As for the former, the lack of significance of the variable *ADV* (the net trade balances) does not allow us to establish a relationship between industrial international competitiveness and the propensity of taking on either an NCI or a controlling interest. Actually, from the previous descriptive analysis, we know that in most of the FDI-intensive sectors, controlling interests are prevalent and a straightforward association with net trade balances could not be found (although in the case of data processing equipment, NCI are actually associated with negative trade balances).

On the other hand, with respect to the role of destination industries' barriers to entry, we found that the coefficient of the concentration ratio (*DCO*) is not significant: apparently there is no relationship between the monopoly degree within a destination industry and the probability of taking on either NCI or controlling interests.

Finally, the country-specific variable for our sample is per capita income (*LY*), that can be interpreted as a proxy of both the development and the technological level of the host country and appears in the equation with a negative sign. A probable explanation is that governmental policies of lower income countries favour NCI (possibly with grants, contributions and other facilities) in order to enhance the technological transfer within the country. Generally speaking, the greater the attraction of these policies, the greater the probability that the impact of other factors – and especially market forces – on the choice between controlling and non-controlling interests may on the whole be weakened.

Although not completely satisfactory, the results of the statistical analysis are nevertheless quite promising. Expanding the database for this sample to new firm, industry and country specific variables (e.g., destination industry R&D, advertising intensity, international and institutional barriers to entry and qualitative information on firms' goals) should enable us to set up a clearer pattern of the behaviour of Italian companies abroad and possibly direct us to draw testable structural hypotheses.

3.4.2 The choice of ownership forms in intra-industry FDI

At this point, it is interesting to assess separately the propensity of having NCI according to the different nature of FDI: horizontal or diversified.

Horizontal FDI are actually the cases to which the EC Commission has dedicated most attention for their higher potential detrimental effects on competition (see Jacquemin, Buigues and Ilzkovitz, 1989).

In this subsection, the logit model (3.1) has been used in order to assess the probability of taking on NCI within the intra-industry subsample, and results are shown in table 3.3, col. 3.

As we can see, when FDI are horizontal, all the variables that were significant within the whole sample keep their significance, and some other variables become significant, allowing us to add further insights to the analysis.

Among the firm-specific factors, the size of the investing firms (*LPSIZE*) is inversely correlated to the propensity of having NCI. This result is consistent with what emerged in previous research concerning US FDI in the 1960s (Stopford and Wells, 1972) and 1970s (Gomes-Casseres, 1988) and the Italian FDI at the beginning of the 1980s (Rolli, 1988). The major propensity towards NCI shown by smaller firms may depend on a series of difficulties that the firms face in order to grow, due to the scarcity of the available resources (according to Penrose's approach). This scarcity may concern financial, technological and managerial resources, as well as the knowledge of foreign markets, while market failures may prevent the overcoming of similar difficulties. Therefore investors, who see the opportunity of foreign growth in order to exploit the resources that are already partly available, might be forced to leave the control of the subsidiary to partners with greater resources and a greater knowledge of markets.

The 'degree of multinationalisation' (*PMULT*) is also negatively related to the propensity towards NCI. Such a result seems to confirm the limits that the knowledge of foreign markets puts upon the probability that Italian firms hold control in foreign subsidiaries.

Among the country-specific factors, the per capita income of the host countries (*LY*) is negatively related to non-controlling forms. This relationship could depend on the fact that lower income countries try to promote forms of inward foreign investment that make easier the transfer of technology and managerial skills in favour of local firms.

Let us now consider the relationships that have emerged with reference to industry-specific factors, in particular the intensity of R&D expenditures (*ORD*) and Pavitt's dummies. The results of the logit analysis suggest a non-linear relationship between *ORD* and the probability of

NCI. In general, the propensity to NCI is positively associated with R&D intensity and, in the case of horizontal FDI, the magnitude of the coefficient of *ORD* increases markedly with respect to the full sample (see previous subsection). This may depend on the fact that – after having controlled for the Pavitt typologies – an increasing effort in R&D raises the need for technological complementarities: if market failures prevent firms from directly acquiring these resources, the search for partners increases. In this context, market failures may affect the acquisition of financial resources for R&D and the assessment of the related risk. The estimated coefficients of the Pavitt's dummies leads us however to be more precise about our conclusions on the relationship between the R&D effort and the probability of NCI. The coefficient of the science-based industries – assessed with respect to traditional sectors – is negative and significant: this means that, *ceteris paribus*, the science-based industries show a propensity to NCI which is systematically lower than that shown by traditional sectors. Similar results – although not so marked – are shown by specialised suppliers and by scale-intensive sectors. In both cases the coefficient has a negative sign, but its magnitude is much lower and, in the former case, it does not reach statistical significance. These results seem to be consistent with what is predicted by the theory of internalisation of technological knowledge (Buckley and Casson, 1976). In fact, the technologically advanced industries are engaged more than the traditional sectors in forms of R&D (i.e., basic long-term research) which are subject to a higher degree of dissipation in case of opportunistic behaviour by potential partners: thus for a given level of R&D these industries show a lower propensity to NCI.

In conclusion, when Italian firms carry out horizontal forms of integration with their FDI, they choose the ownership structure of the foreign subsidiary so as to overcome market failures and take into account the different institutional contexts linked with location. The search for solutions suggested by organisational efficiency seems to emerge, with potentially positive effects on the levels of competitiveness of Italian investors. On the other hand, the lack of significance of the concentration coefficient does not enable us to be more conclusive about the relationships between ownership forms and competition levels.

3.4.3 The choice of ownership forms in inter-industry FDI

In this subsection we examine the probability that firms adopt NCI when taking on diversified FDI.

The usual logit analysis has been applied to the subsample of inter-industry FDI, and the results are shown in table 3.3, col. 4.

It clearly emerges that, when FDI are diversified, the firms' criteria for choosing NCI seem to be completely different from those mentioned above for the horizontal case.

Almost all the variables previously mentioned lose their significance. Both *LPSALES* and *PMULT* are no longer significant. Apparently, in these cases cooperative forms of production are favourably considered by Italian companies independently of their size and experience. This could show that in the case of diversified growth, the information asymmetries that the Italian investors meet are higher than those found in the case of horizontal expansion and affect not only the smaller firms with a minor foreign involvement, but also the larger and more expert ones. The inverse relationship between the per capita income of the host country and the propensity towards NCI has also lost its significance. A possible explanation of this result may be that when FDI's aim is diversification, the host countries perceive fewer opportunities to acquire knowledge from the foreign investor and thus maintain a more neutral attitude towards the forms of control.

Even the R&D intensity of the origin industry of Italian investors no longer seems to have any influence on the propensity towards NCI. Instead, the coefficients of the Pavitt's dummies for the destination industry invert the signs they showed in the horizontal subsample, and are all positive. These coefficients are statistically significant both for science-based sectors and specialised suppliers. In contrast to horizontal growth, in the case of diversification, firms may have relatively fewer ownership advantages to protect, and thus the benefits deriving from acquiring resources via partnership may overcome the risk of dissipation of their own resources. When destination industries are science based, the aim of NCI may be the acquisition of technologies in highly dynamic and innovative firms. When destination industries are specialised suppliers, the products are mostly aimed at satisfying the specific needs of the users, and thus it is probable that the need for a thorough knowledge of the local markets encourages cooperation with local majority partners.

To sum up, apart from the effects exerted by certain types of destination industries, in the case of diversification, FDI seems to take on the non-controlling form more randomly than in the case of horizontal FDI, with reference to the size, foreign experience and technological level of the investing firm. As in horizontal FDI, the choice of NCI can respond to the need for overcoming transactional difficulties in the growth process. The net effect on efficiency, and hence competitiveness, is dubious, mostly for conglomerate mergers, that often prove to be unsuccessful in the long run. The relationship with competition is also difficult to assess. On the one hand, diversified mergers are not altering concentration levels within individual industries, and for this reason they are usually not considered detrimental to competition. On the other hand, such mergers may increase multimarket contacts between firms, and for this reason increasing collusion may result. NCI, making diversification growth easier, may have all these contrasting effects.

3.4.4 The choice of corporate strategies in FDI

When we applied the logit analysis to the full sample of Italian FDI, we noticed that the propensity to NCI was positively and significantly related to diversification. This result has suggested further investigation of which variables diversification abroad may be connected to.

In this subsection we have again carried out the logit analysis on the full sample, using as the dependent variable the probability that Italian FDI are of the inter-industry type (model (3.2)) (see table 3, col. 5).

Obviously, the variable *NCI* is still positively associated with the probability of diversification. The negative correlation between *DIV* and the age of the FDI confirms the growing importance of diversification strategies in time. The coefficients of *LPSIZE* and *PMULT* are both positive and significant: as expected, the probability to diversify increases with the size and the foreign experience of the firms.

As far as technology is concerned, the probability of diversifying abroad does not seem to be significantly affected by the R&D intensity of the *origin* industry. This result does not allow us to confirm – at an international level – what is predicted in general by Penrose (1959) and Chandler (1978) and by the theories of economies of scope and transactional difficulties linked to the exploitation of technological knowledge (Teece, 1980).[5] On the other hand, given the particular difficulties that going abroad implies, it is more likely that R&D-intensive firms diversify at first domestically and only then expand their diversification abroad.[6]

With regard to *destination* industries, the technological intensity seems however to discourage diversification. In fact, diversification is discouraged – vis-à-vis horizontal growth – when the destination industries are different from traditional sectors. For these industries, the Pavitt's dummies coefficients are all negative: they are significant for both science-based and scale-intensive sectors. This result shows that when the technological complexity and the risks associated with large-scale production are high, firms prefer to carry out FDI in already established industries, instead of entering new ones. In this context, R&D intensity and high minimum efficient scale really seem to act as a barrier to entry, even for the firms that already operate in industries with such characteristics. Another variable negatively associated with the probability of diversification (vis-à-vis horizontal expansion) is the concentration ratio of the destination sectors. The fact that horizontal investments (and not diversified ones) are more likely to happen in highly concentrated sectors, raises some questions about the possible outcomes in terms of competition.

Finally, the trade advantages of Italy towards industries and countries (*ADV*) are negatively related to the propensity to diversify and, therefore, are positively related to horizontal growth. Indeed, it is not surprising that Italian firms carry out horizontal FDI rather than diversified ones in order to exploit the competitive advantages they enjoy in international trade.

In conclusion, our results confirm an expected finding: horizontal FDI rather than diversified ones are more closely linked to variables connected with competition and competitiveness.

3.5 Technological agreements and the process of internationalisation of Italy

The previous analysis has already pointed out that R&D intensity is related in different ways to the propensity to take on NCI abroad. In fact, NCI normally have an agreement content, whereas technological agreements are a larger category, which includes non-equity forms. In order to identify possible relations between technology and international competitiveness and competition, we go deeper into the role played by technological agreements within the process of internationalisation of Italian industry.

Our database (see appendix) contains information about international technological agreements of Italian firms in the second half of the 1980s using a definition of technological agreements very close to other contributions on the matter (Chesnais, 1988; Hagedoorn, 1989; Cainarca *et al.* 1989). By technological agreements, we mean a continuous and cooperative partnership in the R&D field, regardless of the stage of the innovative process being considered, from the pre-competitive stage to the competitive one.

Basically, we have divided all technological agreements into two broad typologies: 'pure' and 'impure' technological agreements, and we analyse our data accordingly (see table 3.4).

3.5.1 'Pure' technological agreements

Pure technological agreements can be viewed as 'simple' agreements, in that there is only a technological goal. We can divide this typology into two categories, with regard to the stage of R&D involved: basic R&D and development R&D.

As for cooperation in basic R&D, the role of governmental R&D

Table 3.4. *Number of technological agreements between Italian and foreign firms (1986–90)*

Pure technological agreements		Impure technological agreements			
Basic R&D	Development R&D	TM	TC	TCM	Total
14	42	78	39	41	214

Note: TM: technological–manufacturing; TC: technological–commercial; TCM: technological–commercial–manufacturing.
Source: CERIS–CNR.

institutes, universities and national international R&D programmes is crucial. In 70 per cent of cases at least one state-owned firm, R&D institute or university is present; moreover, 35 per cent of these agreements have received national or international financial support.[7]

In our analysis only 6 per cent of the total number of agreements are in this pre-competitive stage of R&D, perhaps due to difficulties in the appropriability of technology and the widespread existence of opportunistic behaviour. In order to avoid the latter, there is often a sort of 'open' consortium in which all the main competitors in that field are involved, and the findings are usually spread throughout the (European) industrial system.

The second category of pure technological agreements concerns cooperation both in the stage of development R&D, and in agreements about the worldwide diffusion of an industrial standard.[8]

Especially in agreements concerning the industrial standards, cooperation among the most important competitors is a key factor in order to involve all the business areas and to avoid the creation of an alternative standard. This is confirmed by the fact that the highest percentage of multipartner cooperations is found in this category of technological initiatives: there are, on average, 3.7 firms per agreement. On the contrary in the sample as a whole the average is only 2.4.

3.5.2 'Impure' technological agreements

This category covers 'complex' agreements, in that the R&D goal is linked to other aspects of the initiative, such as marketing or manufacturing. Of course, in this category too, the technological goal is more important than the others (otherwise, the initiative would be considered only as a manufacturing or commercial agreement).

First of all, we find technological–manufacturing (TM) agreements in which the R&D function is strictly linked to a manufacturing goal through an acquisition of knowhow (using licences, patents or industrial rights), or by a coproduction agreement of a 'new product' (where the knowhow coming from all the partners is necessary for the joint production), or by a bidding consortium, in which barriers to entry are based on technology and not on economies of scale (this is the main difference between TM agreements and a common bidding consortium).[9]

The TM category is the most important in our sample (35 per cent of cases), perhaps because of the possibility offered by TM agreements to overcome, at the same time, both scale and technological barriers. Even the evolution of legal contracts concerning patents and industrial rights has positively affected the diffusion of TM operations.

Secondly, we find technological–commercial (TC) agreements in which the R&D function is strictly linked to the marketing of innovations. At this point of the innovative process, the improvement of relatively new products that have to be customised according to the necessity of the customer-partner, is very important. It is worthwhile to stress that in this process of customisation, the seller-partner needs the knowhow of the customer-partner in order to improve the final product, and this is the main difference between TC agreements and customised market transactions.[10] In the analysis of TC agreements, private investments play a key role: only one out of thirty-nine cases has received financial support.

Thirdly, we find a further category in which both TM and TC agreements are joined. Even in these technological–commercial–manufacturing (TCM) agreements R&D has a leading role, but it cannot be separated from other motives of the strategic alliance which is the basis of this kind of cooperation (Olleros and Macdonald, 1988). The importance of R&D in TCM agreements derives both from the position of the business in the innovation chain (in the first steps of the process), and from the technological barriers to entry (a high barrier cannot be overcome by one single firm).

In this category we can find numerous joint ventures (twenty-seven out of sixty-two), and equity agreements.[11]

As a matter of fact, we could identify another category of agreements in which the R&D function is linked to the financial aspect of the operation. These technological–financial (TF) agreements are generally composed of venture capital and corporate venture capital operations. Together with the main goal of technological acquisition, the operation can also produce financial profit. As in our analysis there are very few cases of TF agreements, due to a lack of efficiency and transparency of the stock market in Italy, we have not considered this category of agreements.[12]

3.5.3 Geographical and sectoral distribution, technological flow and forms of technological agreements

Our analysis shows that technological agreements follow a different pattern of geographical relationships according to the type of agreement. The following observations are made:

(i) the importance of the USA in basic R&D agreements and in TCM agreements, mainly due to the technological flow coming (traditionally) from the US market;

(ii) the role played by the EEC in development R&D agreements, because of EEC R&D programmes, and in TM agreements, due to the expectations of the completion of the European internal market;

(iii) the flow of technology towards Eastern European countries by means of TC agreements.

When possible, in each geographical partnership, we have identified the direction of the technological flow: from Italy to abroad, from abroad to Italy or a bilateral relationship (see table 3.5). We notice that the inward flow mostly comes from the USA (above all in pure R&D agreements), whereas the outward flow is equally shared among the USA, the EEC and Eastern Europe.

As far as sectoral distribution is concerned, it is worth underlining the huge amount of operations in the defence industry within the TP agreements. The main findings of the reclassification of our sample according to Pavitt's taxonomy, are the importance of high-tech industries in the pure R&D agreements and the relevant role played by specialised industries in the TP agreements.

The forms of technological agreements confirm the preference given to equity forms in impure R&D cooperation (especially in TCM cases) and to non-equity initiatives in the pure technological ones (especially in basic R&D agreements).

3.6 New forms of international involvement: possible outcomes in terms of competition

Bearing in mind the findings in previous sections, we can now turn to the point raised at the beginning of the chapter: which outcomes may be derived from the pattern of Italian FDI – and especially new forms of foreign involvement – in terms of competition?

From the previous analysis it turns out that a large proportion of investments – mostly horizontal ones – are in industries which, at the international level, are among the most concentrated (vehicles, rubber, food and drink, data processing and electronics) and have been more

Table 3.5. *Geographical distribution of technological flow between Italian and foreign firms*

	Italy → World					Italy ← World					Italy ←→ World					
	T	TC	TCM	TM	Total	T	TC	TCM	TM	Total	T	TC	TCM	TM	Total	Total
EEC	–	3	–	1	4	–	3	4	7	14	7	3	4	21	35	53
USA	–	4	1	1	6	9	2	5	7	23	8	3	4	5	20	49
Japan	–	–	–	–	–	2	–	5	1	8	–	–	–	–	–	8
East Europe	2	6	–	1	9	–	–	–	–	–	1	–	–	–	1	10
Other Europe	1	1	–	–	2	1	1	–	2	4	2	–	–	3	5	11
Other World	–	1	–	1	2	1	–	2	3	6	–	–	–	3	3	11
Total	3	15	1	4	23	13	6	16	20	55	18	6	8	32	64	142

Notes: T: pure technological; TC: technological–commercial; TCM: technological–commercial–manufacturing; TM: technological–manufacturing.
Source: CERIS–CNR.

affected by merger activity. It is in fact reasonable to assume that in these sectors, monopoly power and merger activity are interrelated, with causality running in both directions, although monopolisation can hardly be attributed to the Italian multinationals, given their comparatively small size. Taking all this into account, it is not surprising that Italian companies also engaged in international production in those industries, quite independently of their trade performance, in order to respond to the need to follow the basic trends of the international industrial reorganisation, so as not to lose ground vis-à-vis the leading multinationals.

Supposing this is the main goal of most Italian FDI, in order to assess the possible outcomes of these investments on the competitive process, it might be useful to use the classification of industries that the EC Commission produced in order to analyse the effects of mergers and the implication for competition policy (Jacquemin, Buigues and Ilzkovitz, 1989). This classification assigns industries to four groups according to whether or not merger activity may lead to a reduction in competition and/or efficiency gains.[13] Therefore we split the FDI (pointing out if they were non-controlling or controlling interests) and the technological agreements into four groups (see figure 3.1).

Eighty-five per cent of the 445 listed FDI and 82 per cent of total agreements are included in the classified industries. As for the first and fourth groups where the danger of monopolisation is guarded against by the Commission, we see that only 33 per cent of the foreign investments and a very low number of agreements are included. Moreover, given the already mentioned small size of Italian multinationals, we would expect a process of re-equilibrisation of market power vis-à-vis the leading corporations rather than a reduction of competition. Interestingly, however, when we consider the ownership structure of the FDI in these groups, we note a (comparatively) greater propensity to hold controlling interests vis-à-vis the industries included in the other two.

The tendency to hold control that characterises the mergers in these industries leads us to conclude that Italian firms do their utmost to protect or to increase their market shares in precisely those sectors that offer greater benefits in terms of monopoly power. Such patterns of behaviour seem consistent with the fact that, in these sectors, Italian firms establish a very low number of technological agreements: in fact external contractual relationships are often compatible with rivalry among partners, and feature greater instability than control forms.

The great majority of both FDI and agreements are assigned to the third group[14] which, according to the Commission, implies less danger of monopolisation and greater prospects of substantial efficiency gains from mergers and mainly includes growth and highly innovative industries

Danger of monopolisation

GROUP 1:

Danger of a reduction of competition and little prospect of efficiency gains.

Percentage of foreign direct investments:	15.9
Spec. of non-controlling interests:	0.8
Percentage of technological agreements:	0.9

GROUP 4:

Possibility of efficiency gains but also of a danger of monopolisation.

Percentage of foreign direct investments:	16.6
Spec. of non-controlling interests:	0.8
Percentage of technological agreements:	3.5

Efficiency gains

GROUP 2:

Less danger of reduction of competition, but little prospect of efficiency gains.

Percentage of foreign direct investments:	24.1
Spec. of non-controlling interests:	1.1
Percentage of technological agreements:	16.5
Percentage of classified FDI:	85.0
Percentage of classified Agreements:	82.3

GROUP 3:

Less danger of monopolisation and prospect of substantial efficiency gains

Percentage of foreign direct investments:	43.4
Spec. of non-controlling interests:	1.1
Percentage of technological agreements:	79.1

Figure 3.1 Distribution of Italian FDI according to the EEC classification of industries for merger control purposes

Source: Jacquemin, Buigues and Ilzkovitz (1989).

where the competition from US and Japanese companies is strong. Apparently, then, external strategies carried out by most Italian companies should not endanger competition, but have positive effects in terms of efficiency gains. This result should be strengthened both by the fact that the enterprises enjoy a weak monopoly power and that in science-based industries (as shown by the net trade balances) Italian companies seem to be engaged in follow-the-leader strategies, in an effort to be on more advanced technological trajectories.

3.7 Concluding remarks

This chapter has analysed the role of FDI – and especially NCI – and of technological agreements in enhancing the process of internationalisation of the Italian manufacturing industry within OECD countries. Particularly, the main features of this process have been related to the issues of competitiveness and competition.

With respect to the relationship between the pattern of outward FDI and industry trade performance, we could not find a clear indication that Italian companies engage in international production to exploit their competitive advantages. Although in many FDI-intensive industries the corporate external strategies are actually consistent with international competitiveness (such as in mechanical and electrical engineering, rubber and plastics, etc.), we also found important instances of opposite behaviours (e.g., in chemicals, information technology and the food industry). Furthermore, the choice of the ownership structure of the subsidiary seems to be quite independent of industry trade peformance, being mostly oriented to take on control whenever possible.

In order to investigate companies' heterogeneous behaviour, we focused on corporate choice with respect to the ownership structure of foreign investments by relating the probability that the parent company takes on an NCI (instead of a majority interest) to a set of variables capturing firm, industry and country effects.

The empirical results of the logit analysis for the whole sample of Italian NCI in OECD countries have emphasised the role of firm-specific effects and, above all, that (on the basis of the current data-set) the decision of taking on NCI cannot be assessed as a voluntary and strategic choice, although diversification policies seem to matter to a certain extent. (Again the idea that NCI represent a sort of 'last resort strategy' emerges.) As for industry-specific effects, it is noticeable that neither the concentration ratios of the destination industries nor industry trade performance are significantly related to the probability of taking on NCI or controlling interests. Apparently, then, monopoly power does not seem to affect the choice of the control form (maybe because of the small size and consequent harmlessness of Italian multinationals) nor do competitive advantages provide any strategic guidance in this respect.

The importance of firm-specific factors in connection with the choice of the ownership structure of the subsidiary is particularly relevant within intra-industry NCI. In these cases both size and international experience of the parent firm are negatively correlated with the propensity to hold NCI. This suggests that smaller and less-informed firms adopt this form of ownership in order to overcome market failures, integrating and thus complementing their available resources.

The logit analysis seems to highlight a complex relationship between the R&D intensity and the probability of holding NCI. On the one hand, after having controlled for the technological features of industries (as expressed by the Pavitt dummies), the propensity to NCI increases with the R&D intensity, suggesting the existence of market failures associated with the acquiring of financial resources and with the risks involved in R&D. On the other hand, the most technologically advanced industries tend to be, *ceteris paribus*, more cautious towards NCI, consistent with what is predicted by the theory of internalisation of technological knowledge.

As far as inter-industry FDI are concerned, Italian firms seem to choose their ownership structure with fewer restrictions in connection with their size, foreign experience and technological level. As diversification implies information asymmetries that are greater than in horizontal expansion, NCI are possibly chosen in order to overcome these asymmetries, independently of the firm-specific variables examined. Whereas R&D intensity of the origin industry is no longer relevant, the Pavitt typology of the destination industry affects significantly the propensity towards NCI. It is worthwhile to notice that the signs of these effects are now positive, whereas within horizontal FDI they were negative. This may indicate that, in the case of diversification, the ownership advantages that investing firms have to protect are fewer, and thus the pooling of resources via partnerships may not be discouraged by the risk of dissipation.

The probability of diversification through FDI, vis-à-vis horizontal expansion, has also been assessed. Firstly, the analysis pointed out that in concentrated sectors, horizontal FDI are more likely to happen than diversified ones: this finding seems to indicate the propensity by the Italian firms to use FDI in order to strengthen their market power within the international oligopolies. Secondly, it has been shown that competitive advantages that Italian firms enjoy in international trade are better exploited through horizontal, rather than diversified FDI. Finally, it emerged that when destination industries are characterised by technological complexity and high economies of scale, horizontal growth is more likely than diversification.

All this has led us to consider technological agreements as a viable choice to overcome R&D and scale barriers. The analysis has shown both the difficulties in organizing R&D agreements between private firms and the diffusion of innovations by means of inward technological flows. However, the internationalisation process of Italian industry links firms' R&D strategy to the exploitation of economies of scale and scope. This fact is confirmed by the predominant amount of 'impure' technological agreements, such as the agreements related to manufacturing or marketing aspects. The expectations linked to the completion of the EC market can be considered one of the main reasons for this kind of operation.

Referring to the effects on competition of the Italian process of internationalisation, we observed, first of all, that a large part of FDI are located in industries characterised by high levels of concentration and merger activity. After having classified the investments and the technological agreements according to CEC classification of industries for merger control purposes, however, it turned out that many fell into a group that is favourably viewed by the Commission, due to probable increases in both efficiency and competitiveness (vis-à-vis US and Japanese multinationals). On the other hand, as for the external corporate strategies within industries where the danger of monopolisation is higher, we noticed a greater propensity to take on controlling interests, thus highlighting the Italian companies' attempts to exploit all the advantages that monopoly power can offer. That positive effects on Italian competitiveness can derive from this heterogeneous pattern of behaviours, depends greatly on the willingness of the companies and, above all, their capacity to exploit within national boundaries the skills and knowledge acquired abroad. On the whole, however, a greater involvement of Italian firms in international production – in that it increases their size and, possibly, market shares – should have positive net effects for international competition. Due to the comparatively small size of Italian competitors (also within concentrated markets), this process should in fact increase rivalry among firms and break down existing oligopolistic patterns in many industries.

Appendix

Sources of data

The main source that we used to identify Italian FDI was the REPRINT database (Cominotti and Mariotti, 1989), which lists 678 foreign subsidiaries (both controlling and non-controlling interests) of Italian companies worldwide in 1987.

For each subsidiary the following data are reported: three-digit industry (ISTAT–NACE classification), class sizes in terms of employees and of sales, year of the first investment by an Italian firm, name of the parent company, form of the investment (controlling, parithetical, minority), name of the business groups to which the parent company is affiliated. Nearly 450 FDI were found to be located in the OECD countries.

In order to estimate the statistics presented in section 4, further enquiries were necessary both to have more precise figures of subsidiaries' sales and to collect information not provided by that source. All the data referring to the parent companies (sales, exports, three-digit industry) had to be collected from other sources, mainly from company reports.

In Italy, a large number of FDI arc carried out by firms that are affiliated to wider business groups, which normally operate in many different industries. A problem we had to face was to which industry a parent company affiliated to such groups should be attributed. When (and it was the most common case) FDI have been carried out in an industry that was already established within the group, we attributed the parent company to the same industry of the foreign subsidiary: i.e., these operations have been considered cases of intra-industry (horizontal) growth. On the contrary, when FDI actually enabled the group to enter a new industry, or significantly widened its presence in an industry which was relatively marginal, we attributed the parent company to the prevalent industry of the group, and thus the operation was considered a case of inter-industry (diversified) growth.

Host countries' per capita incomes are based on OECD sources, and Italian import–export figures by industry and country were derived from OECD and ISCO (Istituto Nazionale per lo Studio della Congiuntura, see Martelli, 1988) sources.

For EEC and US concentration ratios, figures have been obtained from Yamawaki, Sleuwaegen and Weiss (1989) and Scherer (1985) respectively. For a few industries, not considered in these sources, an ad hoc enquiry was necessary.

Due to lack of information about some of the variables, the sample considered in our study has been correspondingly reduced: the number of cases retained goes from a minimum of 307 to a maximum of 356.

The sources used in order to study Italian FDI cannot give us information about the goal of the FDI and, in particular, if there is a technological motive in the investment. For this reason, and bearing in mind the importance of the internationalisation of technology in the 1980s, we built a new database focused on technological agreements. This is composed of more than 200 international technological agreements of Italian firms in the second half of the 1980s. The principal sources are national financial newspapers and reviews, but some complementary information coming directly from the firms involved were added.

In each record of the database, we collected the main characteristics of the partners (name, controlling group, industry, country), of the agreements (typology, name, industry, date, object, modification) and, finally, of the technological process involved in the agreement (technological flow, public financial support, stage of the R&D process).

It is worthwhile underlining that the importance of technology in international competition is generally emphasised by newspapers, in the sense that they try to consider as technological almost all the economic and industrial initiatives in the international field. On the contrary, a closer study reveals that many operations labelled as 'technological agreements' are, in fact, manufacturing or marketing agreements, or more simply, market transactions. With the aim of overcoming these limitations, we have only considered initiatives that have a precise technological goal.

Notes

Paper prepared under CNR Project 'Servizi e strutture per l'internazionalizzazione delle imprese' and within the European Competitiveness Network organised by WZB, Berlin. We thank the participants of the European Competitiveness Workshop at WZB, Berlin, and particularly Kirsty Hughes, John Hagedoorn and Hideki Yamawaki for helpful comments. We also thank Livio Tonello for helping us with the data and the CERIS staff for the editing. Although this paper has been jointly produced, sections 2, 3, 4.1 and 6 are by Laura Rondi, sections 4.2, 4.3 and 4.4 are by Gianluigi Alzona and section 5 is by Giampaolo Vitali.

1 Some of the problems concerning the EC Commission attitude toward European cross-frontier merger activity are discussed by Kay, chapter 8, this volume.

2 From a recent study on the process of internationalisation in the leading OECD countries, this (unfavourable) situation is a peculiarity of Italy (see Perrucci, 1990).

3 This result does not take into account the international trade position in those industries where Italian companies did not invest (about 40 out of 120 three-digit sectors).

4 The specialisation index for non-controlling interests in an industry *i*, is defined as: $(\mathrm{NCI}_i/\mathrm{FDI}_i)/(\sum_i \mathrm{NCI}/\sum_i \mathrm{FDI})$.

5 For empirical evidence see MacDonald (1985).

6 As we point out in the appendix, we consider as horizontal FDI all the cases where the parent company investment in a foreign subsidiary expanded a line of business already established within the firm, owing to a previous choice of diversification.

7 Examples of this category are the participation of Fiat in the Prometheus project (electronic-for-automotive R&D project), and the agreement between Fidia and Georgetown University in the pharmaceutical sector.

8 Examples of this category are the agreement between Selenia and GEC in the electronic sector and the participation of RAI and Seleco in the R&D programme on European HD television.

9 Examples of this category are agreements between Ansaldo and UTDC in the production of the People Mover (automatic city train), Magneti Marelli and Autodisplay in the production of a new generation of 'computers' for cars, and Aeritalia with the European consortium Eurofighter for the EFA military plane.

10 An example of this category is the agreement between Italtel and Apple in order to adapt Italtel electronic switchboards to Macintosh PCs.

11 Examples are SESAM, the joint venture of Comau and Digital Equipment in the robotic sector and the cross-minority interests of Italtel and AT&T in the telecommunication industry.

12 However, it is important to remember the birth of some new venture capitalists, such as Innovare and Finbiotech, and also that Olivetti has carried out some operations in the USA in the field of corporate venture capital.

13 Although the assumptions underlying this classification may be criticised in some respect (see Kay, chapter 8, this volume), this framework seems to be nonetheless instrumental and workable for our purposes.

14 It may be quite obvious that 43 per cent of technological agreements fall into this group. However, technological agreements were defined to include agreements in all industries that have an R&D motivation also with reference to marketing and manufacturing aspects (see section 5).

References

Buckley, P. and Casson, M., 1976. *The Future of the Multinational Enterprise*, London: Macmillan.

Cainarca, G., Colombo, M., Mariotti, S., Ciborra, C., De Michelis, G. and Losano, M., 1989. *Tecnologie dell'informazione e accordi tra imprese*, Milan: Edizioni Comunità.

Cantwell, J., 1989. *Technological Innovation and Multinational Corporations*, Oxford: Basil Blackwell.

Chandler, A. D., 1978. 'The United States: evolution of enterprise', in P. Mathias and M. M. Postan (eds.), *The Cambridge Economic History of Europe*, Cambridge: Cambridge University Press.

Chesnais, F., 1988. 'Technical co-operation agreements between firms', *STI Review*, December.

Cominotti, R. and Mariotti, S. (eds.), 1989. *Italia multinazionale, II Rapporto R&D*, Milan: Edizione de Il Sole 24 Ore.

Cowling, K. and Sudgen, R., 1987. *Transnational Monopoly Capitalism*, Brighton: Wheatsheaf Books.

Dunning, J. H., 1977. 'Trade location of economic activity, and the MNE: a search for an eclectic approach', in B. Ohlin, P. O. Hesselborn and P. M. Wijkman (eds.), *The International Allocation of Economic Activity*, London: Macmillan.

1981. *International Production and the Multinational Enterprise*, London: Allen and Unwin.

Gomes-Casseres, B., 1988. 'Joint ventures cycles: the evolution of ownership strategies of US multinational enterprises', in F. Contractor and R. Lorange (eds.), *Cooperative Strategies in International Business*, Lexington: Lexington Books.

Graham, E., 1985. 'Intra-industry direct investment, market structure, firm rivalry and technological performance', in A. Erdilek (ed.), *Multinationals and Mutual Invaders: Intra-industry Direct Foreign Investment*, London: Croom Helm.

Hagedoorn, J., 1989. 'Theory of analysis of partnerships in production and innovation', MERIT working paper no. 6.

Hughes, K., 1990. 'Competition and competitiveness in the European economies', mimeo, Berlin: Wissenschaftszentrum.

Jacquemin, A., Buigues, P. and Ilzkovitz, F., 1989. 'Horizontal mergers and competition policy in the European Community', *Economia Europea*, May, 40.

Kay, N. M., 1992. 'Mergers, acquisitions and the completion of the internal market', chapter 8, this volume.

Kogut, B., 1989. 'The stability of joint ventures: reciprocity and competitive rivalry', *Journal of Industrial Economics*, December, 38.

MacDonald, J. M., 1985. 'R&D and the directions of diversification', *Review of Economics and Statistics*, November, 64.

Martelli, B. M., 1988. 'Il commercio dell'Italia per aree geografiche e settori merceologici', *Rassegna di lavori dell'ISCO*, December, 10.

Olleros, F. J. and Macdonald, R. J., 1988. 'Strategic alliances: managing complementarity to capitalise on emerging technologies', *Technovation*, 7.

Pavitt, K., 1984. 'Sectoral patterns of technical change: towards a taxonomy and a theory', *Research Policy*, 13.

Penrose, E. T., 1959. *The Theory of the Growth of the Firm*, London: Basil Blackwell.

Perrucci, A., 1990. *Il processo di internazionalizzazione nei maggiori paesi Ocse*, Milan: Angelil.

Richardson, G. B., 1972. 'The organization of industry', *Economic Journal*, 82.

Rolli, V., 1988. 'Le joint ventures internazionali delle imprese italiane: una verifica econometrica', *Quaderni Sardi di Economia*, 3.

Scherer, F. M., 1985. *Industrial Market Structure and Economic Performance*, Chicago: Rand-McNally.

Stopford, J. M. and Wells, L. T., 1972. *Managing the Multinational Enterprise*, New York: Basic Books.

Teece, D. J., 1980. 'Economies of scope and the scope of the enterprise', *Journal of Economic Behaviour and Organisation*, 1.

Williamson, O., 1975. *Markets and Hierarchies: Analysis and Antitrust Implications: A Study in the Economics of Internal Organizations*, New York: Free-Press/Macmillan.

1983. 'Mitigating contractual hazards: using hostages to support exchanges', *American Economic Review*, 73.

Yamawaki, H., Sleuwaegen, L. and Weiss, L., 1989. 'Industry competition and the formation of the European market', in L. Weiss (ed.), *Concentration and Price*, Cambridge, MA: MIT Press.

4 Strategic technology partnering and international corporate strategies

JOHN HAGEDOORN AND JOS SCHAKENRAAD

4.1 Introduction

In this chapter we address a number of issues pertinent to the internationalisation of the economy, related corporate strategies and in particular the extent to which (international) strategic technology alliances are applied by companies from Europe, Japan and the USA. In order to achieve a better understanding of the international setting of strategic technology alliances we will first broaden the picture of our analysis before we come to the main question of our present contribution, i.e., to what extent European companies differ from their major competitors in their strategic technology partnering behaviour as a major force in corporate internationalisation strategies. In that context we will understand strategic technology partnerships as those inter-firm agreements aimed at the long-term perspective of the product-market position of at least one partner through a joint effort of which common innovative activities are at least part of the agreement.

In the next section we will consider the general background for the issue of internationalisation through a brief discussion of key aspects of phenomena such as the international catching-up strategies of Europe and Japan after the Second World War through foreign direct investment, the changes in international trade, the transformations in the international market structure and the internationalisation of technology flows. Section 3 presents some descriptive information on general trends in strategic technology alliances during the eighties and the sectoral breakdown of these agreements and in section 4 we will analyse trends in the internationalisation of strategic technology partnering. The analysis is based on material from the MERIT–CATI databank which contains information on thousands of strategic technology partnerships (see appendix 1). A major question will be to what extent strategic technology alliances have become more internationally or even globally oriented. If the economy at large has become more internationally oriented and if there is a trend towards global competition, as so often stressed in the literature, it seems interesting to find out whether this is also reflected in the pattern of (international) strategic technology partnering. In section 4 we also enter into the question whether European companies follow a pattern of internationalisation in their strategic technology alliances that is different from their main competitors from the USA and Japan. Finally, section 5 briefly discusses the consequences of our findings for understanding global competition and the competitive positioning of European companies.

4.2 The growing internationalisation of the economy

A number of economic developments taking place during the seventies and eighties changed the international economic system considerably. Although some of these developments had already taken off during the preceding years, it was during the past two decades in particular that a growing internationalisation of the economy became more and more apparent. These changes in the economy in terms of a growing internationalisation are extensively reported in a large number of economic studies (see for instance Cantwell, 1989; Chandler, 1986; Chesnais, 1988; Dunning, 1988a,b; Franko, 1989; Soete, 1991; UNCTC, 1988), which enables us to introduce briefly only some of the major developments.

During the fifties and sixties when the world economy was still largely dominated by US companies, European and Japanese firms began to increase their efforts to catch up with their US competitors. In this catching-up strategy European and Japanese firms initially used exports as the major source of their endeavour to improve their international competitive position, whereas US companies concentrated in particular on foreign direct investment. In general this catching-up strategy by Europe and Japan has to a large extent been successful as, during the sixties and seventies, the international economy gradually changed with a declining share of US companies and an increasing share of European and Japanese companies in international markets.

In the seventies and eighties the international distribution of foreign direct investment also changed considerably (see figure 4.1). The USA transformed from a major home country for foreign direct investment to a major host country. This transformation was mainly caused by the growth of investments in the USA made by European and Japanese multinationals. For the EC we notice the enormous increase in outward foreign direct investment during the eighties, which well exceeds the inflow. In the same period Japanese companies also began to increase

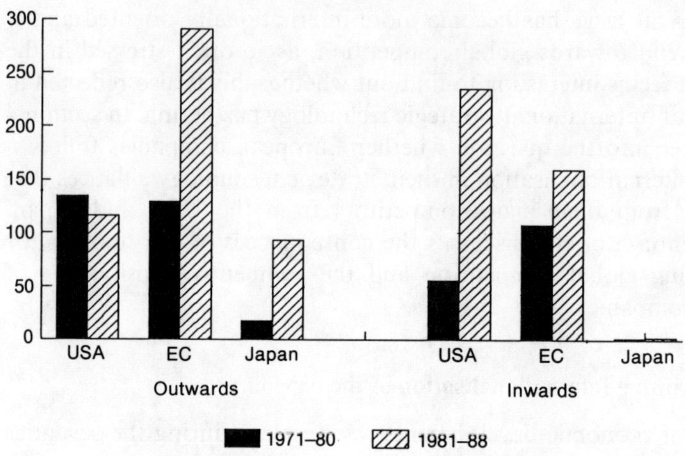

Figure 4.1 Cumulative foreign direct investment flows (inwards and outwards) for the USA, the EC and Japan, 1971–80 and 1981–88 (in millions of current dollars).
Source: OECD, 1990.

their foreign direct investment towards both the USA and Europe. If we compare Japan with the other economic blocs it is striking that its outward flows of foreign direct investment have increased substantially, whereas its inward flows remain almost non-existent.

Changes in the direction of foreign direct investment, and the pattern of internationalisation that follow from them, did not only affect fixed assets in manufacturing and property: although still at a low level in absolute terms, the international distribution of foreign direct investment in R&D activities is changing as well. During the eighties many European companies increased their investments in R&D in the USA, whereas many US companies also enlarged their R&D investments in Europe and Japan. In recent years we have also witnessed an increase of this particular category of foreign direct investment by Japanese companies in both the USA and Europe (see Chesnais, 1988).

Apart from a growth in international trade, which after a period of rapid increase actually decreased again during the eighties, and an expansion of foreign direct investment, the internationalisation of the economy is also apparent in changes in the international market structure. If the international distribution of the group of the world's largest companies is considered, one can observe a drastic change during the past three decades (see Glickman and Woodward, 1990). For instance, the dominance of US companies in the group of the fifty worldwide largest companies has disappeared within thirty years. At the end of the fifties nearly 90 per cent of these world's largest companies were US-based, with only six European enterprises among them. In recent years 'only' twenty companies on the list of largest companies are US-based, which equals the number of European firms. At present Japan has six companies on the list whereas it had none at the end of the fifties. These changes do not strictly imply a process of internationalisation because the composition of the group of the world's largest companies might have changed due to growth of companies within their home markets. However, as this redistribution of, and changes in, economic strength in favour of non-US companies took place in a period of increased international competition, it reveals some fundamental changes in the international market structure.

To a certain extent the explanation for this growing role of Japanese and European companies and the increasing significance of their foreign investments in recent years can be found in the large financial surpluses that were located in Japan, the FRG and some other European countries. These current account surpluses and the excess of domestic saving over domestic investment have provided at least part of a solid financial basis for the international expansion of companies from Japan and Europe.

It is worth mentioning that this internationalisation of the economy is not only attributable to the behaviour of the world's largest companies, suggesting a 'tight' international oligopoly. On the contrary, recent research (UNCTC, 1988) suggests that the international role played by the group of largest multinational companies, in terms of their foreign sales, has remained unchanged or even declined during the past decade. This stagnation in the activities of the group of largest companies, however, has been more than compensated by the group of smaller multinational companies that appear to account for a rising share of the growth of internationalisation in recent years.

Taking a look at the evolution of the world economy at large, and the industrialised world in particular, it is clear that this internationalisation appears to stand out amongst many economic developments and European companies do appear to play a substantial role in this process. The following trends represent a general characterisation of this process:

an increase of exports and imports of goods and services;
growing outward and inward flows of direct investment;
an internationalisation of technology flows;
the internationalisation of monetary and financial systems.

It is against this general background of internationalisation and growing interrelatedness of economic systems that we have to understand the economic rationale for internationalisation from the perspective of individual firms. This general evolution is both an objective development facing companies and a result of their individual and collective behaviour. Consequently, internationally operating companies are not to be seen as 'passive reactors' but much more as active participants setting the scene for many international and often oligopolistic markets. Due to recent technological changes, and in particular the speed and complexity of technological development which are so extensively discussed in the literature, many of these international markets have become more complex. In that particular context we have to view (international) strategic technology inter-firm partnering as part of the process of internationalisation and growing complexity of economic systems where companies create alliances to monitor new developments, enter foreign and/or new markets, and jointly develop new complex technologies; see Hagedoorn and Schakenraad (1990b,c) for more extensive discussion of motives for strategic technology partnering.

4.3 General trends in strategic technology alliances during the eighties

Various studies demonstrate that the number of strategic alliances has increased significantly during the 1980s (see for instance Chesnais, 1988; Contractor and Lorange, 1988; Haklisch, 1986; Hergert and Morris, 1988; Hladik, 1985; OECD, 1986). In some of our previous contributions we reported on general trends in strategic technology alliances in core technologies since the early seventies (see Hagedoorn and Schakenraad, 1990a,b). For core technologies such as information technologies, biotechnology and new materials we found that during the seventies strategic technology partnering was at a relatively low level in information technology and almost non-existent in new materials and biotechnology. However, the first half of the eighties marks a short period of rapid increase, followed by a period of stabilisation in the growth of new agreements, with a tendency towards levelling off during the late 1980s.

In the present chapter we are able to give an overview of the growth of strategic technology alliances in a larger number of sectors other than core technologies. We will restrict our analysis to the eighties, but we expect the general pattern of the pre-eighties period with a low level of strategic technology partnering, as found in our previous analyses, to prevail in virtually every industrial sector or field of technology. As shown in figure 4.2 the general historical pattern of newly established strategic technology alliances in our databank demonstrates that the first years of the eighties are characterised by a somewhat stable increase of new agreements, followed by a sharp increase during the mid-eighties, which is followed by a slower rate of increase during the final years of the eighties. However, in those later years the annual number of newly established

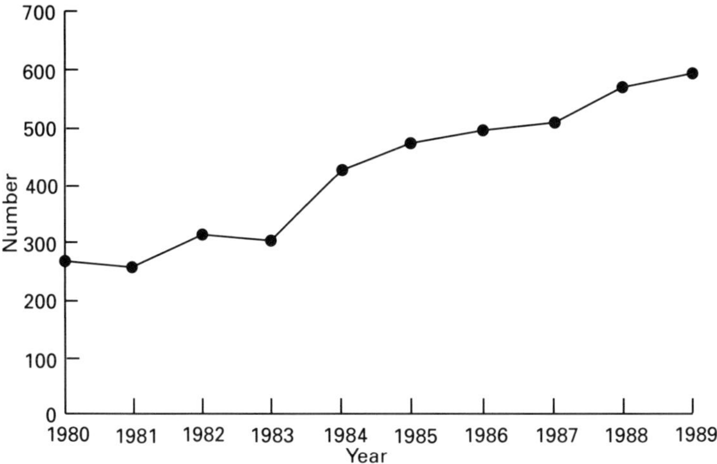

Figure 4.2 Growth of newly established strategic technology alliances in all fields, 1980–89.
Source: MERIT–CATI.

strategic technology alliances is still over twice the number found in the early eighties. If one compares the first half of the decade with the second half it is found that over 60 per cent of all alliances have been made since 1985.

Within this population of newly established strategic technology alliances some fields clearly take a more dominant position than others. As shown in figure 4.3 information technology is the largest field of strategic alliances with 41.2 per cent from a total of almost 4,200 strategic technology alliances in our databank. It is followed by biotechnology with 20.2 per cent, new materials with 10.3 per cent, chemicals 9.8 per cent, and automotive and aviation/defence approximately 5 per cent each. In other words, core technologies such as information technology, biotechnology and new materials take a combined share of more than 70 per cent of all strategic technology alliances established during the eighties. Other fields of technology or industry appear to play a role of minor importance in strategic technology partnering. Apparently the emergence of so-called new 'technological paradigms' related to core technologies have come to affect a growing number of companies through strategic technology partnerships in the first place.

In figures 4.4 and 4.5 we present the historical development of inter-firm cooperation at a less aggregated level. In figure 4.4 it is shown that both biotechnology and new materials demonstrate a pattern of general

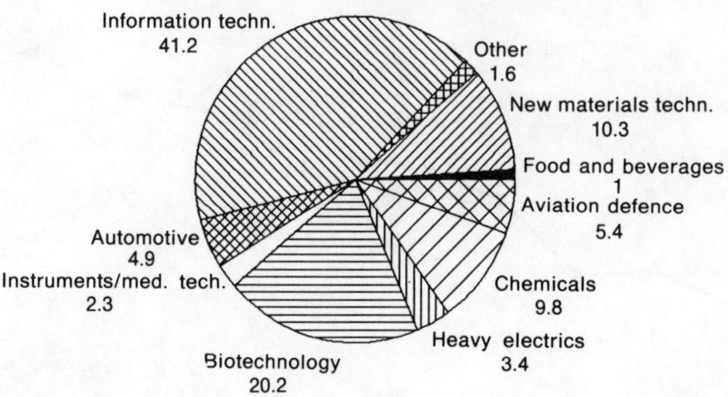

Figure 4.3 Distribution of strategic technology alliances in sectors, 1980–89 by percentage.
Source: MERIT–CATI.

growth in the number of new agreements up to 1987–8 after which there is a relative decrease in numbers of new strategic technology alliances. In information technology, by far the largest field in these core technologies, we see a long-term growth in strategic alliances, with a relatively steep rise during the first half of the eighties, followed by a short period of stabilisation after which the number of new alliances increases again. It seems that for the other fields where strategic technology partnering occurs, the growth in new agreements took place during the final years of the decade, after the number of new agreements had been quite stable throughout the other years of the period.

An explanation for these different growth patterns is somewhat difficult to offer. A disaggregated analysis of trends in strategic alliances in information technology presented elsewhere (Hagedoorn and Schakenraad, 1992), reveals that in most subfields the growth in technology partnering has stabilised with the exception of one major field of growth in inter-firm partnering – software. This particular growth pattern can to a large extent be attributed to the crucial role and increasing importance of software in linking different subfields such as computers, telecommunications, industrial automation and microelectronics. As far as the relative stagnation in strategic technology alliances in new materials is concerned we find it difficult to provide a clear explanation, apart from the general observation that, in this field as in so many other sectors, costs and problems related to the management of alliances might have created a more careful attitude from companies (see also Hagedoorn and Schakenraad, 1991a). For biotechnology the recent decline in new alliances can be explained through particular market structural aspects of inter-firm alli-

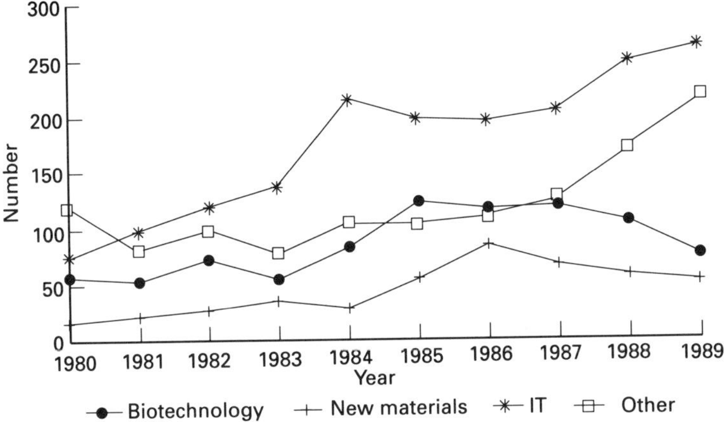

Figure 4.4 Growth of newly established strategic technology alliances in core technologies and other fields, 1980–89.
Source: MERIT–CATI.

ances in that field and a related decline in the number of certain modes of cooperation. Until the later years of the eighties a substantial part of strategic technology alliances in biotechnology was constituted of agreements made between large, multinational companies and relatively small, specialised R&D intensive firms (Hagedoorn and Schakenraad, 1990b). Minority shareholding, research contracts, or a combination of both, were major modes of cooperation between these groups of companies. However, the number of these agreements has decreased substantially in recent years. Many of the small, R&D intensive firms have been taken over by their former partners, have gone bankrupt, or are in serious economic difficulty. Consequently, a number of major cooperating companies have disappeared from the scene leading to a smaller number of potential partnerships, in particular for the modes of cooperation mentioned above.

In figure 4.4 we have already seen that non-core technologies or 'other fields of industry' show an increase in newly established strategic alliances during the second half of the eighties. This increase is in particular due to new strategic technology alliances in chemicals and, to a lesser degree, the automotive industry. In figure 4.5 both these fields first show a rather shallow curve, indicating a constant growth of new alliances, followed by a sharp increase, particularly for chemicals, during the later years of the decade. Also in aviation and defence we see a stable growth pattern with some additional growth since 1986. In heavy electrical equipment, food and beverages, and instrumentation and medical technology the general

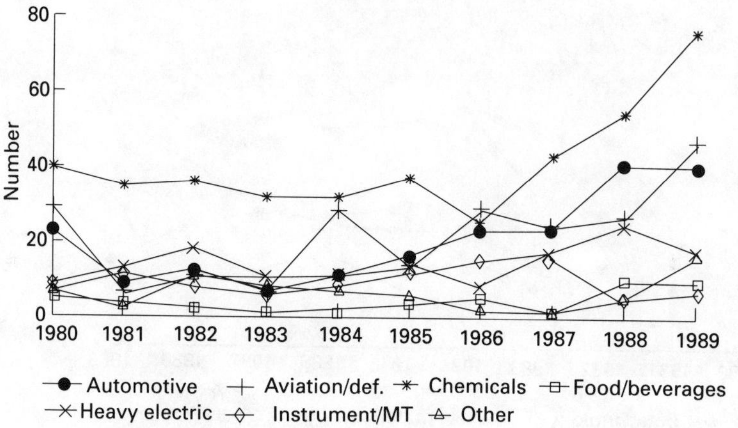

Figure 4.5 Growth of newly established strategic technology alliances in several fields of technology, 1980–89.
Source: MERIT–CATI.

pattern is one of gradual growth with a few ups and downs. The upsurge of strategic technology partnerships in chemicals, in terms of an almost doubling of the number of new agreements made in 1989 compared with the numbers of alliances made annually during the first half of the eighties, can largely be explained through post-restructuring developments in the international chemical industry. In recent years we see a growth in the number of research joint ventures and joint R&D agreements in chemicals, examples of offensive strategic agreements, which take the place of the purely defensive excess capacity-cutting agreements which characterised so much of inter-firm cooperation in chemicals during the seventies and the first half of the eighties.

So far the general pattern and trends in strategic technology partnering show that this phenomenon has become more popular in the past decade. We found that over 70 per cent of these partnerships were made in three major new core technologies, information technology, biotechnology and new materials. Although inter-sectoral differences do occur, the period of the eighties is characterised by a rapid increase of new alliances followed by a gradual decrease in the growth rate during the second half of the decade.

4.4 International and global aspects of strategic technology alliances

A number of contributions from both the management literature (see Ohmae, 1985; 1990; de Woot, 1990) and industrial (international) economics (see Cantwell, 1989; Chesnais, 1988; Contractor and Lorange, 1988; Dunning, 1988a,b; Mytelka, 1991) stress the role that strategic technology partnering plays in the internationalisation strategies of companies. If one accepts that the economy at large is becoming more internationalised one could expect a growth in international strategic technology alliances as well. In that context Ohmae (1985, 1990) emphasises the dominant role that companies from the Triad (USA, Japan and Europe) play in these international strategic technology partnerships.

In figure 4.6 we present the international distribution of strategic alliances during the first and second halves of the eighties in the three Triad regions (i.e., Europe (EC and EFTA countries), Japan and the USA) and non-Triad countries. We are aware that this 'unification' of Europe abstracts from many differences among countries regarding their economic structure. However, as far as economic key variables are concerned, variation in performance is relatively high for almost any entity whether one studies countries, regions, sectors or even individual firms. Also this does not only affect Europe; a similar degree of variation can be expected for the USA and even in Japan. Furthermore, attention in the present debate is indeed concentrated on competition among these three major blocs and related issues such as international strategic alliances.

Regarding the issue of the possible dominance of the Triad it is clear that, in the international scene for strategic technology partnering, the share of alliances with and between companies from non-Triad countries is limited to less than 10 per cent of the total number of alliances. Furthermore, this share even decreased during the second half of the eighties and a closer analysis reveals that the majority of these non-Triad alliances are related to a relatively small number of newly industrialised countries from South-East Asia.

If we look at the possible growth of the international strategic technology alliances, we will find that on the one hand there is a clear growth in absolute numbers (see appendix 2), but on the other hand, due to an overall growth, their relative share has not increased. It is obvious from figure 4.6 that intra-US cooperation takes the largest share in both periods (with 23 and 25.3 per cent), it is followed by European–US technology partnering (approximately 22 per cent), intra-European cooperation (17 and 20 per cent) and strategic alliances between companies from the USA and Japan with 11 and 14 per cent. Technology alliances between Europe and Japan, intra-Japanese cooperation and non-Triad partnering take on average a share of between 5 and 10 per cent. Although the importance of international strategic technology partnering should not be denied, it is indisputable that the share of international alliances has not increased. During the second half of the

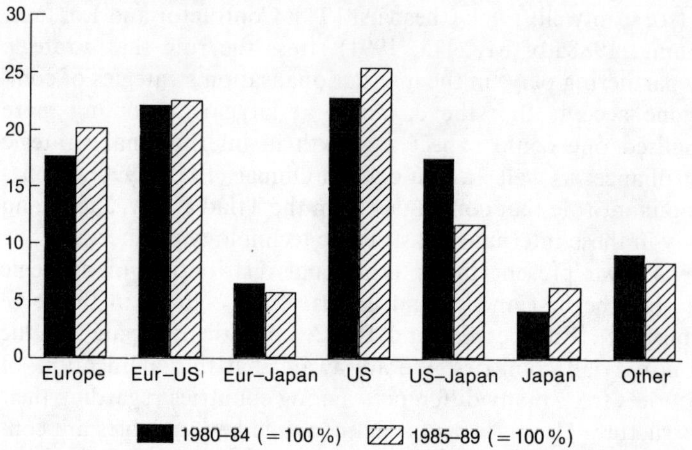

Figure 4.6 International distribution of strategic technology alliances, 1980–84 and 1985–89 by percentage.
Source: MERIT–CATI.

eighties, intra-bloc partnering, i.e., intra-European, intra-US and intra-Japanese technology alliances, has raised its proportion in all new alliances. The proportion of 'international' alliances, i.e., between companies from two international regions, has decreased with the exception of European–US technology partnering which has remained almost stable with an insignificant increase from 22.1 to 22.5 per cent.

It is not that surprising that this distribution and the general trends differ for separate fields of technology and/or industries. The exact figures regarding the international distribution of strategic technology alliances for a large number of industries and fields of technology are given in appendix 2. The main differences and peculiarities with regard to sectoral differences and changes during the eighties are presented in table 4.1. As we can see in this table the largest area of technology partnering, i.e., intra-US cooperation, is dominating the most important core technologies, i.e., information technology and biotechnology, whereas its share in new materials, chemicals, food and beverages and heavy electrical equipment is below average. Alliances between European and US companies are well represented in information technology and in instrumentation and medical technology; the share of their strategic alliances in food and beverages and in the automotive industry is clearly below average. In intra-European cooperation more 'traditional' sectors such as aviation and defence, food and beverages, and heavy electrical equipment stand out as major fields of alliances; the share of European alliances is rather

Table 4.1. *Specific features of the international distribution of strategic technology alliances*

	Large share or increase	Small share or decrease
Intra-USA (average 24%)	information technology from 22 to 30% biotech 36%	new materials 16% automotive 10% chemicals 13% food and beverages on average but decrease from 28 to 14% heavy electr, eq. 12%
Europe–USA (average 22%)	instr. and med. techn. 30%	food and beverages 16% automotive 17%
Intra-Europe (average 19%)	information technology from 13 to 20% aviation/defence 34% food and beverages 26% heavy electr. eq. 35%	automotive from 29 to 12%
USA–Japan (average 14%)	automotive 24% instr. and med. techn. 23%	aviation/defence 4% food and beverages 5% heavy electr. eq. from 15 to 5% information technology from 20 to 12%
Europe–Japan (average 6%)	automotive 11%	information technology from 9 to 5% biotech 3% aviation/defence non-existent
Intra-Japan (average 5%)	new materials from 5 to 23%	
Others, non-Triad (average 9%)	chemicals 21% automotive 17%	

Source: MERIT–CATI, see also appendix 2.

small in automotive technology. In recent years intra-European strategic technology alliances in information technology have increased. Our present material does not include alliances made in the context of European programmes such as Esprit and Eureka, but it is beyond doubt that intra-European technology cooperation in information technology has increased significantly in an attempt to counter the deteriorating competitive position of European companies vis-à-vis their US, and in particular their Japanese, competitors. In the collaboration between European and Japanese firms, which is but a small area compared to other (inter)-national combinations, only automotive stands out as a fairly relevant field of collaboration. In industrial automation European–Japanese strategic technology alliances have decreased from 21 per cent during the first half of the eighties to 6 per cent during the second half. In biotechnology, and in aviation and defence these European–Japanese partnerships are almost non-existent or very small. Strategic technology partnering between the USA and Japan is concentrated in fields such as automotive technology and instrumentation and medical technology. The share of US–Japanese alliances in information technology has dropped from 21 per cent in the first half of the eighties to a mere 12 per cent during the second half of the decade. US–Japanese cooperation is underrepresented in fields such as aviation, food and beverages, and heavy electrical equipment. Intra-Japanese strategic technology partnering is relatively small with the exception of cooperation in new materials where the share of Japanese strategic technology alliances has risen from 5 per cent to over 23 per cent in the second half of the eighties. As already pointed out above, strategic technology partnering is dominated by the Triad: Europe, USA and Japan; non-Triad alliances play only a limited role with the exception of strategic technology partnering in chemicals and automotive technology.

From the perspective of corporate behaviour we can understand (international) strategic technology partnering in the light of the internationalisation of innovative capabilities of companies. We can follow a wide range of contributions, such as those made by Cantwell, 1989; Casson, 1987; Dunning, 1988a,b; and Teece, 1986, in their understanding of multinational companies capitalising on both their market entry capabilities and their internationalisation of innovation and production. Internationalisation enables companies to use local sources of supply through externalisation in the sense of outsourcing part of their vertically related activities to local suppliers as well as engaging in market entry arrangements. For research activities internationalisation allows multinational companies to tap into local scientific and technological sources either through internalisation and investment or through contractual arrangements. Until recently, international companies would undertake research only close to or within their home countries. As indicated at the end of section 2, and as demonstrated by leading multinationals establishing research laboratories in several countries, an increasing number of firms are gradually spreading their R&D, in particular their development activities, internationally. However, economies of scale and economies of scope for research activities can limit the spread of such facilities. Therefore we can expect that the internationalisation of R&D through international strategic technology alliances will still be at a moderate level compared with partnerships which are more

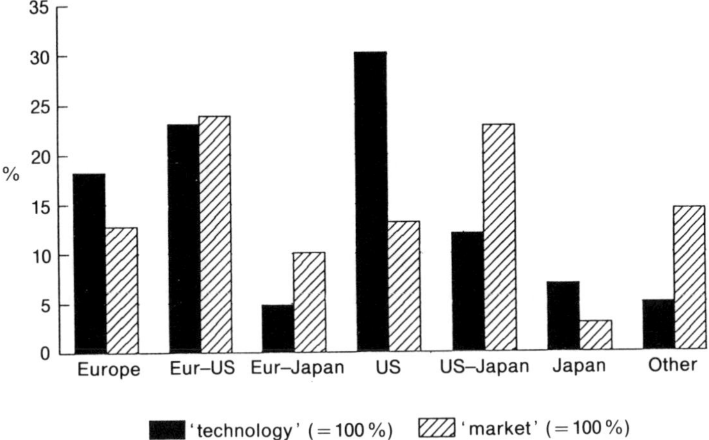

Figure 4.7 International distribution of technology and market-dominated strategic technology alliances 1980–89 by percentage.
Source: MERIT–CATI.

directly related to commercial activities such as market entry arrangements.

Our data enable us to differentiate strategic technology partnerships into alliances that are primarily related to R&D, which we label as technology dominated alliances, and strategic alliances for which market access, despite their technology content, is still more important. Such an analysis can teach us for instance whether strategic alliances of a more R&D oriented nature are more internationally focused or concentrated within each region of the Triad. The relevant distribution is given in figure 4.7; the outcomes for subperiods did not show very large differences, which allows us to present only the distribution for the period of the eighties as a whole. Our background statistical material as presented in appendix 3 shows that the share of market related alliances decreased slightly from 34 to 31 per cent, the share of R&D dominated technology alliances increased from 51 per cent during the first half of the decade to 63 per cent during the second half.

In figure 4.7 we can see that R&D centred technology alliances are most apparent in intra-US alliances and in partnering between European and US companies, and intra-European alliances. In general it can be stated that, with the exception of European–US agreements, intra-bloc partnering is inclined to be of a more 'pure' technology dominated character, whereas market related strategic technology alliances are more internationally oriented. (Additional material not presented in this chapter shows that this holds for practically all fields of technology or sectors of industry.)

So, confirming the implicit hypothesis discussed above, R&D driven alliances tend to be less international and still closer to the original home bases of companies. Apparently, the international character of strategic technology partnering is more apparent when companies use these alliances for their international market access activities.

In the next step in our analysis we will take a closer look at the pattern of internationalisation of strategic technology alliances from the perspective of companies. In the management and business-studies literature in particular, a debate has emerged about the direction and character of the internationalisation of corporate behaviour (see Bartlett, 1986; Ghoshal, 1987; Kogut, 1989; Ohmae, 1985; Porter, 1986, 1990). If this debate is related to corporate behaviour regarding strategic technology partnering the main question is then: does the share of international and global alliances of companies engaged in strategic technology partnering gradually increase? In other words, we will have to find out whether a possible globalisation of the economy and a globalisation of corporate strategies do show up in the international pattern of collaborating firms. A first impression of this relationship is given in figure 4.8. Contrary to the previous empirical material the object of study is not the alliances as such but the companies involved.

In order to analyse the international character of collaborative corporate strategies we have made a distinction between companies with a regional technology partnering strategy, an international strategy and a global technology partnering strategy:

Companies that follow a regional strategy are those of which over 60 per cent of their alliances are made with partners from their own international region, i.e., within Europe, Japan, the USA or, for non-Triad companies, their own country.

An international strategy refers to those remaining companies whose non-regional alliances are over 60 per cent found in one other international region.

Companies with global technology partnering strategies constitute the 'residual' of companies with a relatively large share of strategic technology alliances in a number of international regions.

As we can see in appendix 4, the number of internationally and globally partnering companies in our databank has increased by approximately 50 per cent if we compare the first half of the eighties with the second half. However, as the total number of collaborating companies has also increased, little has changed in relative terms (see figure 4.8). During the first half of the eighties more than 50 per cent of the

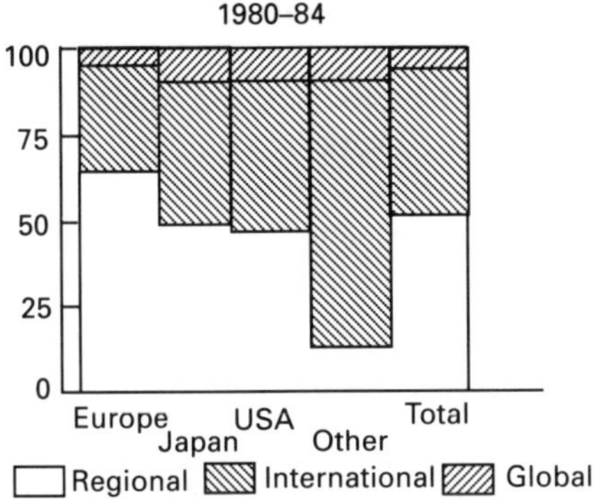

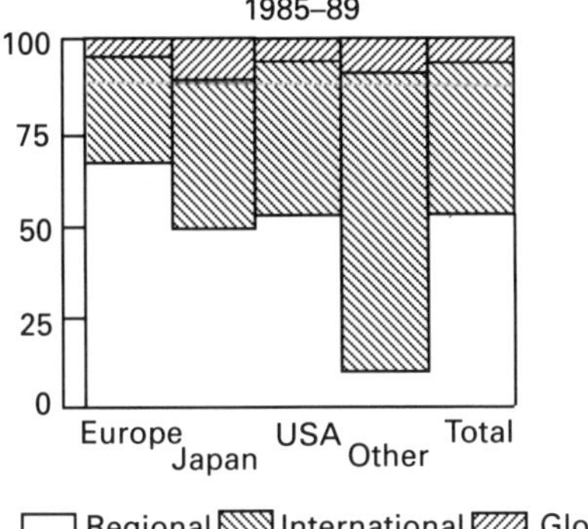

Figure 4.8 International distribution of companies with regional, international and global technology partnering strategies, 1980–84 and 1985–89 by percentage. Source: MERIT–CATI.

collaborating firms followed a regional strategy, over 40 per cent can be characterised as having an international strategy, whereas only 6.5 per cent of the companies appear to follow a global technology partnering strategy. By and large very little seems to have changed in the relative position of each of these strategies during the second half of the eighties.

If we look at the distribution of strategies according to region, we notice that some differences do occur; one has to be somewhat careful with this comparison because Europe, i.e., EC and EFTA countries, is the world's largest market and a comparison of the three regions in terms of the pattern of internationalisation is certainly not in favour of Europe. It is obvious that in both periods European companies have on average a partnering strategy which is most 'regionally' and least globally oriented.

Two-thirds of the European companies in our databank follow a regional strategy in their technology alliances, only about half of the Japanese and US companies are that clearly focused on their own region. Approximately 30 per cent of the European companies and 40 per cent of the Japanese and US companies have a technology partnering strategy that we can characterise as international. In particular Japanese companies appear to follow a global strategy with a share that has increased from nearly 9 per cent during the first half of the eighties to 10.5 per cent during the second half. They are followed by US companies of which the proportion of companies with a global partnering strategy has decreased from 8.1 to 7.3 per cent. Finally, although their share has slightly increased during the second half of the eighties, only 3.6 per cent of the European companies follow a global partnering strategy.

4.5 Some concluding remarks

In this chapter we have made an attempt to understand strategic technology alliances in the context of the process of internationalisation that characterises economic development in the postwar period. Major changes in that period are the growth of European and Japanese foreign direct investment, partly replacing international trade, the internationalisation of R&D and technology flows and, as a part of all this, the growing role being played by Japanese and European firms.

Against this general background of increased international competition one has to understand the policy of leading international companies with respect to corporate flexibility which is seen as compulsory for their successful operation. Strategic alliances can play a major role in achieving this flexibility through the choice of a variety of partners in a number of activities of an internationally operating firm. For strategic technology alliances we have made a distinction between several internationally oriented strategies, with global strategy characterised by a more or less balanced distribution of worldwide technology alliances.

If we look at our empirical findings we have to conclude that strategic technology alliances in the eighties probably did play a role in the process of internationalisation of the economy but their importance should not be overstated. In absolute numbers strategic technology alliances related to international and global presence have increased during the eighties, but so have more regionally and domestically related alliances. During the eighties there has been no increase of the share of inter-regional or international alliances in strategic technology partnerships. Furthermore, for R&D related strategic technology alliances we found that intraregional partnering i.e., cooperation within Europe, the USA or Japan, has gained even more importance. As far as the technology partnering strategies of companies are concerned, only in 6 per cent of the companies that we studied did we find a true global partnering strategy. In particular European companies were found to be least globally oriented in their strategic technology alliances compared to their main competitors i.e., Japanese and US companies.

The consequences of these findings for the competitive positioning of European companies vis-à-vis their global competitors are at present not that obvious. The economic effects of strategic technology partnering on companies are difficult to disentangle and such a complicated issue is beyond the scope of our present contribution (see Hagedoorn and Schakenraad, 1991b). It is obvious that there are dangers in inter-firm cooperation both internationally and domestically. There are examples of true joint efforts where companies build real alliances and where we will see a win–win situation. However, there are also many examples of strategic technology alliances where one of the partners attempts to extract technology or to gain market access on the account of the other(s). Despite these dangers strategic technology partnering can enhance the flexibility of a company through partnering as a monitoring device and also through incorporating a wider variety of technological sources than its intrinsic ones. In particular for those companies that have not achieved the position of market leader but which are still relevant players, strategic technology alliances with competent partners can improve their competitive position.

However, as we have seen, US and Japanese companies tend to be more internationally and globally oriented in their technology alliances than their European competitors. The latter are, on average, more 'regional' in their collaborative strategy, which is not a major problem for those fields of technology where Europe plays a leading role. For those sectors where European companies are in general not at the leading edge of technological development, and many studies suggest that this is the case in quite a number of sectors, a very strong emphasis on intra-European technology partnering could, in the long run, be a dangerous strategy for those European companies that are forced to compete in global markets. Many European companies have improved their international competitive position during the seventies and eighties. For a further improvement in particular in global markets an intelligent utilisation of strategic alliances could very well be beneficial. It has to be stressed that these partnerships are not to be seen as panaceas as even a very rational and intelligent application of them can only partly contribute to the improvement of the competitive positioning of European companies.

Appendix 1 The cooperative agreements and technology indicators (CATI) information system

The CATI databank is a relational database which contains separate data files that can be linked to each other and provide (dis)aggregate and combined information from several files. So far information on nearly 10,000 cooperative agreements involving some 3,500 different parent companies has been collected.

Systematic collection of inter-firm alliances started in 1986. If available, many sources from earlier years were consulted enabling us to take a retrospective view. In order to collect inter-firm alliances we consulted various sources, of which the most important are newspaper and journal articles, books dealing with the subject, and in particular specialist journals which report on business events. Company annual reports, the *Financial Times Industrial Companies Yearbook* and Dun & Bradstreet's *Who Owns Whom* provide information about dissolved equity ventures and investments, as well as ventures that we did not register when surveying alliances.

This method of information gathering which we might call 'literature-based alliance counting' has its drawbacks and limitations:

In general we have only come to know those arrangements that are made public by the companies themselves.

Newspaper and journal reports are likely to be incomplete, especially when they are historical and/or regard firms from countries outside the scope of the journal. Furthermore, in earlier years some journals simply did not exist whereas existing periodicals might grasp the collaboration subject less thoroughly.

A low profile of small firms without well-established names is likely to have their collaborative links excluded.

Some journals emphasise fashionable items, such as superconductivity or HDTV, while interest in 'outdated' topics such as solar and wind energy seems to fade away.

The fact that we read mainly articles written in English probably causes some bias and distortion as well.

Another problem is that information about the dissolution of agreements is not systematically published. This is in particular true for licensing and customer–supplier relationships. On the other hand, research contracts and joint product developments have often disclosed time schedules. Equity joint venture and dissolutions of investments are published rather systematically in specialist journals.

One final problem is that the number of customer–supplier relations and licensing agreements is subject to a fierce underestimation due to the fact that these more casual agreements are little reported publicly, even in the professional literature.

All together, these handicaps in the first place lead to a skewed distribution of modes of cooperation, followed by some geographic – i.e., Anglo-Saxon – bias. Next, we have to reckon with a possible underestimation of certain technological fields and finally, there is some overrepresentation of large firms.

Despite these shortcomings, which are largely unsolvable even in a situation of extensive and large-scale data collection, we think we have been able to produce a clear picture of the joint efforts of many companies. This enables us to perform empirical research which goes beyond case studies or general statements. Some of the weaknesses of the database can easily be avoided by focusing on the more reliable parts, such as strategic alliances.

The databank contains information on each agreement and some information on companies participating in these agreements. The first entity is the inter-firm cooperative agreement. We define cooperative agreements as common interests between independent (industrial) partners which are not connected through (majority) ownership. In the CATI database only those inter-firm agreements that contain some arrangements for transferring technology or joint research are being collected. Joint research pacts, second-sourcing and licensing agreements are clear-cut examples. We also collect information on joint ventures in which new technology is received from at least one of the partners, or joint ventures having some R&D programme. Mere production or marketing joint ventures are excluded. In other words, our analysis is primarily related to technology cooperation. We are discussing those forms of cooperation and agreements for which a combined innovative activity or an exchange of technology is at least part of the agreement. Consequently, partnerships are omitted that regulate no more than the sharing of production facilities, the setting of standards, collusive behaviour in price-setting and raising entry barriers – although all of these may be side effects of inter-firm cooperation as we define it.

We regard as a relevant input of information for each alliance: the number of companies involved; names of companies (or important subsidiaries); year of establishment, time-horizon, duration and year of dissolution; capital investments and involvement of banks and research institutes or universities; field(s) of technology; modes of cooperation; and some comment or available information about progress. Depending on the very form of cooperation we collect information on the operational context; the name of the agreement or project; equity sharing; the direction of capital or technology flows; the degree of participation in case of minority holdings; some information about motives underlying the alliance; the character of cooperation, such as basic research, applied research, or product development possibly associated with production and/or marketing arrangements. In some cases we also indicate who has benefited most.

Appendix 2 Distribution of strategic technology alliances within and between economic blocs, 1980–1984 and 1985–1989

Table 4A.1. *Distribution of strategic technology alliances within and between economic blocs, for biotechnology, new materials, IT, and other technologies, 1980–84 and 1985–89*

	Biotechnology			New materials			Information technology			Other technologies			Total		
	80–84	85–89	total	80–84	85–89	total	80–84	85–89	total	80–84	85–89	total	80–84	85–89	total
Europe	47 14.8	95 18.0	142 16.8	29 23.4	44 14.4	73 17.0	85 13.3	217 19.9	302 17.5	115 24.1	173 24.4	288 24.3	276 17.7	529 20.1	805 19.2
Europe –USA	58 18.2	124 23.5	182 21.5	32 25.8	52 17.0	84 19.5	158 24.6	256 23.5	414 23.9	97 20.3	161 22.7	258 21.7	345 22.1	593 22.5	938 22.4
Europe –Japan	5 1.6	20 3.8	25 3.0	15 12.1	23 7.5	38 8.8	57 8.9	57 5.2	114 6.6	24 5.0	50 7.0	74 6.2	101 6.5	150 5.7	251 6.0
USA	125 39.3	179 33.9	304 35.9	16 12.9	54 17.6	70 16.3	142 22.2	323 29.7	465 26.9	74 15.5	111 15.6	185 15.6	357 22.9	667 25.3	1024 24.4
USA –Japan	45 14.2	54 10.2	99 11.7	16 12.9	40 13.1	56 13.0	133 20.7	132 12.1	265 15.3	80 16.8	83 11.7	163 13.7	274 17.6	309 11.7	583 13.9
Japan	11 3.5	33 6.3	44 5.2	7 5.6	71 23.2	78 18.1	29 4.5	35 3.2	64 3.7	13 3.8	24 3.4	42 3.5	65 4.2	163 6.2	228 5.4
Other	27 8.5	23 4.4	50 5.9	9 7.3	22 7.2	31 7.2	37 5.8	68 6.3	105 6.1	69 14.5	108 15.2	177 14.9	142 9.1	221 8.4	363 8.7
	318 100%	528 100%	846 100%	124 100%	306 100%	430 100%	641 100%	1088 100%	1729 100%	477 100%	710 100%	1187 100%	1560 100%	2632 100%	4192 100%

Source: MERIT–CATI.

Table 4A.2. *Distribution of strategic technology alliances within and between economic blocs, for other technologies, 1980–84 and 1985–89*

	Automotive			Aviation/defence			Chemicals		
	80–84	85–89	total	80–84	85–89	total	80–84	85–89	total
Europe	18 29.0	18 12.6	36 17.6	25 28.7	53 37.6	78 34.2	34 19.4	42 17.9	76 18.5
Europe–USA	10 16.1	24 16.8	34 16.6	24 27.6	31 22.0	55 24.1	31 17.7	54 23.0	85 20.7
Europe–Japan	6 9.7	16 11.2	22 10.7	1 1.1	0 0.0	1 0.4	14 8.0	21 8.9	35 8.5
USA	2 3.2	17 11.9	19 9.3	21 24.1	41 29.1	62 27.2	21 12.0	31 13.2	52 12.7
USA–Japan	10 16.1	39 27.3	49 23.9	7 8.0	3 2.1	10 4.4	35 20.0	28 11.9	63 15.4
Japan	2 3.2	7 4.9	9 4.4	2 2.3	4 2.8	6 2.6	6 3.4	6 2.6	12 2.9
Other	14 22.6	22 15.4	36 17.6	7 8.0	9 6.4	16 7.0	34 19.4	53 22.6	87 21.2
	62 100%	143 100%	205 100%	87 100%	141 100%	228 100%	175 100%	235 100%	410 100%
	Food & beverages			**Heavy electric/energy**			**Instruments/MT**		
	80–84	85–89	total	80–84	85–89	total	80–84	85–89	total
Europe	3 21.4	8 28.6	11 26.2	19 31.1	30 37.5	49 34.8	6 14.3	13 24.5	19 20.0
Europe–USA	3 21.4	4 14.3	7 16.7	13 21.3	22 27.5	35 24.8	9 21.4	19 35.8	28 29.5
Europe–Japan	2 14.3	2 7.1	4 9.5	0 0.0	4 5.0	4 2.8	0 0.0	6 11.3	6 6.3
USA	4 28.6	4 14.3	8 19.0	11 18.0	6 7.5	17 12.1	8 19.0	9 17.0	17 17.9
USA–Japan	0 0.0	2 7.1	2 4.8	9 14.8	4 5.0	13 9.2	17 40.5	5 9.4	22 23.2
Japan	0 0.0	0 0.0	0 0.0	4 6.6	6 7.5	10 7.1	2 4.8	1 1.9	3 3.2
Other	2 14.3	8 28.6	10 23.8	5 8.2	8 10.0	13 9.2	0 0.0	0 0.0	0 0.0
	14 100%	28 100%	42 100%	61 100%	80 100%	141 100%	42 100%	53 100%	95 100%

Source: MERIT–CATI.

Appendix 3. 'Market' versus 'technology' motives for newly established strategic technology alliances, by sector, 1980–1984 and 1985–1989

	Market access/			R&D/technology/		
	80–84	85–89	total	80–84	85–89	total
Biotechnology	9%	15%	13%	70%	86%	80%
New materials technology	44%	26%	31%	47%	73%	66%
Information technology	44%	36%	39%	50%	61%	57%
Automotive	45%	55%	52%	47%	41%	43%
Aviation/defence	13%	16%	15%	66%	62%	63%
Chemicals	50%	51%	51%	22%	36%	30%
Food and beverages	57%	36%	43%	29%	21%	24%
Heavy electrical equipment	23%	24%	23%	59%	30%	43%
Instruments/medical technology	36%	23%	28%	57%	76%	67%
Other	17%	30%	23%	17%	17%	17%
Total	34%	31%	32%	51%	63%	58%

Source: MERIT–CATI.

Appendix 4. Regionalisation, internationalisation and globalisation of strategic technology linkages, for companies, by sector, by economic bloc, 1980–1984 and 1985–1989

	European firms		American firms		Japanese firms		Other		Total	
	80–84	85–89	80–84	85–89	80–84	85–89	80–84	85–89	80–84	85–89
Regional	351 66.4	516 67.1	269 47.4	486 52.7	103 50.2	133 50.0	22 14.2	26 10.0	745 51.2	1161 52.3
International	162 30.6	225 29.3	252 44.4	369 40.0	84 41.0	105 39.5	118 76.1	210 80.5	616 42.3	909 41.0
Global	16 3.0	28 3.6	46 8.1	67 7.3	18 8.8	28 10.5	15 9.7	25 9.6	95 6.5	148 6.7
	529 100%	769 100%	567 100%	922 100%	205 100%	266 100%	155 100%	261 100%	1456 100%	2218 100%

Source: MERIT–CATI.

Note

This paper is one of a series of papers in a research project on 'Inter-company Cooperation and Technological Development' at MERIT. This research focuses on the empirical analysis of changes in industry structures and global trends in different modes of inter-firm strategic technology alliances in a large number of fields of technology. Research for this paper was partly financed by the MONITOR-FAST programme of the Directorate General XII of the Commission of the European Communities. We wish to thank Kirsty Hughes, Christine Oughton, and other members of the WZB Workshop on European Competitiveness for comments.

References

Bartlett, C. A. 1986. 'Building and managing the transnational: the organizational challenge', in M. E. Porter (ed.), *Competition in Global Industries*, Boston: HBS Press.

Cantwell, J. 1989. *Technological Innovation and Multinational Corporations*, Oxford: Basil Blackwell.

Casson, M. 1987. *The Firm and the Market*, Oxford: Basil Blackwell.

Chandler, A. D. Jr. 1986. 'The evolution of modern global competition', in M. E. Porter (ed.), *Competition in Global Industries*, Boston: HBS Press.

Chesnais, F. 1988. 'Multinational enterprises and the international diffusion of technology', in G. Dosi, C. Freeman, R. Nelson, G. Silverberg and L. Soete (eds.), *Technical Change and Economic Theory*, London: Pinter.

Contractor, F. J. and Lorange, P. 1988. *Cooperative Strategies in International Business*, Lexington: Lexington Books.

Dunning, J. H. 1988a. *Explaining International Production*, London: Unwin Hyman.

1988b. *Multinationals, Technology and Competitiveness*, London: Unwin Hyman.

Franko, L. G. 1989. 'Global corporate competition: who's winning, who's losing, and the R&D factor as a reason why', *Strategic Management Journal*, 10.

Ghoshal, S. 1987. 'Global strategy: an organizing framework', *Strategic Management Journal*, 8.

Glickman, N. J. and Woodward, D. P. 1990. *The New Competitors*, New York: Basic Books.

Hagedoorn, J. and Schakenraad, J. 1990a. 'Strategic partnering and technological cooperation', in B. Dankbaar, J. Groenewegen and H. Schenk (eds.), *Perspectives in Industrial Economics*, Dordrecht: Kluwer.

1990b. 'Inter-firm partnerships and cooperative strategies in core technologies', in C. Freeman and L. Soete (eds.), *New Explorations in the Economics of Technical Change*, London: Pinter.

1990c. *Technology Cooperation, Strategic Alliances and their Motives: Brother, Can You Spare a Dime, or Do You Have a Light?*, MERIT paper.

1991a. 'Inter-firm partnerships for generic technologies – the case of new materials', *Technovation*, 11 (7).

1991b. *The Economic Effects of Strategic Partnerships and Technology Cooperation*, MERIT paper.

1992. 'Leading companies and networks of strategic alliances in information technologies', *Research Policy*, 21.

Haklisch, C. S. 1986. *Technical Alliances in the Semiconductor Industry*, New York: mimeo NYU, New York.

Hergert, M. and Morris, D. 1988. 'Trends in international collaborative agreements', in F. J. Contractor, and P. Lorange (eds.), *Cooperative Strategies in International Business*, Lexington: Lexington Books.

Hladik, K. J. 1985. *International Joint Ventures*, Lexington: Lexington Books.

Kogut, B. 1989. 'A note on global strategies', *Strategic Management Journal*, 10.

Mytelka, L. K. 1991. *Strategic Partnerships and the World Economy*, London: Pinter.

OECD 1986. *Technical Cooperation Agreements Between Firms: Some Initial Data and Analysis*, Paris: OECD.

1990. *Industrial Policy in OECD Countries, Annual Review*, Paris: OECD.

Ohmae, K. 1985. *Triad Power*, New York: Free Press.

1990. *The Borderless World*, New York: Harper Business.

Porter, M. 1986 (ed.). *Competition in Global Industries*, Boston: HBS Press.

1990. *The Competitive Advantage of Nations*, New York: Free Press.

Soete, L. 1991. *Technology in a Changing World*, Paris: OECD.

Teece, D. J. 1986. 'Transactions cost economics and the multinational enterprise: an assessment', *Journal of Economic Organization and Behavior*, 7.

UNCTC 1988. *Transnational Corporations in World Development – Trends and Prospects*, New York: United Nations.

de Woot, P. 1990 (ed.). *High Technology Europe: Strategic Issues for Global Competitiveness*, Oxford: Basil Blackwell.

5 Corporate control and competitiveness: the French case

DANIELLE GALLIANO and ALAIN ALCOUFFE

5.1 Introduction

O. E. Williamson has convincingly argued that the organisation of firms should be taken into consideration to explain Japanese and American economic performance (Williamson, 1985). Recent advances in the theory of the firm have also emphasised the role of a number of factors in competitiveness. The presence of these factors is supposed to explain why plant and equipment earn more profits if they are owned by one corporation rather than by another. These factors include particular technological skills, complementary assets and efficient routines (Dosi *et al.*, 1991). It can be argued that the corporate control and its efficiency are central features of organisation and are skills which analysis of competitiveness must take into account.

The protection that surrounded domestic capital markets and the control of foreign investment flows have given specific characteristics to corporate control in the individual European countries. West Germany and France, to quote but two countries, present marked contrasts. The superior postwar performance of German firms has often been attributed to the close relation between banks and industry (Cable, 1985). In France, the existence of 'groups' of firms, connecting non-financial and financial companies and benefiting from administrative influences, has given rise to industrial achievement, but has been accused of having weakened smaller businesses (LEREP, 1987).

The aim of this chapter is to analyse the role of corporate control as an intermediation between ownership and management. We concentrate on the French M-form of organisation – the groups – and ask why more and more firms (of different size) are adopting this kind of structure. Our hypothesis is that this form is associated with better performance related to internal efficiency (and thus gives a competitive advantage).

In section 2 attention is given to the special historical features of the

French case. We conclude that not much attention has been paid to the influence of size in the comparisons between groups and independent firms. In section 3, our hypothesis is confronted with empirical evidence using data collected on food industries.

5.2 French group structure and efficiency

During the two last decades, despite the lack of a legal definition of 'groups', several studies have introduced this notion to take into account the way in which the organisation of large firms evolved. Investigations by LEREP (a team of economists based in Toulouse) analysed the structure of the 500 largest firms between 1964 and 1984 (LEREP, 1987). As the ownership, control and structure of large firms were severely hit by public policies during the eighties it is necessary to present a historical survey of French groups.

The first analysis of the control of the 500 largest firms proved that the control categories used by Berle and Means in their seminal book did not fit the French case. In the latter, family control and majority control remained predominant, although sets of firms appeared to have a scattered ownership and to be connected through financial links. These links may take various intricate forms so that the ownership and control of each firm had to be scrutinised in order to delimit the different 'groups' that can be defined as a set of companies in hierarchic order, tied together by financial links and controlled by one centre. Do the French groups belong to the Multidivisional-form or the Holding-form of firm categories that appear frequently in the economic literature? The question arises because every 'unit' belonging to a 'group' remains legally autonomous and because in many cases control does not require majority ownership. If we are to observe the distinction made by Cable (1987, p. 13) that relative to the M-form firm the H-form 'though divisionalised, lacks the requisite general office functions', it appears that all firms involved in French groups are controlled by a headquarters in an outside unit that performs most (if not all) 'general office functions', i.e., long term strategic decisions, choice of top management and connection with the capital market and the banking system. In this sense, several French groups can be traced back to the second part of the nineteenth century. But they grew significantly between the years 1960 and 1970. During these years, the major French groups exhibited special features:

(a) a great number of shareholders of the parent company, each holding less than 10 per cent of the stock, but among them a few could be presumed to be interested in the control, without playing a decisive part;

Table 5.1. *The evolution of control over the 500 largest French firms*

	Family Control	State Control	Technocratical Control	Co-operative control	Foreign control	Total
1975						
Percentage of capital	30.4	35.4	17.2	1.0	16.0	243 billion FF
Number of firms	212	53	70	20	88	443[a]
1981						
Percentage of capital	17.2	54.5	14.1	0.8	13.4	500 billion FF
Number of firms	158	83	62	24	140	467[a]
1984						
Percentage of firms	18.6	58.3	14.1	1.0	15.3	520 billion FF
Number of firms	151	135	32	24	133	475[a]

Note: [a] The number of firms is less than 500 because several firms are under joint control.

(b) a board of directors without any link with owners and often coopted from the upper level of civil servants;
(c) minority control of most of the affiliates of the group.

This special mixture distinguishes 'groups' from firms under management control and was labelled by Morin (1975) 'technocratic control'. This kind of structure developed from the two historical models of technocratic groups (Paribas and Suez) and became the usual form connected with external growth for the larger firms during the 1970s.

The nationalisation of 1981 involved few parent firms but as the heads of the major groups were involved, the consequences spread through a large part of the French economy. The restructuring of the nationalised firms, and then the privatisation of 1986, have modified the shape of French groups. Minority control became ever less due to fear of take-overs, while the global concentration of capital decreased in the French economy. Nevertheless, the group structure continues to spread outside the top 100 or 200 largest firms presumably because of their internal efficiency in the French surroundings.

The hypothesis put forward here is that, at least in theory, the group organisation of firms induces more efficiency than the traditional structure of the independent firm. This enhanced efficiency represents an organisational advantage, connected to a group structure.

The issue of the efficiency of different types of organisation has in the majority of publications been directed mainly towards testing the

Table 5.2. *The evolution of the type of control over the 500 largest French firms*

	1975	1981	1984
Majority ownership	49.00	55.80	60.40
Minority control	37.80	30.60	27.80
Management control	2.00	2.40	2.40
Cooperatives	4.00	4.60	4.40
Joint control	7.20	6.60	5.00
	100	100	100

Note: All figures denote the percentage among the 500 largest French firms.
Sources: Tables 5.1 and 5.2 are taken from LEREP (1987 p. 31).

superiority of the multidivisional structure, thus developing the early work of Coase, Williamson and Chandler. In this context, numerous studies have been carried out in the framework of various national economies; the USA, the UK and Japan have been the main targets, while European countries and in particular France (where the H or holding structure tends to predominate) have rarely come under scrutiny.

The superiority of the multidivisional structure over the unified structure is generally agreed on, although often there are reservations, such as in the case of the USA (Teece, 1981; Chandler, 1982) and the UK (Thompson 1983). The tests have been less conclusive for West Germany (Cable and Dirrheimer, 1983; Bühner, 1985). The different conclusions may stem from choices made concerning samples, efficiency criteria and statistical and econometric methods. Moreover, as Cable (1987) has pointed out 'the M-form is not culture-free'. Results are sometimes markedly influenced by certain national characeristics, such as national industrial legislation (the H-form is banned by anti-trust legislation in Japan) or the workings of industrial and banking systems (e.g., the role of the Deutsche Bank in West Germany).

Moreover the majority of quantitative studies are based on samples restricted to the major firms of a given nation. Results are, therefore, influenced by the effects of size (Chang and Choi, 1988) and, furthermore, the specific characteristics resulting from membership of a particular industrial sector are not taken into account.

Tests on group structure of firms within the French economy are even fewer. Two main reasons explain why there has been little development of quantitative studies in France. The first stems from the fact that, until 1986, French 'groups', unlike their American counterparts, had no legal existence. It was not until a law of January 1985 concerning consolidated accounts, and its application in 1986, that it was first possible to distinguish the legal existence of the group entity. Affiliates were, until that time, considered as autonomous, and they maintain their legal independence today.

Secondly it was only in 1980 that French censuses took into account the existence of groups of firms. The investigation into financial linkages between firms (the so-called 'Enquête Liaisons Financières; ELF') carried out by the French National Institute of Statistics (INSEE) documented the financial linkages existing between firms present on French territory.[1] This study permitted an exhaustive reconstitution of current groups and an assessment of their role in the French system of production (Thollon Pommerol, 1982).

Concerning the efficiency of French groups, reference must be made to the work of Encaoua and Jacquemin (1982) who studied 319 of the major French groups. The objective was to analyse the respective influence of efficiency and market power in the predominance of the group structure in certain sectors of French industry. In industries where the predominance of groups was not the result of organisational factors (economies of scale, internationalisation, extensive capital requirements, etc.), the quest for monopoly control became the central determining factor.

Still closer to our theme: a recent study conducted by Beau (1991) on the effects of membership of a group on the results of French firms. This study compares two samples of 800 affiliates and independents, with comparable size and sector characteristics. Within this framework the author reaches the conclusion that the organisational efficiency of groups was greater than that of independent firms. The group-controlled firms were distinguished by higher labour productivity and financial yield, indicative of greater efficiency in the management of the means of production. Their financial health is again greater than for the independents. On the other hand, the conclusions are somewhat ambiguous when it comes to economic performance.

5.3 The test of the organisational advantage: the case of the French food industry

In order to develop and enhance this type of work our quantitative study on the French situation concentrated on two objectives. On the one hand we aimed to neutralise the sector effect by working on only one major French production sector, while on the other hand we chose to work on an exhaustive population of firms, taking into account all the groups and independent firms working in the sector under scrutiny.

The food sector is characterised by a variety of types of groups, ranging from the small structure resembling the traditional firm, to the major industrial and financial groups. This diversity makes it possible to avoid several forms of bias, in particular that of an excessive influence or predominance of a particular type of group.

The data on which this chapter is based were collected by INSEE, which provided us with specific information on the groups and independent firms in the food sector.[2] This information allowed us to determine the control of each firm under scrutiny so that the 'groups' in the following analysis include firms under minority control.

The empirical handling of these data was aimed at comparing structural and performance characteristics in the following ways:

In relation to the economic units studied, by comparing the results of independent firms with groups of companies of the same size; this will help to identify the *effect of organisation* on efficiency.

In relation to firms, by comparing the results of controlled firms with those of independent firms of the same size. In this case, the comparison of the two types of unit will make it possible to underline the *effect of structure* on efficiency.

The food industry being composed of several subsectors, there remains to be tested, thirdly, the existence of an influence of sectoral factors – *the intra-sector effect.*

5.3.1 Organisational effect

The group structure theoretically makes it possible to maintain a fine balance between the costs of transactions and organisational costs. Market related transaction costs are diminished by internalising resources and functions within the groups. On the same lines the multifirm structure makes possible better management of the centralisation/decentralisation of strategic and operational decisions and minimisation of organisational costs. This latter aspect tends to favour, from an efficiency standpoint, structuring by groups of firms, rather than a legally unified multidivisional set-up. Management through profit centres takes place at two levels: that of the divisions in terms of products/markets, and that of legal units making up the affiliates and partly owned subsidiaries. The legal separation of units within a given group also provides significant flexibility in choices of strategic involvement or withdrawal. These various organisational advantages play a significant role as far as the independent firm is concerned, even if the two organisations are of equivalent size.

The financial linkage enquiry (by the French National Institute of Statistics) made it possible to identify 172 groups controlling 481 firms in

Table 5.3. *Structure and performance of groups and independent firms*

	Independents				Groups				
Size category	20 < 200	200 < 500	500 < 1000	Total	20 < 200	200 < 500	500 < 1000	< 1000	Total
Number of firms	2318	107	27	2452	15	27	35	39	116
Mean figures:[a]									
Employees	52	295	611	68	158	319	696	4153	1701
Pre-tax turnover	64 093	362 821	744 381	84 620	361 767	621 802	1 035 537	5 542 884	2 367 512
Export turnover	6587	44 843	90 292	9 179	96 424	98 699	109 907	921 956	378 571
Capital by head	261	281	219	260	574	434	326	372	371
Value added (VA)	11 573	63 540	112 158	14 950	71 837	93 010	166 474	1 273 609	509 364
Gross Cash Flow (GCF)	3417	18 187	32 426	4381	28 713	35 690	50 298	478 350	188 021
Margins (GCF/VA)	29.5	28.5	28.9	29.3	40.0	38.4	30.2	37.6	36.9
Gross Margins (GCF/GVA)	31.5	29.9	28.5	30.9	49.9	40.6	32.6	39.0	38.6
Labour Productivity	1227	1229	1216	1226	2281	1943	1487	1334	1391
Salary	145	147	141	145	203	172	158	184	181

Note: [a] In thousands of current francs; GVA: Gross value added; Gross Cash Flow: 'Excédent brut d'exploitation'.
Source: EAE ELF, 1987.

the food industry and a further 708 firms whose main activity lies in other industrial sectors. These units represent 17 per cent of the 2,934 foodstuff firms listed in 1987. Among these 172 groups, 116 have a production base in foodstuff and 66 have as their main activity trading or other branches of production. The latter were excluded from the first part of the study in order to avoid any sector-based bias which they might have introduced.

The analysis of structural characteristics and performance brings to light significant discrepancies between groups and independent firms (see table 5.3). The major groups, with over 1,000 employees, strongly affect the overall mean values of the sector through their superiority over both smaller groups and independent firms. These groups largely dominate the French foodstuff sector through their economic weight and their strategic dynamic (Galliano, 1990). However at this level, as there are no longer independent firms of the same size, direct comparisons are not possible, but the 'survivor' argument suggests that groups have greater organisational efficiency.

On the other hand when comparing similar sizes, whatever the size category in terms of total labour force, groups distinguish themselves by greater economic profitability, by higher performance in terms of turnover and exports, and by better productivity. The discrepancies in structure and performance increase as size diminishes. These discrepancies are already considerable between groups and independent firms in the 500–1,000 employee category. The turnover and the gross operating profit of these groups together with the value added created by their activity are 50 per cent higher. They have higher margins and are more competitive in exports. These groups are characterised by greater operating capital compared to number of employees (326 as against 219). The productivity of their employees is greater (+22 per cent) and goes hand in hand with higher remuneration.

These discrepancies grow for units of 200 to 500 employees. In the last resort it is the small groups of fewer than 200 employees which possess the most noticeable organisational advantage over independent firms. Their turnover, their added value, and their gross operating profits are around three times higher and their productivity per capita is markedly greater (+50 per cent). These small groups are distinguished by a high level of capitalisation and a strong export dynamic compared to independent firms of the same size. Even within the groups they are outstanding for their above average margins and productivity. These small groups are few in number and of less significant economic strength than larger groups. They do however represent, for many independent small and medium sized firms, the organisational advantage of a group company structure. For these firms, the changeover generally stems from their growth phase of planning and the drawing up of strategic objectives, which require a group structure. It thus becomes the best organisational solution to cater for an internal growth phase which they manage by means of a divisional reorganisation of their activities into affiliated profit centres. At the same time it becomes inherently part of the external growth process. This is particularly true in the case of cooperatives which, through a growing involvement in the private sector, create or acquire affiliates and thus become the heads of groups.

In the food industry, group creation took place as follows: 40 per cent of the new groups have fewer than 500 employees and 42 per cent are medium sized groups with between 500 and 2,000 employees. These 'new groups' often result from the fact that independent firms merge into small groups, affiliating their different activities in the context of a multidivisional evolution. At the same time, merging (either with an existing group or with another independent) remains the main avenue by which medium sized groups are created. This type of strategic choice results in most cases from the need for growth in an environment of uncertainty subject to pressures stemming from the concentration of industrial power.

This organisational efficiency of the group structure, which can be clearly seen for medium and small sized units, fits in well with the Williamson analytical framework. Management by profit centres (i.e., controlled companies) allows for increased responsibilities at the level of the entity which is subject to management by objectives. This is different from what happens in the independent firm where the distribution of responsibilities frequently amounts to no more than control by one management team or even one manager alone.

5.3.2 *Structural effect*

Belonging to a group introduces for a firm another more structural aspect of this type of organisational efficiency. The foodstuff firms under group control possess very different characteristics from those of independent firms. In terms of structures, they are distinguished by a noticeably greater size, whatever the variables, and by a larger capital by head ratio. The latter is correlated with a higher rate of remuneration due to a relatively higher technological level and a more qualified labour force. Their performances are in every case better than those of independent firms. These observations are confirmed by a comparison between affiliates and independents within identical size categories. In the case of firms with less than 200 employees, their results in terms of turnover, value added, and gross cash flow, are almost 2.5 times greater. Their export competitiveness is almost 3 times greater. Their profitability (new and

Table 5.4. *Structure and performance of firms according to type of control*

Size category	20 < 200		200 < 500		500 < 1000		< 1000	Total	
	Ind	Affil	Ind	Affil	Ind	Affil	Affil	Ind	Affil
Number of firms	2318	252	107	120	27	68	42	2452	482
Mean figures:[a]									
Employees	52	88	295	322	611	687	2173	68	412
Pre-tax turnover	64 093	160 875	362 821	554 190	744 381	1 082 348	3 068 291	84 620	642 140
Export turnover	6587	22 049	44 843	97 403	90 292	164 447	457 860	9179	98 451
Capital by head	261	416	281	384	219	361	427	260	402
Value added (VA)	11 573	25 645	63 590	94 775	112 158	201 718	1 073 513	14 950	159 004
Gross cash flow (GCF)	3417	9142	18 187	35 598	32 426	70 463	288 078	4381	48 685
Margins (GCF/VA)	29.5	35.6	28.5	37.6	28.9	34.9	26.8	29.3	30.6
Gross Margins (GCF/GVA)	31.5	39.5	30.0	39.6	28.5	37.4	41.2	30.9	39.9
Labour Productivity	1227	1821	1229	1716	1216	1574	1411	1226	1555
Salary	145	167	147	175	141	177	190	145	181

Notes: As table 5.3.
Field: Affiliates and independent firms in the foodstuff industry.
Source: INSEE (EAE ELF, 1987).

gross margins) is clearly higher (+6 and +8 per cent) as is their productivity (+50 per cent). For the 200–500 and 500–1,000 size categories the same divergences can be seen; if they are slightly smaller, they are nevertheless even more significant since the comparisons are between units of the same size. The economic data of the firms remain, according to the variables, from 1.5 to 2 times greater. The divergence is even wider for the margins (+9 per cent).

Small and medium sized companies under group control thus seem to benefit from considerable advantages in terms of structure and performance compared with independents. Belonging to a group particularly affects the smaller units and the divergences tend to increase as size diminishes. Small and medium firms of less than 200 employees enjoy organisational advantages together with synergetic advantages within their parent company as far as trade, technology and social welfare are concerned; advantages which are theoretically not available to independents of the same size. The export propensity criterion is a particularly eloquent example of this type of organisational edge.

This superiority seems not to depend on a given global economic context, since the study of the situation carried out in 1980 underlined the same divergences between the two types of economic agent. Developments between 1980 and 1987 may even have tended to amplify them, particularly as far as margins are concerned. The affiliates and the independents being compared within similar size categories and within the same sector, these results would seem to confirm the existence of an organisational advantage connected to integration in a group.

5.3.3 *Intra-sector effect*

Taken globally, the foodstuff groups possess greater organisational efficiency than independent firms. However, since the food industry consists of thirty-nine subsectors with varying characteristics, their heterogeneity could play a role in this differentiation.

In fact, for the great majority of the sectors (twenty-two out of thirty-nine), the above conclusions are confirmed. Controlled firms continue to be structurally superior and to perform better. Included among these sectors are: cattle slaughterhouses, the milk industry, animal foodstuffs, the sugar industry and chocolate and confectionery.

For another smaller category (nine sectors), the characteristics highlighted are similar for the two types of firm. There are only six sectors in which independent firms do better, although this phenomenon must be qualified by taking into account the size categories of the firms. In fact small, controlled firms (fewer than 500 employees) maintain their organisational advantage within these sectors. Their turnover, their export competitiveness and their value added are almost 3 times greater. They are distinguished by higher capitalisation (342 as opposed to 213 MF) and generate higher margins (32.0 as against 29.2). It is only because of the firms in the 500–1,000 range that the groups come off worse in these sectors.

5.3.4 The growth dynamic in food firms: 1980–87

The analysis of structural characteristics and performance allows us to underline the comparative advantage of groups. Some of the supposed grounds for this superiority have been put forward in section 2 of this chapter. These initial points can be developed by means of statistical observation of their evolution during the last few years. The growth dynamic of these groups is indicative of considerable structural and strategic flexibility, a characteristic which has modified their internal organisation and, by the same token, their role in the food industry.

Internally, the most significant phenomenon has been the increasing inclusion of small and medium firms into the productive organisation of groups. Those most frequently concerned are those of medium size. We have witnessed a noticeable deconcentration of group productive structures to the detriment of companies employing over 1,000 in favour of those with between 200 and 1,000 employees. The latter are responsible for almost 50 per cent of group turnover as opposed to 32 per cent in 1980. On the other hand, in spite of their number, the weight of the smaller affiliates remains quite stable (14 per cent in 1987, 12 per cent in 1980). This predilection for medium size units contrasts with the setting up of industrial heavyweights in the sixties. It is symptomatic of a new departure in internal group organisation, indicating a search for a new efficiency in the context of the flattening out of productivity gains experienced by the foodstuff sector since the seventies.

This economic deconcentration of affiliates is not synonymous with a reduction in size of the groups. If the number of small groups is increasing, so too is the weight of the big foodstuff leaders. The number of major groups with over 5,000 employees rose from 15 to 21 between 1980 and 1987. Nor does this economic deconcentration imply a concomitant financial deconcentration. There is a distinct dominance by oligopolies (i.e., where the weight of the four leaders is greater than 50 per cent of the turnover of the market): this is the case in twenty-seven industries out of thirty-nine. This dominance is increasing since the corresponding figure for 1980 was twenty-three. These oligopolies represent one of the characteristics of the increasing prevalence of groups in the sector.

This process of economic deconcentration accompanied by financial concentration is closely correlated with another facet of the efficiency of groups: that of their financial flexibility, particularly their ability to withdraw from unprofitable or non-strategic assets. This flexibility also draws attention to the process of mergers and takeovers. This external growth strategy has been the outstanding element in the growth dynamic of the foodstuff groups in the period 1970–87. It concerned particularly the most successful independent firms. These new affiliates are characterised by an average size, whatever the variable taken into account (employees, fixed assets, gross value added or turnover) which is 4 to 6 times greater than that of the independents. Their export and gross cash flow results are almost 5 times greater.

5.4 Conclusion

In a period when uncertainty has played a more and more significant part in economic dynamics, groups have been able to demonstrate both the potential deriving from the specific nature of their structure and organisation, and their ability to adapt in situations where flexibility becomes a requirement. In our study, we compared classical firms and groups of similar size in order to isolate the influence of organisation. The results suggest that groups are more efficient than independent firms. The groups and firms under inspection belonged to the food industry, a sector with a wide range of sizes and low monopoly power. Group advantages are likely to be greater in industries with important economies of scale and scope, such as telecommunications, aeronautics or sectors supporting important costs of R&D, marketing or information. Hints in this direction are also to be found in studies of French groups (Encaoua and Jacquemin, 1982), or Italian groups (Alzona and de Castro, 1991).

French industrial groups exhibit some features belonging to those US corporations organised on a multidivisional basis and others similar to Japanese firms, so they stand on an intermediate level between the H mode and the J mode described in Aoki (1990). The hierarchical separation between planning (headquarters) and implemental operation is not so deep as in the divisions of US corporations, and coordination between operating units uses informal channels as in the J mode. These features are to be related to the demarcation criterion of a group used in our study: a group is formed by the financial links between industrial companies acting under common control, though remaining legally autonomous entities.

The potential benefits of this structure are to be found in financing conditions, coordination and flexibility.

5.4.1 Corporate financing

The group increases the range of possibilities by which activities can be funded without risks for the controlling block. If the controlling unit owns a sufficient part of the stock of an affiliate or has disposal of it, this affiliate can raise funds by issuing new shares that will not threaten the control. Besides this, the group can choose the best fitted of its subsidiaries for this operation. This advantage will be greater if minority stockholders cannot prevent reallocation of resources among the affiliates, that is if the group can organise a kind of financial internal market. Mayer (1988) has shown that there are great differences between corporate financing in the great industrialised countries. Equity markets have provided, during the period under inspection, a higher share of corporate financing that occurred in other countries (it is of interest to note that French and Japanese financing structures are very similar; only trade credit is more developed in Japan than it is in France (−1 per cent in France, −10 per cent in Japan)). These results are not surprising: the group structure is especially designed to raise funds without diluting control and, by these means, groups are able to coordinate more economic activities than the initial properties will allow them. Nevertheless capital costs hang heavily on the institutional surroundings so that it is difficult to draw conclusions about the relative efficiency, from these discrepancies.

5.4.2 Coordination

Chandler (1982) has emphasised that the French groups developed activities in a greater number of different industries than the other European or US corporations did. This multisectoral structure mirrors the group ability to coordinate activities and to benefit from economies of scope. Encaoua and Jacquemin (1982) have also showed the 'French industrial groups operate mainly in industries whose characteristics call for internal coordination and require an organisational type which these groups can provide'. But the French group structure also facilitates coordination with outside partners because each affiliate offers possibilities to establish alliances of varying scope.

The efficiency of the groups comes from the various ways by which it permits a reallocation of financial, technological and human resources. Nevertheless groups do not behave as conglomerates because the parent can monopolise the strategic planning. No doubt these advantages could rapidly vanish if legal and/or institutional surroundings change. Yet the financial links between companies inside many groups have been tied for fear of proxy fights whereas the equity market did not appear so efficient at raising funds. The European directive that defines more precisely the accounting rules in groups has also limited the discretionary use of information by the control owners inside and outside. The same holds for industrial relations: at least, in the French state-owned groups, a legal representation of workers and employees has been established.

5.4.3 Flexibility

Aoki (1990) amidst many authors suggested that the comparative efficiency of organisations must be tested in stable, volatile and intermediate environments. Our conclusions are that the French groups can react very quickly to change in markets or technologies. Because they are composed of legally autonomous entities, they have no fixed structure or frontiers and can easily sell companies that are no longer useful to them or buy ones that can add some skills. This ability is especially worthy to cope with the irreversibility costs. The group can move from one industry to another because its entry and exit costs are lower than other kinds of organisation. But this flexibility also depends on the institutional rules that define the relation between property and control. Rapidity and secrecy are often necessary conditions for success or failure of moves, but they could not be obtained if minority stockholders retained more protection and rights. As the greater groups have usually the more scattered stockholders, they would be more affected by legal changes than the smaller ones that have not extensively used the dilution of stocks to raise funds and keep the advantage of financial and administrative flexibility.

The French case is an example of the interactions between mode of organisation and legal surroundings. The European company law of which the seventh European directive (1985) was a cornerstone will eradicate differences in legal surrounding. An adjustment of industrial structure could follow, but the effects of mode of coordination and particular relations between stockholders, managers and employees will still stand.

Notes

1 This investigation will provide us with empirical findings that will support our demonstration.

2 The database is the result of the merger of two investigations carried out by INSEE: on financial linkage (groups, ELF) and the annual investigation into firms (EAE: Enquête Annuelle d'Entreprise), 1980 and 1987.

References

Alzona, G. and de Castro, T., 1991. 'Approche théorique du groupe et l'expérience italienne', in J. P. Gilly (ed.), *L'Europe Industrielle*, La documentation française, Paris.

Aoki, M., 1990. 'Toward an economic model of the Japanese firm', *Journal of Economic Literature*, March.

Beau, D., 1991. 'Les influences de l'appartenance à un groupe sur les structures et les résultats des entreprises industrielles françaises', *Cahiers Economiques et Monétaires*, 38.

Bühner, R., 1985. 'Internal organisation and returns: an empirical analysis of large diversified German corporations', in J. Schwalback (ed.), *Industry Structure and Performance*, WZB, Edition Sigma.

Cable, J., 1985. 'Capital market information and industrial performance: the role of West German banks', *Economic Journal*, March.

Cable, J. R., 1987. 'Organisation form and economic performance', in S. Thompson and M. Wright (eds.), *Internal Organisation, Efficiency and Profit*, P. Allan.

Cable, J. R. and Dirrheimer, M. J., 1983. 'Hierarchies and markets: an empirical test of the multidivisional hypothesis in West Germany', *International Journal of Industrial Organisation*, 1, 1.

Chandler, A. D., 1982. 'The M form: industrial groups, American style', *European Economic Review*, 19, 1.

Chang, S. J. and Choi, U., 1988. 'Strategy, structure and performance of Korean business groups: a transactions cost approach', *Journal of Industrial Economics*, 2.

Dosi, G., Teece, D., and Winter, S., 1991. 'Towards a theory of corporate conference', in: G. Dosi, P. Giannetti and P. A. Toninelli (eds.), *Technology and the Enterprise in a Historical Perspective*, Oxford: Oxford University Press.

Encaoua, D. and Jacquemin, A., 1982. 'Organizational efficiency and monopoly power, the case of French industrial groups', *European Economic Review*, 19.

Galliano, D., 1990. 'La dynamique de croissance des groupes de l'agro-alimentaire', *INSEE Resultats-Système Productif*, 31.

LEREP, 1987. *Propriété et Pouvoir dans l'Industrie*, La documentation française, Paris.

Mayer, C., 1988. 'New issues in corporate finance', *European Economic Review*, 32.

Morin, F., 1975. *La structure du capitalisme français*, Paris: Calmann-Lévy.

Teece, D., 1981. 'Internal organization and economic performance', *Journal of Industrial Economics*, 30, 2.

Thollon Pommerol, V., 1982. 'Les groupes publics et privés', *Economie et statistique*, 147.

Thompson, R. S., 1983. 'Diffusion of the M form structure in the UK: rate of imitation, inter-firm and industry differences', *International Journal of Industrial Organisation*, 1.

Williamson, O. E., 1985. *The Economic Institutions of Capitalism*, New York: Free Press.

Part 2

Technological specialisation and international trade

6 Patterns of technological specialisation and growth of innovative activities in advanced countries

DANIELE ARCHIBUGI AND MARIO PIANTA

6.1 Introduction

Technology is among the determinants of economic competitiveness. It affects a country's performance in several and complex ways, including the degree of research intensity of the economy, the cumulative nature of technological knowledge, the differentiated patterns of sectoral activities, and the characteristics of the national system of innovation.[1] In this chapter, two related topics are addressed: (i) the similarities and differences between the sectoral strengths and weaknesses of national technological activities; (ii) the presence and specialisation of each country in the fields where innovation is more rapid. These issues are addressed using empirical evidence based on patent data at the sectoral level. The next section considers the importance of the specific aspects of national systems of innovation in the context of the increasing globalisation of technological activities. Section 3 describes the distribution of, and the changes in, the technological activities within the OECD area, using as indicators R&D spending and patenting. In section 4 the similarities and differences among the profiles of technological specialisation of advanced countries are examined, developing a measure of 'technological distance'. In section 5 the rates of growth of total patents in the USA in each class are considered as an indicator of the pace of innovation and of international competition in new fields; the activities of each country in such classes are then mapped, showing how the pattern of national specialisation relates to the sectoral trends of world innovation. Finally, section 6 discusses the relevance of these findings for European competitiveness.

6.2 Internationalisation of technology and national specialisation

Technology has become increasingly important in modern economic systems. Advanced countries have become more knowledge-intensive;

international competitiveness, productivity, and rates of growth are linked to the ability to innovate successfully, as illustrated by a large number of empirical analyses.[2]

Mastering technological innovation, however, is not a simple task. National success in innovative capacity requires the combination of different factors, including high quality research, institutions supporting technical advance, and adequate managerial skills. These factors are unevenly distributed across countries, resulting in substantial differences in the quantity, nature and trajectory of the innovations produced. Since innovation is becoming a key factor in competition among countries, nations where barriers to innovation are higher will lose ground relative to their competitors.

To keep its position in international competition, each country has to increase its effort to produce new technology and to adapt and diffuse inventions and innovations. Most countries have perceived this changing environment and have devoted a greater attention to science and technology, with a variety of institutional efforts to support technical advance. At the same time, the benefits received by firms for the innovations they introduce have become less certain: the time span in which an innovation can be exploited has decreased in most new technologies, characterised by rapid obsolescence. The number of firms at the frontier of technical knowledge has also increased, leading in some sectors to greater competition in high technology markets.

Firms have adopted several strategies to obtain the pay-offs of their innovations. These strategies include:

(a) using a given knowhow in different products and processes. This strategy may lead firms to increase both their product diversification and their cooperation with other firms in research and production ventures in new fields;

(b) using the same knowhow in a larger number of markets, with greater exports of products and processes, and transfer of technology. This strategy parallels the rapid growth of firms' international activities, leading to an increasing globalisation of technology markets.

In previous research, we have investigated the effect of globalisation on national technological capabilities, using a variety of patent-based indicators at the sectoral level, focusing on the 1975–88 period. An increasing technological specialisation in the majority of countries has been found (Archibugi and Pianta, 1992b), suggesting that globalisation has not led to an internationally uniform pattern of production of innovations across sectors; on the contrary, each country has further developed its comparative advantages in selected technological niches.

The increasing specialisation in the production of innovations does not necessarily mean that national patterns in the adoption and diffusion of technology and patterns of market demand are equally diverging. In particular, the aggregate picture of the technological and industrial performance of advanced countries shows that a process of convergence is taking place for indicators ranging from countries' R&D intensity to productivity levels.[3] This apparent paradox is related to the ability of national economies to use their different technological resources, and to acquire the knowhow they do not possess from a variety of channels, including trade, patent cross-licensing, international cooperative research projects and many other specific forms of technology transfer.

The internationalisation of technology and the changes in firms' strategies have led to different government responses. In Japan a focus of national effort on selected areas has been encouraged. In Europe greater intra-European technological cooperation has been fostered by recent policies aiming at consolidating a Europe-wide technology base. The US government has long concentrated its resources in military-related fields, and is now searching for alternative policies. Comparative analyses (Nelson, 1984) showed that countries have reacted in different ways to the new technological environment, although an increasing integration between government policies and market processes has been found, with the common objective of improving national competitiveness.

6.3 National performances in technology: some aggregate evidence

Table 6.1 reports some indicators on the distribution of technological activities in the OECD area. While the percentage distribution of R&D and patents reflects the size of each country, the shares of total and industrial R&D in the gross domestic product point out the different technological intensity of advanced countries. The USA, Sweden, Switzerland and Germany[4] devote a share close to 3 per cent of GDP to total R&D activities, while Japan has a 2.7 per cent share and the EEC average is below 2 per cent.

If we focus on the R&D which is financed by and performed in industry, thus excluding government-funded projects (including military R&D), the ranking of countries changes substantially. Switzerland, Japan, Germany and Sweden have a share greater than 1.7 per cent of GDP, while the USA shows a 1.4 per cent value and the EEC average is below 1 per cent.

In terms of the percentage distribution of R&D across countries, the USA accounts for almost half the total R&D activities of the countries considered, but for only 45 per cent of industrial R&D. Conversely, Japan

Table 6.1. *Technological capabilities of advanced countries (by percentage)*

Countries	Total R&D expenditure, 1987	R&D funded and performed in industry, 1987	Total R&D expenditure as a share of GDP, 1987	R&D funded by industry as a share of GDP, 1987	Patents granted in the USA, 1988
USA	49.02	45.44	2.90	1.41	53.01
Japan[a]	16.22	21.56	2.67	1.86	21.17
EEC	27.91	26.74	1.95	0.98	19.76
FRG	8.75	10.48	2.83	1.79	9.58
France	6.16	4.79	2.29	0.93	3.47
UK	6.10	5.35	2.27	1.04	3.40
Italy	3.14	2.47	1.19	0.49	1.41
Netherlands	1.57	1.46	2.33	1.14	1.07
Belgium	0.74	0.98	1.65	1.14	0.39
Denmark	0.37	0.34	1.43	0.68	0.20
Spain	0.79	0.72	0.62	0.30	0.16
Ireland	0.10	0.07[b]	0.94	0.37[b]	0.06
Portugal	0.10	0.05[b]	0.45[b]	0.10[b]	0.01
Greece	0.09	0.03[b]	0.33[b]	0.08[b]	0.01
Switzerland	1.02	1.58[b]	2.88[b]	2.10[b]	1.02
Sweden	1.34	1.49	2.99	1.74	1.63
Austria	0.44	n.a.	1.32	n.a.	0.45
Canada	2.26	1.71	1.36	0.54	1.95
Australia	0.98	0.62[b]	1.19	0.39[b]	0.55
Finland	0.41	0.44	1.73	0.97	0.31
Norway	0.40	0.42	1.81	0.89	0.16
TOTAL[c]	100.0	100.0			

Notes: [a]Data for Japan are the OECD adjusted values; [b]1986; [c]The percentage shares are calculated on the sum of all countries.
Source: CNR–ISRDS elaboration on OECD, MSTI, April 1990 and CHI Research data.

has a share in total R&D equal to 16 per cent while its share of industrial R&D is much higher, at 22 per cent.

The percentage distribution of patents granted in the USA provides a similar picture. Since patents granted to American firms and inventors in their domestic market are considered here, the US share is higher than its share of both total and industrial R&D. Since in the next sections we will use US patenting as a technological indicator at the sectoral level, this factor may bias the data for the USA. Japan's share of patenting in the USA is equal to its share of industrial R&D, while the EEC share in patenting (below 20 per cent) is substantially lower than its R&D share (27 per cent).

Table 6.2. *Rates of growth of R&D and patenting in OECD countries*

	Average annual percentage rates of change			
	R&D expenditure 1979–88[1]	Domestic patents 1979–88[2]	Foreign patents 1979–88[3]	External patents 1979–88[4]
USA	5.30	2.44	6.30	7.50
Japan	8.15[a]	8.30	3.85	11.53
EEC	4.16	1.10	9.38	7.49
FRG	3.58	0.54	4.87	6.79
France	4.86	1.16	5.95	7.64
UK	2.43[c]	0.64	5.49	8.34
Italy	9.43	−11.59[f]	10.01	8.50
Netherlands	3.83[a]	2.00	10.17[f]	6.91
Belgium	4.40[a]	−1.05	10.15	6.38
Denmark	7.18[a]	3.28	7.24	13.47
Spain	10.11	−0.31	11.77	5.06
Ireland	6.06	9.34[a]	3.38	14.12
Portugal	6.76[b]	−6.19	5.33	29.86
Greece	10.30[d]	−0.18	27.88	8.96
Switzerland	4.75[d]	−2.21	9.87	3.38
Sweden	7.71[a]	−2.39	10.12	8.56
Austria	3.95[e]	−0.75	13.51[a]	7.44
Canada	5.60	6.28	2.88	8.31
Australia	6.08[b]	3.26	5.31	17.36

Notes: [1]R&D data are expressed in real terms; [2]Patents by residents of the country; [3]Patents by foreigners in the country; [4]Patents by residents extended in other countries.

[a]1979–87; [b]1978–86; [c]1978–87; [d]1979–86; [e]1981–88; [f]1980–88.

Source: Elaboration on OECD data.

Table 6.2 shows the main trends in technological indicators. In the 1979–88 period R&D expenditure has increased in all countries. In Japan it has grown at an average annual rate (8.1 per cent) which, in real terms, is higher than in both the USA (5.3 per cent) and the European Community (4.1 per cent). Within Europe, countries starting from a low technology intensity, such as Spain, Italy, and Portugal, have grown at a rate higher than average. The slowest growth rate has occurred in the UK.

The greater the resources devoted by each country to science and technology, the more we can expect that it would try to appropriate the benefits in several markets, and patents are one of the methods used by firms to protect their innovations. Domestic patent applications (i.e., patent applications of residents in their own country – see table 6.2, col. 2) increased over the same period at a very slow rate, and in eight countries a decline actually occurred. Conversely, a rapid growth can be found in the number of external patents (i.e., the total number of applications filed by national firms and inventors in other countries – table 6.2, col. 4).[5] One possible explanation is that firms tend to limit their domestic patent applications to inventions of greater commercial potential, while at the same time extending in a greater number of countries the patents actually registered. This pattern is consistent with the findings of research which has shown that, although the number of patents granted in selected countries has declined, the money spent on renewal fees has not.[6]

In parallel, as shown in table 6.2 col. 3, the number of foreign patents (i.e., patent applications filed by foreign applicants in a given country) has significantly increased in all countries. As a consequence of the globalisation of technology, firms also have to cope with increasing pressure from foreign competitors in their domestic market.

A trend towards a globalisation of firms' strategies for appropriability is evident. The aggregate analysis performed in this section does not, however, indicate the direction of the innovative strategies pursued by firms and governments in each country. Not all countries are competing in the same technological markets; their particular path of specialisation is investigated in the next section.

6.4 Similarities and differences in countries' technological specialisations

While aggregate patterns of science and technology activities suggest an increasing convergence among advanced countries in terms of innovative efforts, at the sectoral level different models of specialisation have been identified, with countries concentrating their activities in a few areas of greater strength; a description of national patterns of technological specialisation, based on a variety of patent data, has been provided elsewhere (see Archibugi and Pianta, 1992a; Freeman *et al.*, 1991).

In order to address the question of how similar or different national specialisations are, the sectoral distribution of technological activities has been compared, developing a measure of distance between pairs of countries. The distance between individual countries will be analysed for the periods 1975–81 and 1982–88, using data on the sectoral distribution across forty-one SIC classes of patents granted in the USA.[7]

The method we have used is an application of the chi square statistic. Firstly, the percentage distribution of patents in forty-one non-residual SIC classes (see appendix for their listing) is considered for two countries; the square of the difference between these percentages is calculated for each class, and divided by the share the class holds in the world total

Table 6.3. *Distances between the patterns of technological specialisation of advanced countries*

	Period	USA	Japan	EEC
USA	1	–	22.33	11.18
	2	–	24.64	9.52
Japan	1	22.33	–	24.39
	2	24.64	–	30.22
EEC	1	11.18	24.39	–
	2	9.52	30.22	–

Note: The distance indicator is based on the percentage distribution across forty-one SIC classes of patents granted in the USA to individual countries. The index ranges from 0 to 1,000. Distance values are divided by the maximum possible distance, calculated on the average of the five more extreme cases. Period 1: 1975–81; Period 2: 1982–88.
Source: CNR–ISRDS elaboration on CHI research data.

patents; the sum of these weighted squared differences is the distance indicator used in our analysis. The formula used is the following:

$$D_{ab} = \sum_{i=1}^{n}\{(p_{ia} - p_{ib})2/p_{iw}\}$$

where:

D_{ab} is the distance between country *a* and country *b*;
p_{ia} is the percentage of patents of country *a* in sector *i*;
p_{ib} is the percentage of patents of country *b* in sector *i*;
p_{iw} is the percentage of patents of the world total in sector *i*;
n is equal to forty-one non-residual SIC classes.

The distance index between two countries is equal to zero when they have the same percentage distribution of patents across classes, and it grows rapidly when one country is strong in fields where the other holds few or no patents. The maximum value of the indicator can be calculated[8] and a standardised index, which ranges from 0 to 1000, is obtained dividing the distance values by the maximum, allowing comparisons over time of the relative distance between countries. Table 6.3 shows the distance between the three major regions – the EEC, the USA and Japan – for the late 1970s and the mid-1980s.

The EEC and the USA have the closer sectoral distribution of patenting activities and they become slightly more similar across the two periods (distance indexes of 11 and 9.5). In 1975–81 Japan is much more different

Table 6.4. *Distance between the patterns of technological specialisation of advanced countries*

	Period	USA	Japan	FRG	France	UK	Italy	N'lands	Belgium	Denmark	Spain	Switz.	Sweden	Canada
USA	1	–	22.33	17.40	8.95	12.25	37.00	28.82	46.71	36.13	68.51	56.4	31.85	14.19
	2	–	24.64	17.11	6.89	11.02	35.18	23.36	45.11	37.20	69.06	46.09	29.75	13.84
Japan	1	22.33	–	29.28	23.70	25.79	50.74	43.18	57.48	56.14	104.10	73.21	68.58	56.14
	2	24.64	–	37.93	25.61	30.18	60.86	35.26	85.40	79.02	104.38	76.13	64.80	79.02
FRG	1	17.40	29.28	–	9.62	9.51	13.36	54.04	31.20	42.27	45.05	27.89	43.58	31.89
	2	17.11	37.93	–	12.24	14.74	13.58	48.81	46.09	132.19	40.03	24.02	29.18	28.87
France	1	8.95	23.70	9.62	–	3.24	23.22	32.78	40.09	39.13	51.03	40.04	39.63	22.76
	2	6.89	25.61	12.24	–	5.09	26.53	25.47	41.04	40.85	55.71	35.78	33.78	21.85
UK	1	12.25	25.79	9.51	3.24	–	26.44	78.24	37.50	33.77	53.78	39.02	42.40	27.86
	2	11.02	30.18	14.74	5.09	–	24.37	37.15	33.43	35.33	56.52	32.14	38.55	28.65
Italy	1	37.00	50.74	13.36	23.22	26.44	–	65.36	42.30	44.93	40.49	29.08	63.98	45.67
	2	35.18	60.86	13.58	26.53	24.37	–	64.82	53.61	41.20	38.19	19.79	44.79	42.18
Netherlands	1	28.82	43.18	54.04	32.78	78.24	65.36	–	85.78	75.04	105.82	82.71	79.91	46.56
	2	23.36	35.26	48.81	25.47	37.15	64.82	–	65.38	74.14	119.77	74.82	73.68	41.17
Belgium	1	46.71	57.48	31.20	40.09	37.50	42.30	85.78	–	64.95	84.88	47.47	86.04	68.43
	2	45.11	85.40	46.09	41.04	33.43	53.61	65.38	–	59.65	90.47	53.45	77.72	61.77
Denmark	1	36.13	56.14	42.27	39.13	33.77	44.93	75.04	64.95	–	57.73	53.34	41.58	41.24
	2	37.20	79.02	132.19	40.85	35.33	41.20	74.14	59.65	–	48.95	47.76	36.32	36.09
Spain	1	68.51	104.10	45.05	51.03	53.78	40.49	105.82	84.88	57.73	–	51.99	63.30	55.79
	2	69.06	104.38	40.03	55.71	56.52	38.19	119.77	90.47	48.95	–	60.10	42.30	56.86
Switzerland	1	56.40	73.21	27.89	40.04	39.02	29.08	82.71	47.47	53.34	51.99	–	76.81	79.79
	2	46.09	76.13	24.02	35.78	32.14	19.79	74.82	53.45	47.76	60.10	–	87.65	64.02
Sweden	1	31.85	68.58	43.58	39.63	42.40	63.98	79.91	86.04	41.58	63.30	76.81	–	20.94
	2	29.75	64.80	29.18	33.78	38.55	44.79	73.68	77.72	36.32	42.30	87.65	–	17.11
Canada	1	14.19	56.14	31.89	22.76	27.86	45.67	46.56	68.43	41.24	55.79	79.79	20.94	–
	2	13.84	79.02	28.87	21.85	28.65	42.18	41.17	61.77	36.09	56.86	64.02	17.11	–

Note: The distance indicator is based on the percentage distribution across forty-one SIC classes of patents granted in the USA to individual countries. The index ranges from 0 to 1,000. Distance values are divided by the maximum possible distance, calculated on the average of the five more extreme cases. Period 1: 1975–81; Period 2: 1982–88.
Source: CNR–ISRDS elaboration on CHI research data.

from both the USA (index equal to 22) and the EEC (index equal to 24); in the second period Japan increases substantially its difference from both areas, and in particular that from the EEC (index equal to 30).

Table 6.4 provides the same distance indexes for thirteen advanced countries. The pattern of relative differences emerging from the matrix is fairly complex; the USA has the closest similarities to France, the UK and Canada in both periods. Japan is closest to the USA and France, but with higher distance indexes. Germany has a sectoral distribution of patents similar to France, the UK and Italy. In turn, France and the UK are very close together and are similar to the USA and Germany. Italy is close to Germany, followed at a distance by France, the UK and Switzerland. The remaining countries have very high distance indexes and tend to show closer similarities either to the USA or the major European countries.

In interpreting such patterns of relative difference across countries the impact of countries' size of patenting activities is evident. The larger countries, including the USA, Japan, France, the UK and Germany, distribute their patents across all sectors, resulting in a somewhat closer picture than that resulting from the comparison between small countries which concentrate their patents in few (and different) areas. Smaller countries are very different from one another and tend to be closer to the larger country which shares the same sectoral specialisation. Smaller countries, in other words, appear to have developed a technological specialisation in selected, country-specific 'niches' (see Walsh, 1988; Soete, 1988; Kristensen and Levinsen, 1983); such a position allows small countries to compete in these fields at the international level. Their niches, however, are very different, showing that small nations can be specialised in entirely different areas: it is not just their size that decides the nature of their sectoral strengths and weaknesses.

The impact of selected sectors on national specialisation is also evident from the distance matrix of table 6.4. The strong similarity between France and the UK, and to a lesser extent the USA, is due to the common importance of military-related and state-supported areas (aircraft, guided missiles, ordnance) and of classes such as drugs and medicines and agricultural and other chemicals. Some of these fields are also areas of technological specialisation for Germany, which on the other hand shares with Italy and Switzerland a relative concentration of its patenting in specialised industrial machinery and in some chemical classes. Other types of links among national specialisations can be identified. A relative importance of electronic-related fields appears to be at the root of the similarities shown by Japan, the USA, France and The Netherlands. The USA is also fairly close to Canada, which in turn shows a specialisation profile similar to that of Sweden, with Denmark not too far away; in these linkages the relative importance in all countries of natural resource and agriculture-related activities, as well as of specialised production in fields such as shipbuilding and engineering, appears to be crucial.

It is interesting to note that for almost all pairs of countries the distance index increases over time, suggesting that most countries develop a sectoral distribution of their patenting activities leading to a more distinct national profile, linked to their own economic and technological characteristics, rather than converging to a standard patenting profile for all advanced countries.

From this complex picture of relative similarities and differences a number of lessons can be drawn. First, the differentiated nature of patenting activity leads to a variety of links between pairs of countries, which are based in shared relative specialisations in particular patenting fields. This fragmented pattern of relative similarities makes an overall assessment of the distance between countries difficult, but it highlights the different models of specialisation which are present even within the same country.

Secondly, the ability of large countries to cover most technology fields with their innovative activities means that size (i.e., the aggregate volume of their resources devoted to S&T) is an important factor in this measure of similarity. This leads to a picture of a core made up of the major countries, which are fairly close to one another, while smaller ones appear scattered around them, closer to one of the larger countries, and very different from most of the other smaller ones.

Thirdly, while the analysis of individual countries has shown strong stability in national patterns of specialisation in technology (see Cantwell, 1989), in comparing the relative distance between countries some mobility can be found. The differentiated pattern of sectoral patenting and the combined shifts over time of all countries lead to an overall picture of fairly dynamic relative positions of individual countries. In other words, even within the constraints of the technological capabilities accumulated by each nation over time, countries do shift their relative positions, taking or missing the technological opportunities offered by the changing patterns of innovation.

6.5 The pace of innovation across patent classes

The economic 'quality' and market importance of individual patents is highly skewed; while some have a dramatic economic impact, many patents never become actual innovations. This is true not only for individual patents, but can be extended to patent classes. Patents in certain fields are not related to important (or growing) economic markets, while in other fields patents reflect important advantages in technology as well as in economic competition.

The relevance of individual sectors in the growth of technological activities is analysed in this section. An attempt will be made to relate particular profiles of sectoral specialisation to the patterns of growth of patenting activities. For this purpose, a methodology for identifying the position of each sector in international technological competition has been developed.

The rates of change of patents in each class are used as an indicator of their relative technological importance. A fast growing patent class often corresponds to original developments in scientific and technological knowledge, but it can also be related to increasing competition, or diffusion of already known inventions and innovations. Several case studies (see, among others, Walsh, 1984; Wheal and McNally, 1986; Achilladelis *et al.*, 1987; Trajtenberg, 1990) have shown that fast growing patent classes are generally associated with increasing competition among firms or countries for leadership in selected technological areas. In more general terms, it could be argued that the fields of rapid expansion of patents represent crucial areas at the technological frontier, with a strong impact on the future development of the economy. The classification used in section 3 is not detailed enough to identify the areas of greater technological dynamism. In a classification at the two-digit level, subfields of rapid expansion are often merged with subfields with stagnant or declining rates of change. A pioneering study on fast growing patent classes (Patel and Soete, 1988), for example, focused on the 300 fastest growing subclasses out of a total of 110,000. For our purposes, such a detailed level of disaggregation is not needed. In fact, the countries' position will be assessed here in all the classes and not only in the fast growing subset, requiring a less disaggregated classification.

We have considered the 118 technological fields defined by the three-digit international patent subclasses. Table 6.5 reports the growth rates of total patents in each of the 188 IPC subclasses[9] between the 1975–78 period and the 1985–88 period. We have focused on the two extreme four-year periods in order to identify the most important technological transformations. Growth rates were computed on the total number of patent applications filed in the USA by all countries, since we assume that technological developments occur on a global scale.

Between the two periods considered, total patents have grown by 11.9 per cent. The contribution of individual classes to this trend has been very different, as table 6.5 clearly shows.[10] The growth rates of the 118 classes have been divided into four quartiles, in the following way: 1st quartile (declining): below −10% (30 classes); 2nd quartile (stagnant): from

Table 6.5. *Rates of change of patents in the US – IPC 3-digit classification*
Rates of change between the 1975–78 and 1985–88 periods by percentage (all IPCs combined rate of growth 11.14%)

4th Quartile Fast growing	
Crystal growth[a]	N/A
Disposal of solid waste	485.3
Instrument details	169.2
Bookbinding; albums; special printed matter	101.5
Information storage	94.0
Biochemistry; beer; mutation or genetic engineering	89.6
Computing; calculating; counting	88.4
Optics	77.6
Lighting	66.5
Electric communication technique	62.7
Medical & veterinary science; hygiene	58.5
Refrigeration or cooling; manufacture or storage of ice; liquefaction or solidification of gases	53.1
Layered products	51.7
Footwear	49.9
Hand tools; portable power-driven tools; handles for hand implements; workshop	46.7
Ropes; cables other than electric	45.8
Steam generation	44.9
Electric techniques not otherwise provided for	44.6
Nuclear physics; nuclear engineering	42.0
Positive-displacement machines for liquids; pumps for liquids or elastic fluids	38.6
Educating; cryptography; display; advertising; seals	36.5
Controlling; regulating	34.1
Wearing apparel	32.7
Machine tools; metalworking not otherwise provided for	31.3
Measuring; testing	30.1
Doors, windows, shutters, or roller blinds, in general; ladders	29.9
Heat exchange in general	29.4
Spraying or atomising in general, applying liquids or other fluent materials to surfaces in general	29.1
Saddlery; upholstery	27.4
Headgear	26.6

Table 6.5. (*cont.*)

3rd Quartile Medium growing	
Basic electronic circuitry	25.4
Sewing; embroidering; tufting	24.3
Weapons	23.7
Basic electric elements	23.0
Musical instruments; acoustics	22.3
Printing; lining machines; typewriters; stamps	21.8
Working or preserving wood or similar material; nailing or stapling machines in general	19.6
Generation, conversion, or distribution of electric power	19.0
Butchering; meat treatment; processing poultry or fish	18.3
Earth drilling; mining	17.9
Casting; powder metallurgy	16.4
Drying	15.2
Generating or transmitting mechanical vibrations in general	14.9
Furniture; domestic articles or appliances; coffee mills; spice mills; suction cleaners in general	14.8
Combustion apparatus; combustion processes	14.4
Engineering elements or units; general measures for producing and maintaining effective functioning of machines or installations; thermal insulation in general	14.3
Baking; edible doughs	14.1
Combustion engines; hot-gas or combustion-product engine plants	13.2
Writing and drawing appliances; bureau accessories	12.6
Aircraft; aviation; cosmonautics	11.9
Cements; concrete; artificial stone; ceramics; refractories	11.2
Tobacco; cigars; cigarettes; smokers' requisites	9.9
Photography; cinematography; analogous techniques using waves other than optical electrography; holography	9.7
Land vehicles for travelling other than on rails	9.0
Treatment of water, waste water; sewage or sludge	8.7
Vehicles in general	8.7
Glass, mineral and slag wool	7.0
Locks; keys; window or door fittings; safes	6.9
Storing or distributing gases or liquids	6.2

Table 6.5. (*cont.*)

2nd Quartile Stagnant	
Crushing, pulverising or disintegrating; preparatory treatment of grain for milling	5.6
Machines or engines in general; engine plants in general; steam engines	5.3
Signalling	5.3
Cleaning	3.4
Brushware	2.7
Sports; games; amusements	1.4
Life-saving; fire-fighting	1.0
Hand & travelling articles	0.8
Heating; ranges; ventilating	0.3
Separating solids from solids; sorting	0.0
Ships or other waterborne vessels; related equipment	−0.3
Building	−0.5
Grinding; polishing	−0.6
Liquid handling	−0.8
Conveying; packing; storing; handling thin or filamentary material	−1.5
Electolytic or electophoretic processes; apparatus thereof	−2.4
Petroleum, gas and coke industries; technical gases containing carbon monoxide; fuels; lubricants; peat	−3.0
Separation of solid materials using liquids or using pneumatic tables or jigs; magnetic or electrostatic separation	−3.3
Construction of roads, railways, or bridges	−4.5
Hoisting; lifting; hauling	−5.3
Working treatment of metals	−5.3
Weaving	−5.8
Water supply; sewerage	−7.2
Organic macromolecular compounds; their preparation or chemical working-up; compositions based thereon	−7.4
Paper-making; production of cellulose	−7.7
Natural or artificial threads or fibres; spinning	−7.8
Agriculture; forestry; animal husbandry; hunting; trapping; fishing	−9.3
Animal & vegetable oils, fats, fatty substances and waxes; fatty acids therefrom; detergents; candles	−9.8
Mechanical metalworking without essentially removing material; punching metal	−9.9

Table 6.5. (*cont*).

1st Quartile Declining	
Machines or engines for liquids; wind, spring, weight, or miscellaneous motors	−10.1
Checking devices	−10.7
Furnaces; kilns; ovens; retorts	−12.4
Physical or chemical processes or apparatus in general	−13.1
Ammunition; blasting	−13.3
Making paper articles	−13.6
Foods or foodstuffs; their treatment not included in other classes	−14.1
Metallurgy; ferrous or non-ferrous alloys; treatment of alloys or non-ferrous metals	−14.4
Fluid-pressure actuators; hydraulics or pneumatics in general	−14.6
Skins; hides; pelts; leather	−14.9
Dyes; paints; polishes; natural resins; adhesives; miscellaneous composition; miscellaneous applications of materials	−16.8
Metallurgy of iron	−18.0
Fertilisers; manufacture thereof	−18.3
Centrifugal apparatus or machines for carrying out physical or chemical processes	−18.4
Working of plastics, working of substances in plastic state, in general; working of substances not otherwise provided for	−20.1
Haberdashery; jewellery	−20.7
Working cement, clay, and stone	−21.7
Decorative arts	−23.3
Hand cutting tools; cutting; severing	−24.0
Presses	−24.0
Yarns; mechanical finishing of yarns or ropes warping or beaming	−26.4
Hydraulic engineering; foundations, soilshifting	−26.7
Braiding; lace-making; knitting; trimmings; non-woven fabrics	−29.0
Inorganic chemistry	−29.8
Railways	−30.7
Sugar or starch industry	−30.9
Organic chemistry	−33.2
Treatment of textiles, etc; laundering; flexible materials not otherwise provided for	−40.4
Horology	−42.1
Explosives; matches	−47.1

Note: [a]This new class was introduced after the first period.
Source: CNR–ISRDS elaboration on CHI research data.

Table 6.6. *Share of patent classes in total US patents classified according to their rates of change, 1975–78 and 1985–88 (by percentage)*

	1975–78	1985–88
4th quartile fast growing classes	24.60	33.34
3rd quartile medium growing classes	29.77	31.10
2nd quartile stagnant classes	23.92	20.82
1st quartile declining classes	21.57	14.57

Note: The four groups are based on the three-digit IPC subfields divided into quartiles according to their rates of change. The classes of each group are listed in table 6.5.
Source: CNR–ISRDS elaboration on CHI research data.

−10% to 6% (29 classes); 3rd quartile (medium growing): from 6% to 26% (29 classes); 4th quartile (fast growing): above 26% (30 classes). The list of the fast growing patent classes may raise some questions as to how accurate the identification of the most innovative sectors is. A cross-check via an independent source has been possible, using the highly detailed classification of high technology products developed by ENEA on the basis of the expert opinion of engineers and technicians (see Amendola and Perrucci, 1988).[11] The majority of high technology products identified by such a classification can be found in fast growing patent classes.

The fastest growing fields of patenting include many classes related to microelectronics, such as information storage, computing, optics, electronic communications, controlling and measuring and testing. In the declining classes, on the other hand, organic chemicals and inorganic chemicals are to be found. In more general terms, areas related to the cluster of electronic technologies have grown at higher rates than mechanical and chemical clusters.

Fast growing classes also contain some products generally considered as traditional such as footwear and headgear. It should be borne in mind, however, that the IPC classes include in the same category both products and processes; the results appear less surprising if it is recalled that a substantial number of the patents in footwear relate to, for example, specialised industrial machinery, and that headgear includes helmets.

Table 6.6 reports the share of patents included in each quartile for the periods 1975–78 and 1985–88. The fast growing classes accounted for less than a quarter of all patents in the period 1975–78, but they account for a

Table 6.7. *National technological specialisation and patenting in fast growing classes by percentage (Patents granted in the USA, three-digit IPC classes)*

	Patents in fast growing classes			Correlation coefficients between TRCA indexes 1985–88 and rates of growth of patent classes between 1975–78 and 1985–88[a]
	Distribution across countries	Share in total national patents		
	1985–88	1975–78	1985–88	
USA	53.82	25.52	33.69	0.09
Japan	21.53	24.19	37.10	0.22
EEC	16.55	22.87	28.50	−0.22
FRG	7.68	20.01	27.19	−0.27
France	2.46	26.63	34.68	−0.04
UK	3.53	25.87	34.73	−0.07
Italy	1.17	21.63	28.37	0.00
Netherlands	1.07	25.51	33.44	0.14
Belgium	0.29	18.30	27.68	−0.13
Denmark	0.24	27.90	32.94	−0.14
Spain	0.10	19.15	23.82	−0.17
Canada	1.62	21.88	28.78	−0.15
Switzerland	1.34	18.06	26.75	−0.25
Sweden	1.11	26.18	32.29	−0.17
Australia	0.39	21.88	25.99	−0.15
World	100.00	24.60	33.34	

Note [a]The correlation coefficients have been calculated on 116 classes, excluding the class 'crystal growth', introduced after the first period considered, and the class 'disposal of solid waste', which has very few patents and an extremely high growth rate.
Source: CNR–ISRDS elaboration on CHI research data.

third in 1985–88. We assume that for each country it is an advantage to hold a higher share of patents in the sectors which are growing at an above average rate. However, the importance of many fast growing classes on a country's overall technological activities may be small; an advantage in such fields does not result *per se* in faster growth of patenting activities. Furthermore, it is unlikely that the areas of fast growing innovation correspond to already established new markets and an advantage in leading-edge technologies may not immediately translate into better industrial performances (see Archibugi and Pianta, 1992a, ch. 10).

In order to assess the position of individual countries, two different measures were developed, and the results are shown in table 6.7.

The first measure is the share of a country's patents falling in the fast growing classes in both periods considered. By definition, the share has increased for all countries, and the results have to be compared with the world average share in the two periods (cols 2 and 3); a substantially higher concentration of patents in fast growing classes can be found only for Japan, while in both periods the USA, the UK, France and The Netherlands have, in fast growing classes, a share of their patents which is slightly above the world average. However, such a measure does not take into account the countries' performance in the patent classes belonging to the other groups.

The second measure compares the rates of growth of patent classes (already shown in table 6.5) with an index of specialisation (the Technology Revealed Comparative Advantage index, or TRCA)[12] of a country's patenting activity calculated for the same 118 subclasses. The correlation coefficient between the two vectors (which include data for the 116 subclasses with significant growth rates excluding crystal growth and disposal of solid waste) indicates how close the specialisation pattern of a country is to the sectoral distribution of fast growing classes in world patenting. A positive correlation suggests that the country has the majority of its sectoral strengths in areas which grow faster, and the majority of its sectoral weaknesses in fields with slow growing or declining patenting. The reverse is true for a negative value of the correlation coefficient.

The results, presented in table 6.7, col. 4, show that only Japan has a sectoral pattern of specialisation which exhibits a clear positive relation to the rates of growth of world patenting. This result is partly affected by the dramatic increase of Japanese patents in the USA. The United States is the only other country showing a positive correlation, but very close to zero. Germany and Switzerland have the strongest negative correlation between their sectoral specialisation and the pattern of growth of world patenting; in other words they concentrate their relative strengths in subclasses where world patenting is stagnant or declining. This evidence can be documented in greater detail with the graphic representation of figure 6.1. For each country the TRCA indexes for the 118 subclasses were calculated for the more recent period 1985–88; the indexes were then ranked and each divided into three groups of classes: high, medium and low TRCAs. This information is combined in figure 6.1 with the distribution in four quartiles of the 118 subclasses according to the growth rates of world patenting. Each bar corresponds to a quartile, and is subdivided according to the frequencies of high, medium or low TRCA indexes that are found for those subclasses. The figure shows where a country distributes its relative strengths (top layer) and weaknesses (bottom layer), in fields of patenting ranging from fast growing (right bar) to declining (left bar).

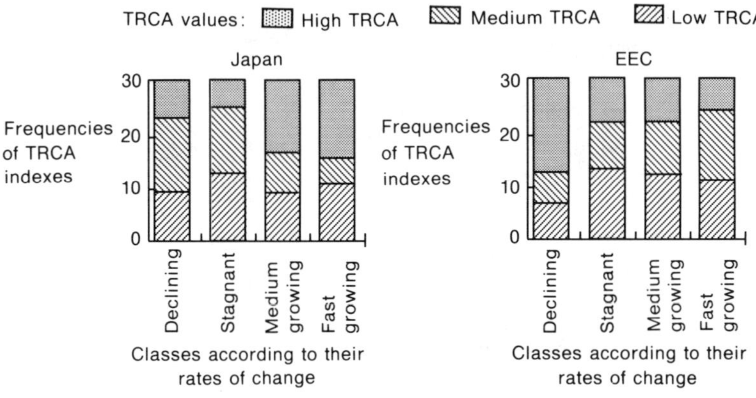

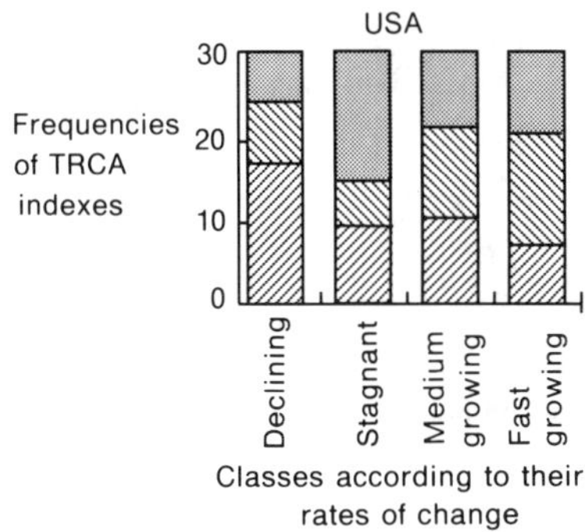

Figure 6.1 Countries' positions in fast growing, medium growing, stagnant and declining technologies, 3 digit IPC patent classes, rates of change 1975–78 to 1985–88.

The EEC has a below average share in fast growing classes in both periods and its position worsens over time. In the second period, in only six (out of thirty) of the fast growing classes is a high specialisation found, while the EEC shows a high specialisation in eighteen out of thirty declining classes.

An opposite pattern is shown by Japan. In the first period Japan had a share of patents in the fast growing classes slightly lower than its share of total patents (see table 6.7), but it later reversed this position, reaching a TRCA index equal to 1.11 in the second period. Japan has a high specialisation in half of the fast growing classes, while in declining classes it has high TRCA indexes in only seven classes out of thirty.

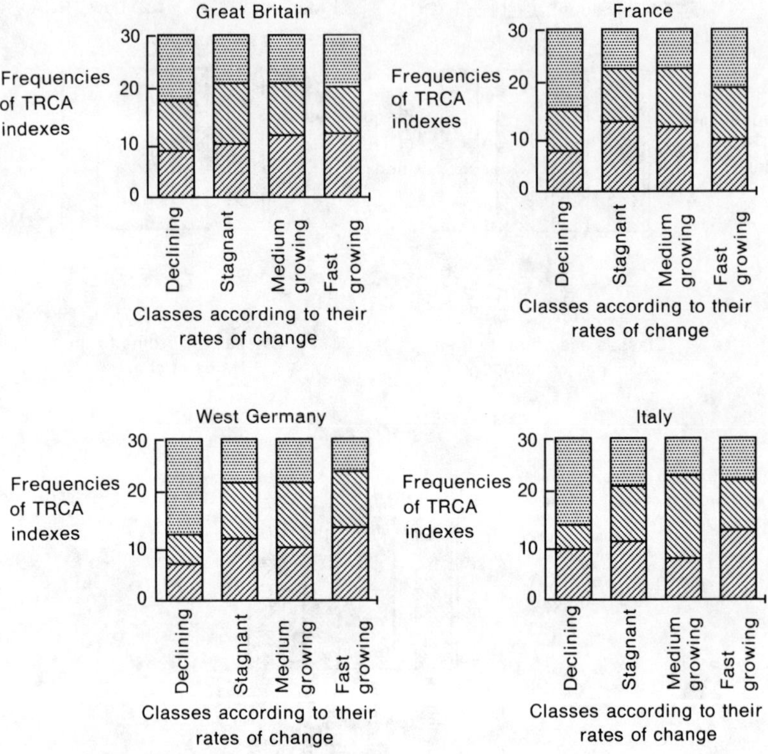

Figure 6.1 (*cont.*)

The results for the USA are biased by the fact that we are here considering US patents in the domestic market. In both periods, however, the US share in fast growing classes is slightly above its total share of patents. In ten (out of thirty) fast growing classes the USA presents high TRCA values, and is highly specialised only in six of the declining classes. This result is somewhat counterintuitive, as the total amount of patents granted to US residents decreased remarkably over the period 1975–88, and one could have expected to find that the sectoral strengths of the USA would occur in classes with a declining rate of change. This result shows the opposite – that the US decline in patenting has mainly affected the less dynamic sectors, while the technological activities in the fields of more intensive competition have been preserved.

The results shown by the EEC are the outcome of differentiated tendencies across individual countries. Since Germany is the largest European patenting country, the aggregate result reflects German patent

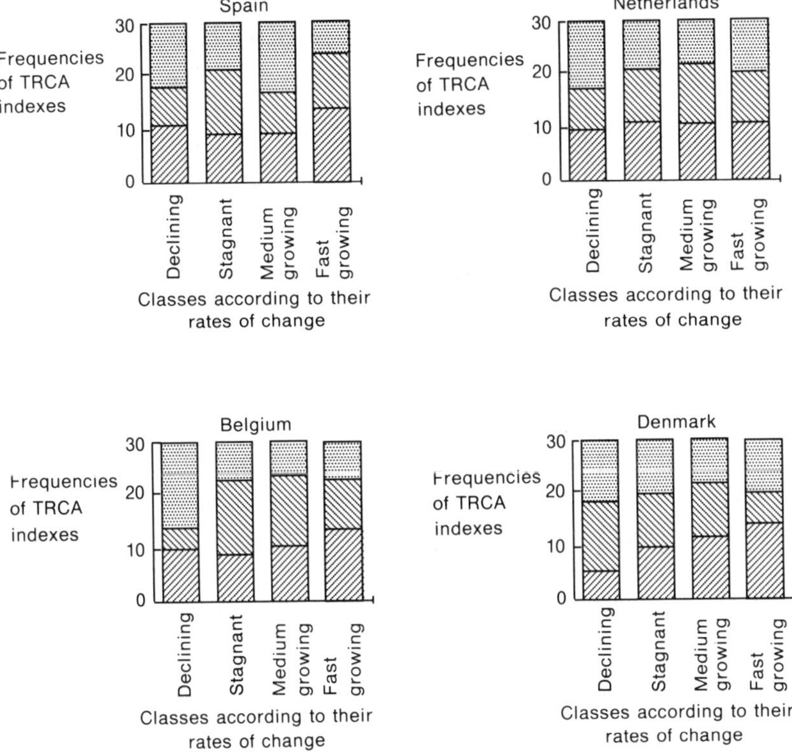

Figure 6.1 (*cont.*)

activity more than that of any other country. In fact, the sectors of German strengths in the fast growing classes are almost the same as those of the EEC as a whole. In both periods, the German share of patents in the fast growing classes is below its share in all patents.

The United Kingdom, on the contrary, shows a robust specialisation in fast growing classes, in spite of the reduction experienced over the last two decades in the total number of patents granted in the USA. As for the USA itself, it could be argued that the reduction in the absolute number of patents may have affected declining classes more than the fast growing ones. The third-largest European country, France, has a share in fast growing classes slightly above its share of total patents, although it has lost ground over the two periods. Finally, Italy has a distribution of its strengths and weaknesses very close to the German and European aggregate, with a concentration in the stagnant and declining patent classes.

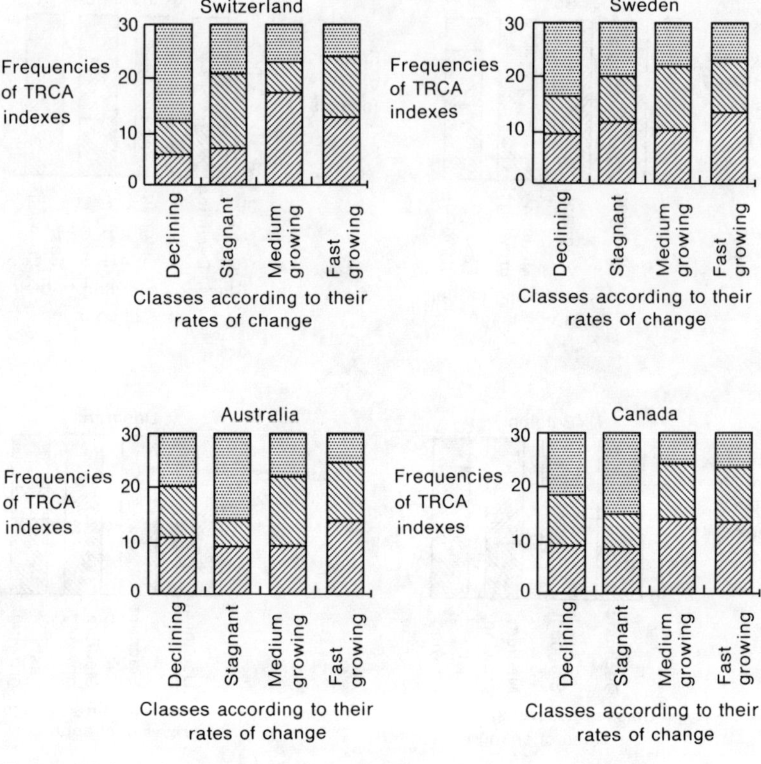

Figure 6.1 (*cont.*)

6.6 Prospects for European competitiveness

The empirical evidence presented in this chapter should be related to the current debate in international technological activities. On the one hand, the international orientation of firms' innovative efforts has increased, with the development of a variety of new forms of acquiring and exchanging knowhow across national borders, including cooperative R&D projects, cross-licensing agreements, joint ventures and even mergers and acquisitions (see the chapter by Hagedoorn and Schakenraad in this volume).

On the other hand, this does not mean that national characteristics do not play a role in the new technological landscape. Firms' strategies are constrained by the comparative advantages of nations (Porter, 1990) when taking strategic decisions about their international activities. In other words, the internationalisation of technology, and the related discussion on 'techno-globalism', does not bring about a larger uniformity among countries in the production of innovations; rather it is more likely to lead to an increasing diversity.

In fact, comparative research on the national systems of organisation of innovation have made it possible to identify the qualitative and institutional differences among countries (see, among others, Nelson, 1984; 1991; Freeman and Lundvall, 1988; Dosi *et al.*, 1988). This body of research has shown the crucial role played by nation-specific factors and institutions in shaping technological change. In this chapter we have provided quantitative evidence which can complement the qualitative analyses noted above, showing that the sectors where countries produce innovations are increasingly divergent.

A great variety in the nature of national systems of innovation is also found within Europe. Indeed, the diversity among countries should be regarded as an advantage, since it may make it possible to develop technological capabilities in different fields. However, in terms of developing a distinct profile of technological specialisation, Europe still appears as an aggregate of disparate countries, some of them rather similar (the UK and France, or to a lesser extent Germany and Italy), others more different (all the smaller ones), and neither a common specialisation profile, nor a clear complementarity is evident. The pattern of growing technological distance among EEC countries does not appear as a clear outcome of either a policy of European integration or of a market-driven process of greater intra-European division of labour.

The prospects for European competitiveness which follow from this analysis of the patterns of technological specialisation and growth of patenting activity are not promising. A large literature has already documented the unsatisfactory nature of European performance in terms of aggregate indicators of innovative activities, and the progressive erosion of its position compared, in particular, to Japan (see, among others, Patel and Pavitt, 1987; Freeman *et al.*, 1991). Such a pattern is qualified by the evidence provided here on the poor European performance in the technological fields where innovations grow faster.

If we look at the European presence in these fields, as identified by fast growing patenting classes, the problems of the European position are evident. A sectoral strength in fast growing classes means a long-term advantage for a country's innovative and economic activities, since the relative share of fast growing patent classes increases over time. Consequently, countries specialised in fast growing classes are likely to increase their share of patents also at the aggregate level, as long as they do not show a decline in their activity in other fields which exceeds their gains in fast growing classes. Once innovations are translated into new, growing markets a similar pattern can also be expected for the countries' shares in world trade.

The EEC position is in sharp contrast with that of Japan. Japan has consistently specialised in fast growing patent classes, indicating that the Japanese sustained growth of patents, experienced over the last twenty years, is also likely to continue in the future. European technological strengths, on the other hand, are not placed in the more dynamic fields, and it is likely that the share of European patents will decrease somewhat in the future. The leading European technological power, Germany, is not specialised in the most dynamic sectors. The UK, which has considerably decreased its share of technological activities, appears to have concentrated its efforts in the fast growing sectors. The US specialisation profile we have measured is biased by the fact that patenting in its domestic market was considered. However, the fact that several US sectoral strengths are located in fast growing classes indicates that the decline in total US patents is concentrated in the less dynamic sectors, suggesting that a restructuring of innovative activities has occurred in the USA.

The evidence provided by these technological indicators cannot be immediately translated into considerations on the developments of European competitiveness. A variety of other factors, besides technology, shape a country's competitive position, and the differences in sectoral specialisations and in the nature of the national systems of innovation may lead to diverging competitive performances starting from a similar technological base. However, international competitiveness of advanced countries is increasingly affected by non-price factors in which technology plays a critical role; even in the sectors where price competition is important, innovation in processes and organisation can be critical for maintaining a competitive edge.

For these reasons the outlook for European technological specialisation and its contribution to competitiveness is not encouraging, even though major changes and an acceleration of intra-European integration in technological activities can be expected after 1992.

Appendix

List of SIC classes used for patent applications in the United States

1 Food and kindred products
2 Textile mill products
3 Industrial inorganic chemistry
4 Industrial organic chemistry
5 Plastic materials and synthetic resins

6 Agricultural and other chemicals
7 Soaps, detergents, cleaners, perfumes, cosmetics & toiletries
8 Paints, varnishes & allied chemicals
9 Miscellaneous chemical products
10 Drugs & medicines
11 Petroleum, natural gas, extraction & refining
12 Rubber & miscellaneous plastic products
13 Stone, clay, glass & concrete products
14 Primary ferrous products
15 Primary & secondary non-ferrous metals
16 Fabricated metal products
17 Engines & turbines
18 Farm & garden machinery & equipment
19 Construction, mining and material handling machinery & equipment
20 Metalworking machinery & equipment
21 Office computing & accounting machines
22 Special industrial machinery, except metalworking machinery
23 General industrial machinery & equipment
24 Refrigeration & service industry machinery
25 Miscellaneous machinery, except electrical
26 Electrical transmission and distribution equipment
27 Electrical industrial apparatus
28 Household appliances
29 Electrical lighting & wiring equipment
30 Miscellaneous electrical machinery, equipment & supplies
31 Radio & television receiving equipment except communication types
32 Electronic components & accessories & communication equipment
33 Motor vehicles & other transportation equipment, except aircraft
34 Guided missiles & space vehicles & parts
35 Ship & boat building & repairing
36 Railroad equipment
37 Motorcycles, bicycles & parts
38 Miscellaneous transportation equipment
39 Ordnance except missiles
40 Aircraft & parts
41 Professional & scientific instruments
42 Unclassified patents
43 Other industries

Notes

This paper is part of a research project on the scientific and technological specialisation of advanced countries jointly financed by the Commission of the

European Communities, DG XII, Science, Research and Development, Service Research Evaluation, and the Italian National Research Council. We are grateful to Patrizia Principessa and Roberto Simonetti for research assistance, and to the other participants of the WZB's network on European Competitiveness for their comments.

1 In previous research on the technological specialisation of advanced countries (Archibugi and Pianta, 1992a and b), we have mapped national sectoral advantages and disadvantages.

2 See, among others, Hughes, 1986, Soete, 1987 and Fagerberg, 1988 for international competitiveness; Baumol *et al.*, 1989 for productivity; and Fagerberg, 1987 for growth rates.

3 See, among a large literature, Dosi *et al.*, 1988; Nelson, 1989; Baumol *et al.*, 1989.

4 Throughout this chapter, data for Germany refer to the former West Germany.

5 A single patent application could therefore be counted more than once if it is extended in more than one country.

6 See Schankerman and Pakes, 1986: 'Part of the decline in the patenting per unit of inventive input may reflect a shift away from "more patents" to "higher quality".'

7 We have shown elsewhere that patenting at the US Patent Office is a reliable indicator of national technological specialisation for most countries, but not for the USA, as patenting activity in the domestic market has a sectoral distribution which is substantially different from that emerging in foreign markets (see Archibugi and Pianta, 1992a and b). In this chapter data on patents granted in the USA are used, and particular caution is therefore needed in interpreting the results for the United States (see also Grupp, 1989).

8 The maximum value of the distance indicator can be extremely high because it is found in the very special case when two countries concentrate all their activity in two different sectors which have the lowest shares of patents in world distribution. In order to avoid erratic values, the average of the five sectors with the lowest shares of world distribution has been considered for calculating the maximum. While such a standardisation does not affect the relative position of countries in a given period, it is required in order to make comparisons over time, as is done in tables 6.3 and 6.4.

9 The size of individual classes is highly skewed; the smallest one, disposal of solid waste, accounts for 0.01 per cent of all patents, while the largest one, basic electric elements, has a share of 6.49 per cent.

10 It should be pointed out that Japanese patents in the USA have shown the greatest increase over the period considered, and therefore the fast growing classes here considered may include fields where Japanese activity is particularly relevant.

11 This 'bottom-up' approach has selected 250 high technology product groups out of a four-digit international trade classification.

12 The TRCA index is equal to the ratio between the share of world patents in a class held by a country, and the share of the country's patents in all classes in the world total.

References

Achilladelis, B., Schwarzkopf, A. and Cines, M., 1987. 'A study of innovation in the pesticide industry: analysis of the innovation record of an industrial sector', *Research Policy*, 16(2–4).

Amendola, G. and Perrucci, A., 1988. *Commercio internazionale e tecnologia: aspetti teorici e problemi di ricerca empirica*, Rome: ENEA.

Archibugi, D. and Pianta, M., 1992a. *The Technological Specialization of Advanced Countries: A Report to the EEC on International Science and Technology Activities*, Boston: Kluwer.

1992b. 'Specialization and size of technological activities in industrial countries: the analysis of patent data', *Research Policy*, 1(21), 79–93.

Baumol, W. J., Blackman, S. A. B. and Wolff, E. N., 1989. *Productivity and American Leadership: the Long View*, Cambridge, MA.: MIT Press.

Cantwell, J., 1989. *Technological Innovation and Multinational Corporations*, Oxford: Basil Blackwell.

Dosi, G., Freeman, C., Nelson, R., Silverberg, G. and Soete, L. (eds.), 1988. *Technical Change and Economic Theory*, London: Frances Pinter.

Fagerberg, J., 1987. 'A technology gap approach to why growth rates differ', *Research Policy*, 16(2–4).

1988. 'International competitiveness', *Economic Journal*, 98, 391.

Freeman, C. and Lundvall, B. A. (eds.), 1988. *Small Countries Facing the Technological Revolution*, London: Pinter.

Freeman, C., Sharp, M. and Walker W. (eds.), 1991. *Technology and the Future of Europe*, London: Pinter.

Grupp, H., 1989. *The Measurement of Technical Performance in the Framework of R&D Intensity, Patent, and Trade Indicator*, Karlsruhe: FhG.

Hughes, K., 1986. *Technology and Exports*, Cambridge: Cambridge University Press.

Kristensen, P. H. and Levinsen, J., 1983. *The Small Countries Squeeze*, Roskilde: Forlaget for Samfundsokonomi og Planlaegning.

Nelson, R., 1984. *High Technology Policies. A Five Nations Comparison*, Washington DC. American Enterprise Institute.

1989. 'US technological leadership: where did it come from and where did it go?', *Research Policy*, 19, 117–132.

ed. 1991. *National Innovation Systems: a Comparative Study*, mimeo, Columbia University.

OECD, 1990. *Report of the Technology Economy Program*, Paris.

Patel, P. and Pavitt, K., 1987. 'Is Western Europe losing the technological race?', *Research Policy*, 16(2–4).

Patel, P. and Soete, L., 1988. *International Comparisons of Activity in Fast-Growing Patent Fields*, Brighton: SPRU.

Porter, M., 1990. *The Competitive Advantage of Nations*, London: Macmillan.

Schankerman, M. and Pakes, A., 1986. 'Estimates of the value of patent rights in European countries during the post-1950 period', *Economic Journal*, 96, 1077–83.

Soete, L., 1987. 'The impact of technological innovation on international trade patterns: the evidence reconsidered', *Research Policy*, 16(2–4).

1988. 'Technical change and international implications for small countries', in Freeman and Lundvall (1988).

Trajtenberg, M., 1990. *Economic Analysis of Product Innovation: The Case of CT Scanners*, Cambridge, MA: Harvard University Press.

Walsh, W., 1984. 'Invention and innovation in the chemical industry: demand pull or discovery push?', *Research Policy*, 13(4).

1988. 'Technology and the competitiveness of small countries: a review', in Freeman and Lundvall (1988).

Wheal, P. R. and McNally, R. M., 1986. 'Patent trend analysis: the case of microgenetic engineering', *Futures*, October.

7 The role of technology, competition and skill in European competitiveness

KIRSTY HUGHES

7.1 Introduction

This chapter analyses the relative international competitiveness of the largest four EC economies compared with their two largest advanced competitors – the USA and Japan. It focuses on international trade performance in manufacturing industry in the period 1980 to 1987. This time scale allows us to assess both levels of relative competitiveness and trends in competitiveness. The chapter aims to provide, firstly, a descriptive analysis of these six economies' trade performance, addressing questions as to the similarity or otherwise of their trade structures, the degree of convergence or divergence in these structures, the patterns of competitiveness and specialisation, and secondly, an econometric analysis aimed at identifying the determinants of the performance of the European economies relative to the USA and Japan.

The analysis also addresses the fairly widely held view, expressed in particular by the European Commission (EC), that the European economies must improve their competitiveness vis-à-vis the USA and Japan and reverse the relative weakening of their competitive position – the 'eurosclerosis' – of the 1980s. The completion of the internal market in 1992 and a focus on high technology are seen as two central routes whereby the European economies can become more competitive. In this chapter we consider the basis for this view by analysing the competitiveness of these six largest OECD economies both to assess the nature of their relative competitive positions and to identify what are the key determinants of their relative competitive performance.

7.2 Patterns of competitiveness in the 1980s

In this section, we assess the structure of, and trends in, the international trade position in manufacturing of the USA, Japan, Germany, France, the UK and Italy between 1980 and 1987. We first focus on the general patterns of competitiveness and then consider the structure in terms of technology intensity and the effects of 1992. The data are export and import data in current US dollars, obtained from the OECD on the four-digit International Standard Industrial Classification, which gives a disaggregation level of eighty manufacturing industries.

One question that may be addressed with these data is whether it is in fact appropriate to treat the EC economies as a group and discuss European competitiveness relative to that of the USA and Japan – i.e., the notion of three competing blocs – or rather whether there are as many and as large differences between the four EC economies considered here as there are between them and the USA and Japan. We can also consider whether the EC economies are performing worse than the USA and Japan or whether and to what extent relative performance also varies over time and across country. Furthermore, we can aim to identify whether or not there is any convergence in either structure or performance during the 1980s. The answers to these questions are important both in policy terms and in assessing the likely effects on different countries of the internal market process and of the impact of the reindustrialisation of the East European economies.

We use two main measures to assess international trade performance – OECD export shares and the net trade balance. Thus, for an individual industry, i, in a country, j, the OECD export share is:

$$XS = X_{ij} / \sum_j X_{ij} \; j = 1, 2, 3 \text{ (the OECD economies)} \qquad (7.1)$$

where X = exports; and the net trade balance is:

$$\frac{X_{ij} - M_{ij}}{X_{ij} + M_{ij}} \qquad (7.2)$$

where M = imports.

Taken together the two measures provide a broad picture of relative international performance, the first giving an indication of competitiveness in a particular world market, the second providing additionally an indication of specialisation as well as performance.

Tables 7.1 and 7.2 present total OECD export shares and net trade balances, respectively, for the six economies under consideration here and for the four EC economies taken as a group (that is summing the four's exports and imports and treating them as one country). In terms of export shares in 1980, Germany has the largest share followed by the USA, Japan, France, the UK and Italy. By 1987 the shares of the USA and the

Table 7.1. *OECD manufacturing export shares*

	France	Germany	Italy	UK	EC4	Japan	USA
1980	9.5	16.9	7.1	8.9	42.4	11.9	15.3
1984	8.0	15.3	6.9	6.8	37.0	16.1	15.8
1987	8.4	18.2	7.4	7.2	41.2	14.7	12.7

Source: see appendix for sources of all data in tables 7.1 to 7.11.

Table 7.2. *Manufacturing net trade balance*

	France	Germany	Italy	UK	EC4	Japan	USA
1980	0.04	0.15	0.08	0.02	0.08	0.46	0.01
1984	0.05	0.17	0.12	−0.10	0.07	0.52	−0.24
1987	−0.02	0.19	0.07	−0.09	0.06	0.47	−0.29

UK have fallen both absolutely and relatively, so that the USA has the third largest share and the UK swaps places with Italy to have the smallest share. The ranking in terms of trends is somewhat different – Japan has the largest increase followed by Germany and Italy. The remaining three lose export share – France loses the least followed by the UK and the USA. Clearly, size *per se* has no direct link to export performances on the basis of these figures.

A similar picture is presented by the net trade balance figures in table 7.2. Here though the levels and trends are more similar. According to the level of the trade balance the countries can be ranked as follows: Japan, Germany, Italy, France, UK, USA. Germany has the largest improvement over the period and only it and Japan have positive changes. By the end of the period France, the UK and the USA all have negative net trade balances.

The overall picture from these two tables is one then of varied performance across the six economies with Japan coming either first or second and the USA coming last, and with Japan, Germany and Italy being the only ones to show positive developments in their competitiveness over the period. This indicates both rather different performances among the four EC economies and considerable difference in the relative positions of their two main competitors, the USA and Japan. The tables also give some indication of the so-called 'eurosclerosis' effect. The four EC economies do all experience deteriorating performance in export shares to 1984

Table 7.3a. *Correlation of export profiles 1980*

	France	Germany	Italy	UK	USA	Japan
France	1.0					
Germany	0.95	1.0				
Italy	0.77	0.77	1.0			
UK	0.79	0.80	0.71	1.0		
USA	0.75	0.81	0.62	0.88	1.0	
Japan	0.84	0.87	0.61	0.60	0.62	1.0

Table 7.3b. *Correlation of export profiles 1987*

	France	Germany	Italy	UK	USA	Japan
France	1.0					
Germany	0.94	1.0				
Italy	0.69	0.72	1.0			
UK	0.84	0.79	0.69	1.0		
USA	0.79	0.75	0.52	0.86	1.0	
Japan	0.83	0.88	0.55	0.69	0.73	1.0

but all subsequently improve again by 1987; however, only Italy and Germany improve to a level better than that of 1980. The pattern with respect to net trade is more varied and there is no support for a general deterioration in the early or mid-1980s from these figures. These figures reject then the view that European performance in general deteriorated with respect to the EC's main competitors – the picture is different depending on whether the comparison is with the USA or Japan and is also different depending which of the four EC economies is considered.

7.2.1 Similarity and convergence

Although, at the level of total manufacturing, the levels of, and trends in, performance vary across these countries quite markedly, it might be expected that these countries would show more similarity in terms of their structure of trade and their relative performance across different manufacturing industries, particularly in the case of the EC economies. In addition to this question of similarity, we can ask whether these economies are becoming more or less similar over time. It has been suggested that as the advanced economies are tending to converge at a macro level that there is a similar convergence at a micro level. To explore these issues

Table 7.4a. *Correlation of net trade balances 1980*

	France	Germany	Italy	UK	USA	Japan
France	1.0					
Germany	0.32	1.0				
Italy	−0.01	0.02	1.0			
UK	0.32	0.55	0.20	1.0		
USA	−0.01	0.56	−0.17	0.40	1.0	
Japan	0.05	0.48	0.40	0.39	0.21	1.0

Table 7.4b. *Correlation of net trade balances 1987*

	France	Germany	Italy	UK	USA	Japan
France	1.0					
Germany	0.23	1.0				
Italy	−0.10	0.02	1.0			
UK	0.22	0.48	−0.03	1.0		
USA	0.01	0.48	−0.38	0.43	1.0	
Japan	0.02	0.57	0.28	0.26	0.05	1.0

further, we look at two sets of correlations – the correlations between countries of the distribution of their exports across the eighty ISIC industries in 1980 and 1987, set out in tables 7.3a and 7.3b, and the correlations between countries of the distribution of their net trade balance across industry in 1980 and 1987, tables 7.4a and 7.4b.

Looking first at the export profile correlations – tables 7.3a and 7.3b – these are mostly fairly high, indicating substantial similarity in the manufacturing export structures of these economies. The highest correlation in both years is that between France and Germany; the lowest correlation in 1980 is between Italy and the USA, and in 1987 between the UK and Japan. This might suggest greater similarity does exist among the EC economies than between these economies and the USA and Japan. A closer inspection of the tables, however, indicates that this is not so. Germany's profile in 1987 is most similar to France then Japan, the UK and the USA. The USA's profile is most similar to the UK and then France and Germany. The UK's highest correlation in both years is with the USA. The country with the lowest correlations is Italy which has the least similar profile to all the other five countries. Thus, though there is indeed similarity, this varies across countries and there is no evidence that the EC four are more similar to each other than to their two main competitors.

The net trade correlations – tables 7.4a and 7.4b – tell a rather different story. These are much lower, in some cases negative. The highest correlation in 1987 is 0.57 between Japan and Germany and the lowest is −0.38 between the USA and Italy. Overall Germany has the most similar net trade pattern to other countries, especially to Japan, the USA and the UK. Most other countries have only low positive correlations apart from that between the UK and the USA. Italy again has the most dissimilar pattern. Together with table 7.3, this suggests that while these six economies do have a similar pattern of export structures, this does not result in similar patterns of competitiveness. Nor where there are similarities in net trade, does this relate in any clear way to performance. Germany, which has the strongest correlations, exhibits these both with the best and the worst – Japan, and the USA and the UK respectively.

The finding of relatively low levels of similarity in net trade is reinforced when we address the question of convergence. The changes in the individual correlations in both sets of tables between 1980 and 1987 are mostly negative. With respect to the export profile correlations, ten decline while five increase. With respect to the net trade correlations, eleven decline, one is unchanged and three increase. At least over this eight-year period to 1987, then, there is no support for a convergence theory with respect to international trade structures or performance patterns, rather we obtain a picture of mild divergence. This finding supports the results of Archibugi and Pianta (1990) who, looking at technological specialisation, similarly find no evidence of convergence, though stronger evidence of dissimilarity than we find here.

The finding of a mild divergence relates to a separate question which is how much change and development there is in a country's trade profile over time. Do successful economies, for example, exhibit more change than unsuccessful economies or do they, rather, continually reinforce and build on success in particular industries? Table 7.5 presents correlations for each country of their export profiles in 1980 and 1987 and of their net trade balances in 1980 and 1987. The correlations are all high, the lowest being for the UK and the USA for both variables. These correlations indicate then a rather low level of change in each country's trade structure and performance profile with relatively little difference between countries in terms of their export profiles, though the UK and the USA's poor performances are picked up in the greater change in their net trade distributions. This is a picture of all countries maintaining a very similar export pattern over the 1980s despite changes in relative and absolute performance across countries. Thus, neither success nor failure would appear to promote swift changes in specialisation in the medium run.

Table 7.5. *Correlation for each country of exports, 1980–1987, and net trade, 1980–1987*

	France	Germany	Italy	UK	EC4	Japan	USA
Exports	0.96	0.97	0.95	0.90	0.98	0.94	0.93
Net Trade Balance	0.93	0.96	0.95	0.83	0.95	0.93	0.83

7.2.2 Technology and trade

One common theme of many commentaries on the competitiveness of the advanced economies is that this competitiveness depends on innovation, particularly in the high technology industries. This has led to calls for government subsidy of research and development (R&D) and, in particular, encouragement for cooperative and collaborative R&D. Section 7.3 looks in more detail at the role of R&D in relative trade performance; here we look at export performance by technology group. In order to do this, the eighty ISIC industries are categorised into three groups – high, medium and low technology according to the OECD's classification (OECD, 1986). This categorisation is, of course, somewhat crude but for our current descriptive purposes it will give us some overview.

Table 7.6 presents each country's OECD export shares – as in table 7.1 but now subdivided by technology group. France and Italy have their highest export shares in the low technology group; Germany has its highest share in the medium technology group, and Japan, the USA and the UK all have their highest shares in the high technology group. Taking the EC four as a group, their highest share is in medium technology and their lowest in high technology. Their combined high technology share is, however, larger than either that of Japan or that of the USA. Looking at trends over time, only Japan shows an increase in its high technology export share, Germany and Japan have an increase in their medium technology export share, and Germany and Italy have an increase in their low technology export share. All other countries lose export share in all groups.

Simple correlations do not, of course, indicate causation. Nevertheless, it is interesting that these simple descriptive statistics do not support a link between technology group and trade performance. Of the three countries relatively specialised in high technology, one – Japan – has good trade performance, while two – the USA and the UK – have the worst trade performances of the six during the 1980s, one – Germany – performs relatively well in medium technology products, while the other – Italy –

Table 7.6. *OECD export shares by technology group (by percentage)*

	France	Germany	Italy	UK	EC4	Japan	USA
High Technology							
1980	7.8	15.6	4.4	10.9	38.6	16.9	24.1
1984	7.0	12.9	4.0	8.3	32.1	24.4	25.5
1987	7.5	14.9	4.3	8.5	35.3	22.7	21.8
Medium Technology							
1980	9.6	20.6	6.4	9.0	45.5	12.8	16.8
1984	7.8	19.0	5.8	6.5	39.2	16.6	16.1
1987	8.3	22.4	6.4	6.7	43.7	16.2	11.6
Low Technology							
1980	10.1	13.4	9.2	8.1	40.8	8.9	9.8
1984	8.9	12.4	9.8	6.2	37.3	10.6	9.7
1987	9.1	14.8	10.8	7.8	41.7	7.5	8.2

performs best in low technology products. Thus, good and bad relative trade performance can be related to both high technology and low technology groups. One interpretation of these results is not that the advanced countries should, therefore, all be specialising in low technology products, but rather that to focus on one characteristic – innovation – is potentially highly misleading and that other characteristics such as quality (related to skill, machinery, management and so forth) may be equally important.

It is also interesting to look at the trends over time in performance in these three technology groups from a different angle. Thus, while Japanese performance may be superior in all groups to that of the EC four, we may ask in which groups is it relatively better or worse and how is that changing over time. To measure this we construct a relative export variable as:

$$RX_{tjk} = (X_{tj}/X_{tk})/(\sum_t X_{tj}/\sum_t X_{tk})\ k \neq j \qquad (7.3)$$

where t = technology group – high, medium or low,
j = Japan, USA, Germany, France, UK or Italy,
k = Japan or USA.

Where $RX > 1$ a country does relatively better in that technology group relative to the USA or Japan than on average. We summarise the results of this exercise here – further details are given in Hughes (1991a). In the high technology group, all the EC countries perform badly relative both to the USA and to Japan. The USA performs well with respect to Japan in the high technology group. There is no strong trend over time in the high technology group. With respect to the medium technology group,

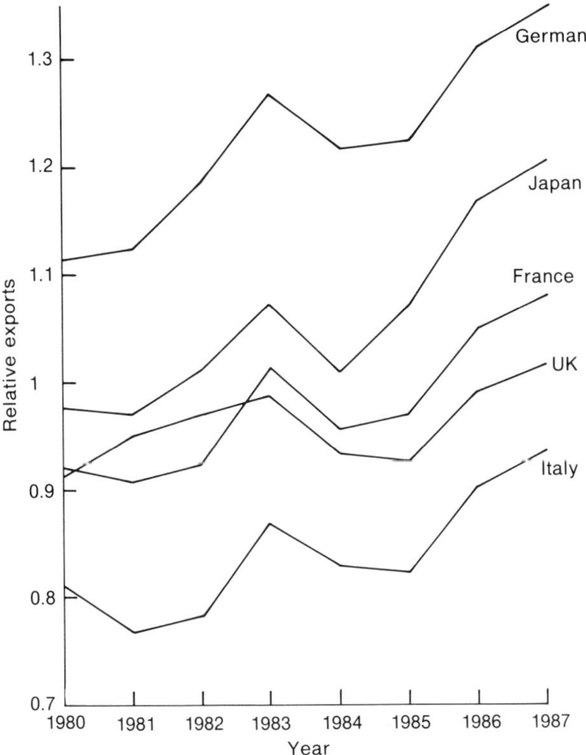

Figure 7.1 Exports relative to the USA in medium technology relative to all sectors.

Germany performs well, having an *RX* index greater than one relative to both the USA and Japan. In the low technology group, all the EC four perform well with respect to both the USA and Japan. The trends over time in the medium and low technology group are also of interest and are set out in figures 7.1 and 7.2. Figure 7.1 sets out *RX* relative to the USA in the medium technology group. For all countries there is a clear upward trend over the 1980s, indicating that the general US loss in competitiveness in the 1980s is particularly pronounced in the medium technology sector. Figure 7.2 sets out *RX* relative to Japan in the low technology group and again shows a clear upward trend for all countries; thus, Japan's performance has become weaker in low technology products relative to its performance in medium and high technology products.

Thus, these figures reinforce the idea that the EC economies perform relatively worse in the high technology group compared with both the

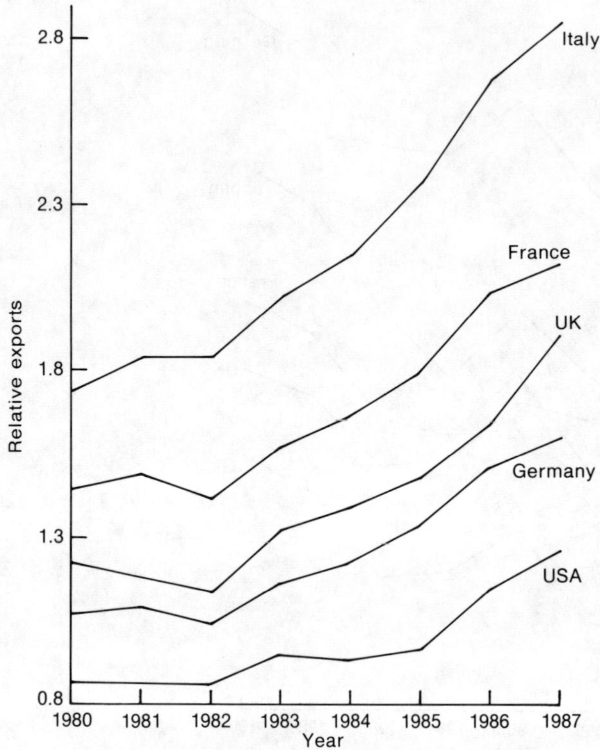

Figure 7.2 Exports relative to Japan in low technology relative to all sectors.

USA and Japan. However, as we have already discussed, there is no simple relationship apparent between performance in a particular technology group and overall trade performance. Further, the two clear trends here are with respect to medium technology in the case of the USA and to low technology in the case of Japan. The US case is particularly interesting, as the medium technology group includes many consumer goods where the USA may be losing important markets, possibly through fluctuations in the dollar exchange rate having more impact on products in this group.

Overall, the data presented here indicate that the four EC economies are specialised in different ways across the three technology groups, and that although all four perform relatively badly with respect to the USA and Japan in high technology, there is no evidence from these data that this damages overall trade performance.

7.2.3 1992 and sensitive sectors

The completion of the EC's internal market under the 1992 programme (EC, 1988) may have a number of effects on the competitiveness of the EC economies vis-à-vis the USA and Japan. These effects depend both on how successful the 1992 programme is in achieving its aim of an EC economy without barriers between countries and on the analysis of the impact of the changes on the existing patterns of and trends in competitiveness. Disagreement exists as to the likely effects of the 1992 process – from the positive estimates of the EC itself (EC, 1988) to those who consider it will have adverse effects (Cutler *et al.*, 1989; Hughes 1990), those who consider the effects will be rather small (Davis *et al.*, 1989) and those who suggest the effects will be positive and larger than estimated by the EC (Baldwin, 1989). It is not possible here to address the many issues that arise in this debate, though some are addressed in chapter 8 (Kay); rather we focus here on the current patterns of competitiveness in those sectors most likely to be affected by the 1992 process.

The EC has argued that certain sectors will be more sensitive to the completion of the internal market than others (Buigues *et al.*, 1990). Those sectors with high or medium non-tariff barriers are identified as more likely to be 'sensitive' to the completion of the internal market than others. Taking the level of non-tariff barriers as its first criterion the EC uses a number of additional criteria, notably the degree of price dispersion, the extent of import penetration and the potential for scale economies, to identify 40 out of 120 sectors on the EC's three-digit NACE classification as sensitive to the completion of the internal market. These sectors account for 50 per cent of value-added. These sectors in particular, then, have suffered, in the EC's view, from a lack of integration relative to the USA and Japan.

In order to compare EC trade performance in these sectors relative to the USA and Japan, it is necessary to reclassify the sectors on to an international concordance. Thus, we aim to identify the EC sensitive sectors among the eighty ISIC sectors for which we have data here, using a NACE–ISIC concordance (further details are given in Hughes, 1991b). An exact concordance is not possible for all sectors, so we identify three groups – twenty ISIC sectors that are sensitive, twenty-one 'mixed' sectors that correspond to both sensitive and insensitive NACE sectors, and thirty-nine insensitive sectors.

Table 7.7 sets out each country's OECD export shares by the three groups of sectors. Of the four EC economies, France, Germany and Italy have their highest export shares in the sensitive sectors. The USA and Japan each have higher export shares in the sensitive sectors than

Table 7.7. *OECD manufacturing export shares by 1992 group (by percentage)*

	France	Germany	Italy	UK	EC4	Japan	USA
Sensitive Sectors							
1980	7.8	15.7	5.8	11.9	41.2	13.4	21.8
1984	7.1	13.7	5.7	8.2	34.6	21.2	22.4
1987	7.4	16.0	6.3	8.9	38.7	18.9	18.9
Mixed Sectors							
1980	10.7	20.1	8.3	8.3	47.4	12.6	14.8
1984	8.6	18.1	7.7	6.2	40.6	16.0	14.9
1987	9.0	21.3	8.2	6.2	45.0	15.2	10.6
Insensitive Sectors							
1980	9.2	13.6	6.7	7.6	37.0	10.1	11.1
1984	8.1	12.7	6.8	6.3	33.9	11.4	11.0
1987	8.4	15.1	7.3	6.4	37.3	9.6	10.0

Germany, though the EC four share is slightly above that of the USA and Japan together. None of the six has their best performance in the insensitive sectors, suggesting that these are sectors where competition from other countries is strong both for the EC four and for the USA and Japan.

Table 7.7 indicates that the USA and Japan perform relatively strongly in the sensitive sectors. This can be interpreted in line with the EC's arguments that these are sectors where various barriers have inhibited competition and efficiency within the EC. The question arises, however, as to who will benefit most from the 1992 process. Will the EC firms benefit most from the changes or will US and Japanese firms be able to build on their existing advantages and benefit more from being able to move freely within a more open EC market? The answer to this question will depend not only on the analysis of the likely effects of 1992 and the controversy surrounding that issue but also on other factors that are influencing the development of relative competitiveness. Some assessment of the importance of other factors can be obtained by looking at trends in performance in these sectors.

Figures 7.3 and 7.4 present a relative export variable – as we constructed it earlier for the technology groups but now constructed for the sensitive sectors. This shows the trends in the export performance of each EC country relative to the USA and Japan in the sensitive sectors relative to all sectors. While all the EC economies perform badly in the sensitive sectors relative to both the USA and Japan, the trends with respect to the two countries are different. Thus, all four EC countries and also the USA are losing competitiveness in the sensitive sectors relative to Japan during

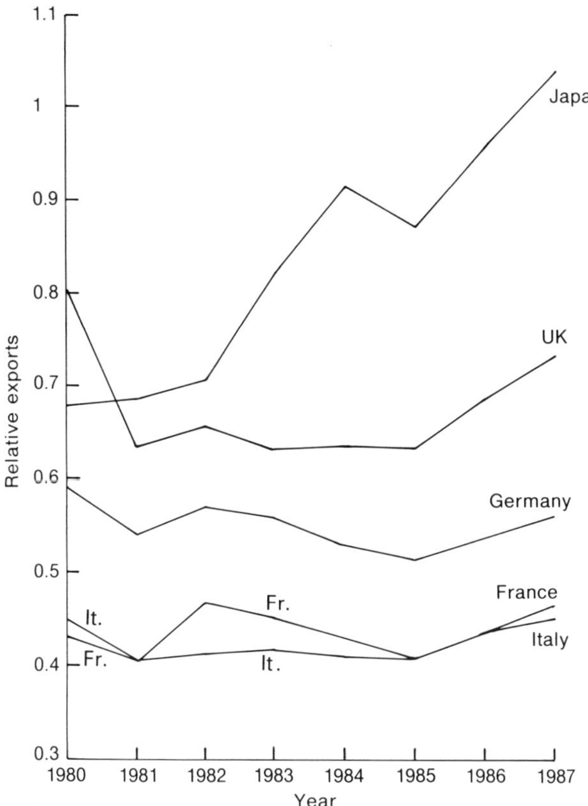

Figure 7.3 Exports relative to the USA in sensitive relative to insensitive sectors.

the 1980s. The USA and the UK have both the highest levels of relative competitiveness in these sectors and the sharpest falls. Relative to the USA in contrast, the four EC countries experience little change in their competitiveness over the period as a whole, though they all show some increase from 1985. Even if the 1992 changes were to benefit the EC economies in these sectors more than the USA and Japan, these figures show that any improvement in EC relative performance might not be sufficient to offset the continuing downward trend in performance in these sectors relative to Japan, though it may with respect to the USA. Overall, then, there is indeed a problem of relative competitiveness of the EC economies in the 1992 sensitive sectors; however, whether 1992 itself will reverse this trend in a dynamic world where other forces are also affecting competitiveness is an open question.

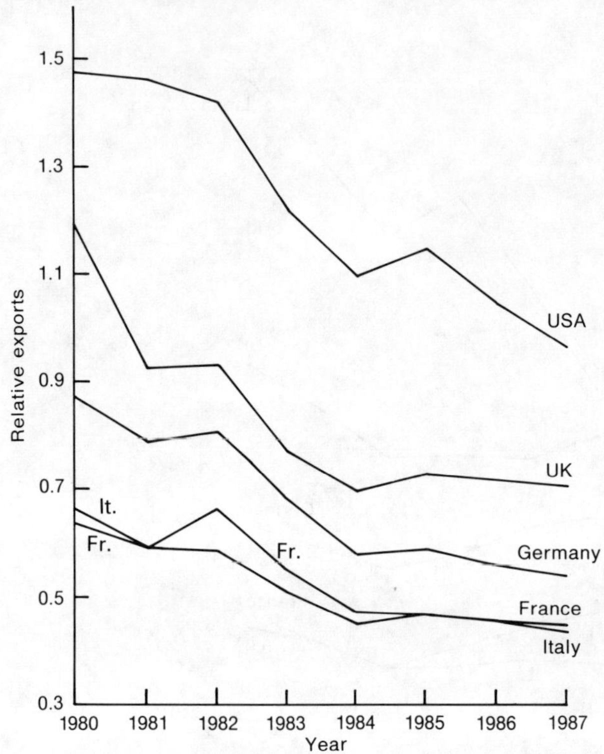

Figure 7.4 Exports relative to Japan in sensitive relative to insensitive sectors.

7.3 Determinants of European trade performance relative to the USA and Japan

In this section, we investigate further the underlying factors determining the trade performance of the main EC economies relative to their two main rivals. The previous discussion has already raised a number of factors that may contribute to an explanation of relative performance such as competition, scale, and innovation. Thus, the main aim of the 1992 programme is meant to be one of raising competition and efficiency. This, according to the EC (EC, 1988), may be achieved through increasing market size by removing barriers, while allowing the achievement where appropriate of higher scale economies. The resulting increase in competition from the completion of the internal market should stimulate both static and dynamic efficiency. The larger market size and competition should also encourage increased R&D and more European cooperation in R&D so improving competitiveness in innovation-intensive industries. As discussed above, however, the simple descriptive statistics do not suggest any clear link between technology-intensity and overall trade performance.

The approach we adopt there is to analyse to what extent the various factors that would, in general, be expected to influence the trade performance of industrialised countries can explain the *relative* performance of each of the four EC economies focused on here with respect to the USA and Japan. Thus, while, for example, innovation may act as a determinant of export performance of each of these six economies, it may or may not help in explaining relative bilateral performance. The main factors that we will consider here can be grouped under four main headings: competition, technology and innovation, human capital and physical capital. We will consider each of these in turn.

The effect of competition on exports is a complex issue. In general increased competition may be expected to increase efficiency which would have a direct positive effect on exports. However, whether more monopolistic industries will restrict exports or otherwise may depend on whether they can segment the domestic and international markets and whether, for example, they are directing excess capacity to export markets. Furthermore, more recent work on market structure and trade suggests both that imperfectly competitive markets may stimulate intra-industry trade (see, for example, Helpman and Krugman, 1986) and that strategic competition on an international level may affect trade in a number of ways (see, for example, Dixit and Kyle, 1985). Thus, there may be direct and indirect effects of competition on trade depending on both efficiency and strategic considerations.

With respect to technology and innovation, there is a large literature that suggests there is a positive relationship between innovation and trade (for a survey, see Hughes, 1986). However, the impact of innovation on trade flows may become less strong for a number of reasons. Firstly, to the extent that much R&D is located in multinationals there may be only a weak relationship between where R&D is carried out and where its impact on production and exports is experienced. Secondly, as trade flows increase and as firms in different countries establish both production and R&D links, the transfer and flow of technological knowledge may be quite swift and again the link between R&D and trade will weaken. Finally, the literature already referred to on strategic competition suggests that R&D may be one strategic weapon firms use in international oligopolistic competition and so the effect of R&D on trade will depend on the dynamics of this international interaction.

A more static aspect of technology already discussed in section 7.2 is the role of scale economies. Scale economies may lead to competitive advantage as larger domestic and export markets allow shifts down the learning curve. The EC's concerns about scale economies would suggest that the EC economies may derive less benefit from scale economies than the USA and Japan and so may not have an advantage in scale-intensive industries.

Human capital of various forms is a factor that is expected to have a positive effect on trade performance and one, in particular, where the industrialised countries may have an advantage. Human capital may also interact with the technology factor to affect competitiveness as well as being a more general determinant of quality and efficiency. Skilled labour, although treated often as an endowment, must of course be trained over time, and differences among the industrialised countries with respect to types, quantities and levels of skills could be expected to affect their relative performance. Finally, physical capital is a further factor endowment variable that may determine export advantage, although conventional wisdom since the Leontief paradox has been that the advanced countries are more likely to have an advantage in physical than human capital industries.

7.3.1 Estimation

To estimate the effects of the various factors considered above on relative export performance, we adopt two measures of competitiveness – the index of revealed comparative advantage (RCA) and the net trade ratio. Since we are concerned with performance relative to the USA and Japan, the two dependent variables are measured for each EC country relative to the USA and to Japan. Thus we take the RCA index of each of the four EC economies relative to the RCA indexes of Japan and the USA. Thus for each country we measure RCA as:

$$\text{RCA} = (X_{ij}/\sum_k X_{ik})/(\sum_i X_{ij}\sum_i\sum_k X_{ik}) \qquad (7.4)$$

where i = industry,
j = France, Germany, Italy, UK, USA or Japan,
k = all the OECD economies.

For each EC country we then construct two versions of each dependent variable: we take each country's RCA index relative to that of Japan and its RCA index relative to that of the USA. Similarly, we take the net trade ratio (exports/imports) of each EC country relative to that of the USA and of Japan. We also construct two similar variables for the USA relative to Japan, both for its RCA and for its net trade.

The data used to measure each country's RCA and net trade ratio are, as in section 7.2, OECD trade data from 1980 to 1987. We construct a set of independent variables to represent the four main characteristics discussed above – competition, innovation, physical capital and human capital. These data are not available for all our economies over this time period and at this level of disaggregation. In order to carry out this comparative exercise we therefore use UK industry data to proxy the various industry characteristics we wish to identify. Further details on data are given in the appendix. The independent variables are as follows:

RDNO = R&D/value-added. This acts as a proxy for innovation.

CR5GO = five firm concentration ratio measured with respect to gross output, as one proxy for competition and the potential for strategic behaviour.

SCALE – minimum efficient scale, measured as mean plant size in the top 50 per cent of net output divided by total net output.

KL = capital–labour ratio. This represents physical capital.

There are four human capital variables to try to capture some of the variety in skilled labour:

NMEMP = operative staff/total employment.

SKMNG = managerial staff/total employment.

SKPT = professional and technical staff/total employment.

FSK = female staff (excluding managerial and professional and technical staff)/total employment.

These data are for 1980 to 1987 except for *SKMNG*, *SKPT* and *FSK* which are available only in 1981. The estimation is carried out as a pooled estimation. *SKMNG*, *SKPT* and *FSK* are assumed to be the same in each year.

The results are reported in tables 7.8 to 7.11. Tables 7.8 and 7.9 report results for the RCA index for Japan and the USA respectively. Tables 7.10 and 7.11 report results for the net trade ratio with respect to Japan and the USA respectively. The estimation is for sixty-eight industries. We discuss each table in turn.

The pooled results in table 7.8 – RCA with respect to Japan – are fairly similar across countries, including, notably, the USA. Thus, to the extent there is a similarity in determinants of trade performance with respect to Japan this is not simply a shared EC phenomenon. All five countries have a negative and significant effect of R&D on RCA, a positive effect of

Table 7.8. *Revealed comparative advantage of each country, relative to Japan, pooled 1980–87*

Country	*RDNO*	*CR5GO*	*SCALE*	*KL*	*NMEMP*	*SKMNG*	*SKPT*	*FSK*	Constant	$\bar{R}^2$
France	−0.82	0.67	−0.05	0.70	−4.21	−1.10	0.19	0.93	−6.23	0.35
	(−11.27)	(3.96)	(−1.31)	(7.34)	(−6.05)	(−4.17)	(1.56)	(8.09)	(−5.56)	
Germany	−0.70	0.43	−0.11	0.53	−3.55	−1.02	0.27	0.73	−5.49	0.29
	(−12.42)	(2.78)	(−3.14)	(6.53)	(−6.38)	(−5.08)	(2.99)	(6.70)	(−6.45)	
Italy	−0.62	0.06	−0.05	0.22	−2.83	−0.78	−0.14	0.57	−5.29	0.25
	(−7.71)	(0.31)	(−1.25)	(2.14)	(−4.06)	(−2.75)	(−1.12)	(4.42)	(−4.57)	
UK	−0.60	0.48	−0.11	0.56	−0.83	−1.29	0.13	1.18	−6.10	0.27
	(−8.50)	(2.83)	(−2.70)	(5.83)	(−7.62)	(−5.09)	(1.13)	(8.58)	(−5.81)	
USA	−0.65	0.40	−0.08	0.50	−5.56	−1.10	0.16	0.69	−6.74	0.27
	(−8.41)	(2.43)	(−2.16)	(4.91)	(−8.33)	(−4.51)	(1.21)	(5.14)	(−6.11)	

Notes: N = 544; all variables are in logs; figures in brackets are *t*-statistics; standard errors are hetero-skedastic consistent.

Table 7.9. *Revealed comparative advantage of each country, relative to USA, pooled 1980–87*

Country	*RDNO*	*CR5GO*	*SCALE*	*KL*	*NMEMP*	*SKMNG*	*SKPT*	*FSK*	Constant	$\bar{R}^2$
France	−0.17	0.27	0.03	0.19	1.36	0.001	0.04	0.23	0.52	0.12
	(−2.57)	(1.94)	(1.11)	(2.74)	(2.78)	(0.01)	(0.47)	(2.38)	(0.61)	
Germany	−0.05	0.03	−0.03	0.27	2.01	0.08	0.12	0.04	1.25	0.10
	(−0.84)	(0.30)	(−1.14)	(0.50)	(6.05)	(0.60)	(1.38)	(0.51)	(2.23)	
Italy	0.03	−0.34	0.02	−0.28	2.73	0.33	−0.30	−0.13	1.46	0.23
	(0.34)	(−1.82)	(0.80)	(−3.54)	(4.98)	(1.37)	(−2.28)	(−0.97)	(1.66)	
UK	0.05	0.09	−0.02	0.06	0.74	−0.19	−0.03	0.49	0.65	0.10
	(0.87)	(0.87)	(−1.05)	(1.07)	(2.34)	(−1.30)	(−0.33)	(1.08)	(1.08)	

Notes: N = 544; all variables are in logs; figures in brackets are *t*-statistics; standard erros are hetero-skedastic consistent.

capital intensity, negative effects of *NMEMP* and *SKMNG* and positive effects of *FSK*. *CR5GO* has a positive and significant effect except in the case of Italy. *SCALE* is always negative but not significant for France or Italy. *SKPT* varies in sign and is only significant – and positive – in the case of Germany. Thus, there are some shared determinants of performance relative to Japan but also some differences. The R&D results are clear and unsurprising – Japan has relatively better performance in R&D-intensive industries. The results for *CR5GO* could indicate either an advantage of all five countries except Japan in strategic competition or alternatively that Japan performs better where competition in general is more intense. The results for physical capital are interesting and show that all five countries have an advantage in physical capital compared to Japan. The scale results are more mixed – certainly there is a negative effect but it is not confined to the EC countries, the USA being one of three to have a significant coefficient.

The results for human capital are mixed. Except for Germany which has a clear relative advantage in professional and technical staff, there is no clear relationship for this variable. *SKMNG* is clearly negative, indicating an advantage for Japan in industries where there is a high proportion of management. This is interesting given the stress on different management techniques and communication methods in Japanese firms. Further, Japan would seem to have an advantage in industries with a high proportion of operative staff. Finally, and of some concern, all countries including the USA have an advantage in industries intensive in female labour that is neither managerial nor professional or technical – if this is a crude proxy for unskilled labour, it implies Japan has an advantage overall in R&D-intensive, management-intensive and skill-intensive industries.

The results with respect to the USA – table 7.9 – are rather different. R&D has a negative effect on France's relative competitiveness with respect to the USA but not for any of the other three countries. All four EC economies have a positive and significant sign on *NMEMP* but otherwise the results vary by country. France has positive signs on *CR5GO*, *KL* and *FSK* – suggesting advantage in physical capital and unskilled labour. Germany in contrast has no other significant coefficients except for *NMEMP*, suggesting these variables cannot distinguish German advantage relative to the USA. The same is true for the UK. Italy has negative coefficients on *CR5GO*, *KL* and *SKPT* indicating a disadvantage in high concentration, capital-intensive and skill-intensive industries.

Table 7.10 presents the results for the net trade ratio relative to Japan. The pooled results are similar to those for RCA – suggesting disadvantage

Table 7.10. *Net trade ratio of each country, relative to Japan, pooled 1980–87*

Country	*RDNO*	*CR5GO*	*SCALE*	*KL*	*NMEMP*	*SKMNG*	*SKPT*	*FSK*	Constant	$\bar{R}^2$
France	−0.81	0.44	−0.04	0.98	−4.98	−1.49	0.23	1.37	−9.11	0.33
	(−7.46)	(2.30)	(−0.92)	(8.77)	(−5.61)	(−4.47)	(1.17)	(9.52)	(−6.59)	
Germany	−0.65	0.37	−0.13	0.76	−4.43	−1.09	0.23	1.12	−7.36	0.31
	(−8.32)	(2.08)	(−3.32)	(8.01)	(−6.70)	(−4.53)	(1.71)	(8.74)	(−7.02)	
Italy	−0.61	−0.63	0.03	0.34	−3.70	−1.01	−0.27	0.91	−7.70	0.29
	(−5.97)	(−2.91)	(0.54)	(2.98)	(−4.47)	(−3.06)	(−1.72)	(6.23)	(−5.84)	
UK	−0.58	0.41	−0.13	0.85	−5.03	−1.61	0.05	1.50	−9.19	0.29
	(−6.05)	(2.16)	(−2.94)	(7.70)	(−6.43)	(−5.38)	(0.31)	(9.70)	(−7.34)	
USA	−0.79	0.55	0.15	0.87	−6.95	−1.42	0.31	1.44	−9.77	0.31
	(−7.12)	(2.54)	(−2.86)	(6.67)	(−7.55)	(−4.53)	(1.74)	(8.38)	(−6.88)	

Notes: N = 544; all variables are in logs; figures in brackets are *t*-statistics; standard errors are hetero-skedastic consistent.

Table 7.11. *Net trade ratio of each country, relative to USA, pooled 1980–87*

Country	*RDNO*	*CR5GO*	*SCALE*	*KL*	*NMEMP*	*SKMNG*	*SKPT*	*FSK*	Constant	$\bar{R}^2$
France	−0.03	−0.11	0.11	0.12	1.97	−0.07	−0.09	−0.07	0.67	0.06
	(−0.26)	(−0.58)	(2.76)	(1.13)	(2.89)	(−0.23)	(−0.77)	(−0.44)	(0.57)	
Germany	0.13	−0.18	0.02	−0.11	2.52	0.33	−0.09	−0.31	2.42	0.10
	(2.05)	(−1.41)	(0.56)	(−1.38)	(5.29)	(1.76)	(−0.88)	(−3.56)	(2.92)	
Italy	0.18	−1.17	0.18	−0.53	3.24	0.41	−0.58	−0.53	2.07	0.25
	(1.38)	(−4.43)	(3.42)	(−4.61)	(4.18)	(1.25)	(−3.66)	(−3.03)	(1.72)	
UK	0.21	−0.13	0.02	−0.02	1.92	−0.19	−0.26	0.06	0.58	0.01
	(31.6)	(−1.11)	(0.67)	(−0.19)	(4.44)	(−0.94)	(−2.76)	(0.57)	(0.70)	

Notes: N = 544; all variables are in logs; figures in brackets are *t*-statistics; standard errors are hetero-skedastic consistent.

of the EC economies and the USA in R&D-intensive industries, management-intensive and skill-intensive industries and with advantages in more concentrated and capital-intensive industries.

Finally, table 7.11 presents the results for the net trade ratio relative to the USA. These results differ from those of table 7.9. In particular, both Germany and the UK have a positive and significant effect of R&D on their relative competitiveness. The UK as well as Italy has a negative and significant effect of *SKPT* while Germany and Italy have a negative and significant effect of *FSK*. Thus, again these results are different from the results with respect to Japan. They also vary in some respects by EC country.

Overall, the results do indicate the importance of the four groups of factors discussed earlier – competition, innovation, human capital and physical capital. However, the results are not the same for the comparison with the USA as with Japan. Relative to Japan, the results do suggest problems with respect to innovation and skill, and possibly competition, but with respect to the USA this is not so. The US results are more varied but there is some indication of positive R&D and skill effects for some countries and types of skilled labour. The results show, then, that it is unwise to generalise about the competitiveness of the EC countries with respect to their main competitors – the determinants vary between the USA and Japan and there is variation across countries. Each country competes internationally with many other countries and weaknesses with respect to one competitor may not indicate a general weakness. Certainly, it is unsafe to generalise about the competitiveness of the EC group of countries relative to the USA and Japan on the basis of these results.

7.4 Conclusion

In this chapter we have analysed the relative international competitiveness of the four largest EC economies with respect to the USA and Japan. A comparison of both their export structures and their competitiveness across industries indicated that while export structures were similar they were diverging during the 1980s. Further, industry competitiveness – measured by the net trade ratio – was not similar across these six countries. The EC economies were not found to be more similar to each other than to the USA and Japan; in fact Italy had the most dissimilar trade structure of the six economies considered here. A descriptive analysis of the level of, and trends in, competitiveness during the 1980s showed that the three most successful economies were Japan, Germany, and Italy, who specialised respectively in high, medium and low technology industries. The two economies with the worst trends in performance – the USA and UK – had their best performance in high technology industries. A comparison of performance in those sectors particularly sensitive to 1992 suggested that there were potential problems for the EC economies. Not only were both the USA and Japan performing better in those sectors but Japan's performance was improving particularly strongly in those sectors over time.

Section 7.3 presented the results of an econometric analysis of the determinants of relative competitiveness with respect to the USA and Japan. The results indicated that most countries had problems with respect both to R&D and to skill with respect to Japan. However, there was variation in the results by country. The results with respect to the USA were much more varied. In the case of relative net trade both Germany and the UK had an advantage with respect to R&D while results for skill vary by country. Overall, the results show both that it is misleading to generalise about the EC countries as a group and, furthermore, that the nature of strengths and weaknesses in competitiveness depends on which of the main competitors is used for a comparison. The results indicate that competitiveness is determined by a variety of factors in ways that vary across countries.

Appendix

The export and import data were obtained from the OECD computer databank. Exports and imports were in thousands of US dollars at current prices. The data for section 7.2 are for eighty four-digit ISICs. However, in order to be compatible with the industry data in section 7.3 five ISICs are dropped and four ISICs are combined into groups containing either two or three ISICs.

The UK data were obtained from a comprehensive database on UK manufacturing industry constructed for 202 four-digit manufacturing industries covering all of manufacturing industry. Further details of its construction are given in M. Andrews *et al.* 'Creating a database for UK Manufacturing in the 1980s' available from myself on request.

To translate the data into the ISIC a concordance table was obtained from the UK Department of Trade and Industry. The 202 industries were aggregated to seventy-three ISICs for which exact concordances existed. Missing variables in individual data series resulted in the final sample size of sixty-eight industries.

SKPT, *SKMNG* and *FSK* were derived from the UK Census of Population 1981. R&D data were obtained from Business Monitor MO14 and British Business for 1981, 1983, 1985, 1986 and 1987. Missing years were calculated by interpolation. Capital stock data were obtained from the Central Statistical Office. The remaining data were obtained from the UK Census of Production 1980 to 1987.

Note

I am grateful to participants at the conference on European Competitiveness for comments. Any errors are the author's responsibility.

References

Archibugi, D. and Pianta, M., 1990. 'The technological specialisation of the EEC, the US and Japan: evidence from patent data', mimeo.

Baldwin, R., 1989. 'On the growth effects of 1992', *Economic Policy*, 9.

Buigues, P., Ilzkovitz, F. and Lebrun, J.-F., 1990. 'The impact of the internal market by industrial sector: the challenge for the member states', *European Economy – Social Europe* (special edition).

Cutler, T., Haslam, C., Williams, J. and Williams, K., 1989. *1992 – the Struggle for Europe*, Berg.

Davis, E., Geroski, P., Kay, J., Manning, A., Smales, C., Smith, S. and Szymanski, S., 1989. *1992: Myths and Realities*, London Business School.

Dixit, A. and Kyle, S., 1985. 'The use of protection and subsidies for entry promotion and deterrence', *American Economic Review*, 75.

EC, 1988. 'The economics of 1992', *European Economy*, 35.

Helpman, E. and Krugman, P., 1986. *Market Structure and Foreign Trade*, Cambridge, MA: MIT Press.

Hughes, K., 1986. *Exports and Technology*, Cambridge: Cambridge University Press.

1990. 'Competition, competitiveness and the European community – a critical analysis of "the economics of 1992"', Discussion Paper FS IV 90–7, Wissenschaftszentrum für Sozialforschung.

1991a. 'Trade structure and competitiveness in the main OECD economies', Discussion Paper FS IV 91–2, Wissenschaftszentrum für Sozialforschung.

1991b. 'Trade performance of the main EC economies relative to the USA and Japan in 1992-sensitive sectors', Discussion Paper FS IV 91–4, Wissenschaftszentrum für Sozialforschung.

OECD, 1986. *Science and Technology Indicators*, 2, OECD (Paris).

Part 3

European integration and structural change

8 Mergers, acquisitions and the completion of the internal market

NEIL KAY

8.1 Introduction

The completion of the internal market targeted for 1992 has stimulated considerable interest in the corporate strategies that will be developed by corporations to cope with the demands and opportunities presented by the emerging European economy. Since the publication of the White Paper on completing the internal market (CEC, 1985), the Commission[1] has been enthusiastic about the role of external strategies such as joint venture and merger in stimulating and reinforcing the effective operation of the completed market. Elsewhere (Kay, 1991) we have argued that the Commission's view that 1992 will directly stimulate industrial activity such as joint venture is misplaced. In this chapter we consider the parallel question of merger in the context of 1992 and conclude that there is serious cause for concern that the acceleration of the rate of cross-frontier merger activity may be to the detriment of the completed market and may reduce both competition and efficiency.

In this chapter we shall argue that the Commission has adopted too permissive an attitude towards European merger and acquisition activity and that there is a real danger that the emerging Europe-wide merger wave may sacrifice some of the gains in productive efficiency and consumer welfare that 1992 is intended to generate. The Commission's policy proposals are dependent on an obsolete theoretical framework, and it recognises but neglects clear and consistent evidence on merger failure.

We shall first consider the foundations of the Commission's approach to merger control and then critically examine this in the light of the available empirical evidence. The relevance of the benchmarks and indicators nominated for merger control purposes will be discussed before consideration is given to the broader context of the development of European competition and the conflicting agendas in which it is set.

8.2 Theory and evidence in merger activity – the Commission's perspective

The Directorate-General for Economic and Financial Affairs (DG II) produced a systematic analysis of the effect of horizontal mergers and the implications for competition policy in 1989 (CEC, 1989). The analysis builds on the idea of an efficiency/monopoly-power trade-off as developed in an early model of O. E. Williamson (1968).[2] The basic model identifies three possible effects resulting from merger: cost savings obtainable from increases in the scale of production (economies of scale),[3] the creation of monopoly power (CEC, 1989 p. 17), or some combination of the two:

> Those who give precedence to the efficiency effects believe that the increased concentration resulting from mergers leads to cost reductions which, other things being equal, allow increases in margins.
>
> Those, on the other hand, who focus more on the dangers of monopolization see the causality as working mainly in the opposite direction: mergers tend to induce price rises, as a result both of increased concentration and the expectation of more collusive behaviour . . .
>
> In fact, it is probable that in many cases mergers simultaneously produce some efficiency gains, notably in the form of cost reductions, and some increase in monopoly power which may manifest itself in higher prices. There is thus the question of a trade-off between the two types of effect. (CED, 1989 p. 18)

Consistent with this, the later section on 'analysis for the purposes of merger control' is introduced with the statement 'The impact of a merger can be of three basic types: it can improve efficiency without any reduction of competition, reduce competition without any gain in efficiency; or have effects at once conducive to efficiency and harmful to competition' (CEC, 1989 p. 45).

The Williamson trade-off has implications for profitability which can be illustrated with the help of table 8.1. The three basic types of merger effects associated with the Williamson trade-off can be analysed in terms of effect on corporate profitability. If efficiency improves without any reduction in competition (case 3 in table 8.1) then profitability increases due to the decrease in costs. On the other hand, if merger reduces competition without any effect on efficiency, then profitability increases, this time due to monopoly power and the raising of price–cost margins (case 1 in table 8.1). Finally, if merger results in efficiency gains *and* increased monopoly power, *both* effects will contribute to increased profitability (case 4).

The three possible outcomes associated with the Williamson trade-off differ in their welfare implications. Outcomes in which efficiency gains are

Table 8.1. *Impact of merger on corporate profitability*

	Efficiency		
	No effect	Costs decrease	Costs increase
Competition:			
No effect	0 (2)	+ (3)	− (5)
Decrease	+ (1)	+ (4)	? (6)

Notes: + profits increase; − profits decrease; 0 no effect on profits; ? net effect on profit uncertain.

more than compensated for in terms of losses due to monopolisation represent a diminution of welfare, while those in which efficiency gains predominate are more likely to be treated as benign and unproblematic. Consequently, much attention has been given to the likelihood of one or other of the effects dominating, and CEC (1989) is consistent in this respect:

> [A]t the present time, judgements as to whether a merger presents a danger of monopolization, potential efficiency gains or a combination of the two must be based on general indicators.
>
> As far as monopoly power is concerned the indicators favouring its emergence are well-known: high market share with a scattered competitive fringe, low import penetration and high entry barriers, demand that is inelastic and also static or only slowly increasing, and a differentiated product, etc.
>
> Among the factors that point to the likelihood of efficiency gains are large-scale economies and learning effects, substantial excess capacity, and high capital intensity and technology content. It is criteria such as these that will be used to examine the present situation in the EC in Part B of this paper. (CEC, 1989 p. 19)

This appears entirely reasonable in the light of the Williamson trade-off model; the Commission's study then goes on in Part B to use indicators of the factors mentioned above to make 'a preliminary classification of industries into those in which mergers – and thus concentration – are likely to have on balance beneficial effects and those in which the overall effect is likely to be negative' (p. 23). The analysis is carried out at three-digit level and results in three major categories of industries classified by likely prospects for merger: (1) those offering little or no prospect of efficiency gains, whether or not competition is reduced, (2) those in which merger activity is *prima facie* beneficial due to potential efficiency gains and little danger of reduction in competition and (3) those likely to produce both efficiency gains and dangers of reduction in competition.

For our purposes, one of the most significant features of this analysis is the assignment of most of the high tech industries (including chemicals, pharmaceuticals, computers, telecommunications, electronics, the motor and aerospace industries, and precision instruments) to the second category of industries, 'in which there is less danger of a reduction of competition and mergers offer real prospects of efficiency gains' (CEC, 1989 p. 29).

We therefore have what appears to be a reasonable and well-balanced perspective on probable effects of mergers, devised from a simple and convincing theoretical framework. The report discusses the proposal for a merger control regulation in the light of this classificatory approach, concluding, for example, that mergers in the high tech sector may enhance and help European industry catch up with American or Japanese rivals.

Unfortunately this approach is simply not supported by the empirical evidence which the report itself cites (pp. 21–2). The problem is that the approach builds on Williamson's simple trade-off model which is itself inconsistent with the body of knowledge on merger effects which has been built up over recent years. We can summarise the problem by emphasising that the three basic merger effects of 'danger of monopolisation, potential efficiency gains or a combination of the two' (CEC, 1989 p. 19) are represented by cases 1, 3 and 4 in table 8.1. As can be seen, *all* three cases lead to increased profitability due to merger effects on demand and/or costs. Case 2 (no effect on efficiency or competition) is neglected in the simple trade-off model since it would be of no interest to a rational profit-maximising firm. The simple trade-off model does not recognise cases 5 and 6, in which merger may have an adverse effect on efficiency and costs.

Thus, increased profitability is a concomitant of merger *whatever* the balance of efficiency versus monopoly power in the Williamson trade-off model. This directly contradicts the empirical evidence cited by CEC (1989):

> A comparative study, directed by Mueller (1980), of results from various EEC countries concerning full legal mergers concluded that . . . the tests of post-merger profitability suggested that the mergers had little or no effect on the profitability of the merging firm in the three to five years following the merger; nor was there any significant difference in the return per share three years after the merger. This confirms the results obtained in many American studies (see Scherer (1980) pp. 138–139).

Further, a comprehensive recent survey of research into the impact of mergers in the UK concludes that most studies looking at their effect on profitability lead to 'the clear impression of a small, variable but negative impact' (Hughes, 1989 p. 79). Another recent survey paper by Mueller (1988) studies the impact of mergers on profitability in a variety of countries and time periods and concludes that 'a ... consistent and dramatic positive effect of mergers on profitability has not been observed' (p. 54). Indeed many studies report neutral or even negative effects on performance, and Thompson (1988) interprets Mueller's survey as indicating that 'mergers actually reduce profitability' (p. 78).

The evidence on mergers' effects on efficiency cited in CEC (1989) is consistent with this depressing performance:

> Detailed studies of the success of mergers in the UK (Meeks (1977); Cowling *et al.* (1980)) confirm that efficiency is rarely increased by merger, and sometimes reduced. Studies by management consultants come to similar disappointing conclusions. Coley and Reinton (1980) looked at US and British companies in the *Fortune* 250 list and the *Financial Times* 500 which in the past had made acquisitions to enter new markets' ... only 23% of the 116 firms analysed were able to recover the cost of their capital or better still the funds invested in the acquisition programme. It also appears that the higher the degree of diversification, the smaller is the likelihood of success. For horizontal mergers in which the acquired firm is not large, however, the success rate is high (45%) (CEC, 1989 p. 21).

Since outcomes in this last study were classified as either success or failure, the last line could be rewritten as 'the failure rate is still high (55%)'. It is a remarkable comment on a consistently dismal message from the empirical literature that the Commission report can take comfort from a 'high' success rate in a small subsample in which the majority of outcomes are still failures.

Dennis Mueller makes a crucial point on one set of studies in which no increases in profitability were reported on average; 'It is difficult to believe that some of these mergers did not result in sufficient increases in market power to generate extra profits. However, the reduction in profits, due to losses in efficiency among the other mergers, were apparently sufficiently great to offset these gains' (Mueller, 1988 p. 54).

This point is an extremely important one which is worth spelling out in some detail. Since mergers increase concentration and reduce actual or potential competition, they will typically have, at best, a neutral effect on monopoly power, and, at worst, an adverse effect on monopoly power. The net effect from this factor would typically be to increase profitability for any group of mergers. Therefore, if any group of mergers report neutral effects on profitability overall, it is natural to conclude that the gains in profitability due to increased monopoly power have been offset by efficiency losses such as those reported in the Coley and Reinton study referred to in CEC (1989).

This has major implications for merger control and competition policy.

It implies a rejection of the simple version of the Williamson trade-off model used by the Commission. In that framework only outcomes in which profitability increases are recognised, that is cases 1, 3 and 4 in table 8.1. Ironically, it means that the three cases *not* recognised by the Commission (2, 5 and 6) are on balance more likely in practice than are the three officially recognised cases. If there is a trade-off, it more commonly appears to involve increased monopoly power and *decreased* efficiency. It also implies a rejection of the comment in CEC (1989): 'the only conclusion to be drawn from the empirical evidence is that a general presumption in favour of (horizontal) mergers is not justified' (p. 22). This is incorrect. A more accurate interpretation would be 'The only conclusion to be drawn from the empirical evidence is that a general presumption *against* (horizontal) mergers is justified'. Even if mergers had no net effect on profitability, the tendency of some mergers to increase concentration and facilitate collusion suggests that on average they would diminish efficiency. The fact that some studies report negative effects on profitability suggests that losses in efficiency in these cases are more than sufficient to compensate for any increases in monopoly power, signalling the probable existence of the twin hazards of increased monopoly power and diminished efficiency. It should also be borne in mind that all these mergers have been allowed through the anti-trust legislative hoops set up by respective national authorities.

One obvious question which is raised by these studies is *why* merger should still be pursued by corporations in view of its consistently disappointing performance measured in terms of profitability. The studies were not generally designed to answer such a question. However, it can be pointed out that the results are easier to reconcile with managerial theories of firms in which growth and size are managerial objectives than with traditional neoclassical profit maximising perspectives.

However there is a further consideration of particular relevance to the issue as to whether or not merger activity will tend to diminish efficiency in the context of 1992. The studies that have been carried out so far have been predominantly concerned with single-country merger and acquisition activity. If it is so difficult to extract efficiency gains from two US firms merging, or a UK firm taking over another UK firm, there is liable to be less hope for European cross-frontier merger, with Italian firms taking over Dutch, and German firms merging with Spanish. It is difficult enough to marry together two different firms in the same country, without the added complications of different cultures, language, legal systems and political conventions. While the evidence at the moment is mostly anecdotal, there is every reason to suppose that the emerging wave of cross-frontier mergers identified in

Table 8.2. *National, community and international industrial mergers (including acquisitions of majority holdings) in the Community in 1983/4, 1984/5, 1985/6, 1986/7, 1987/8*

National [a]					Community [b]					International [c]					Total				
83/4	84/5	85/6	86/7	87/8	83/4	84/5	85/6	86/7	87/8	83/4	84/5	85/6	86/7	87/8	83/4	84/5	85/6	86/7	87/8
101	146	145	211	214	29	44	52	75	111	25	18	30	17	58	155	208	227	303	383

Note: Data gathered by the Commission from the specialist areas: [a] Involving firms from the same member state; [b] Involving firms from different member states; [c] Involving firms from member states and third countries with effects on the common market.

table 8.2 are likely to be even more problematic than are single-nationality amalgamations.

There is one other efficiency defence that can be put forward in favour of a liberal attitude towards mergers, and that concerns the market for corporate control. CEC (1989) argues that the threat of takeover may discipline management and encourage them to pursue profit-oriented behaviour (p. 20). However CEC (1989) also recognises that against this must be set the dangers of short-termism and a concern with financial transactions at the expense of productivity and competitiveness.

In addition it should be pointed out that the market for corporate control is fairly weak or even non-existent in many EC countries, with hostile takeovers being frequently difficult or practically impossible to mount. The relatively well-developed markets for corporate control in the UK and the USA are not typical of the EC situation and therefore the takeover threat argument is of diminished relevance in this context. It is also ironic that this argument is raised in the context of 1992; if the Community does approach market completion, then 1992 should generate increased competitive pressure in product and factor markets, encouraging profit-oriented behaviour and increased efficiency. Since competition in these markets is more direct and focused than the vague possibilities of takeover even in economies where the market for corporate control is well developed, focusing on the efficiency implications of threat of takeover in the EC context seems at best redundant. There appears little need to look to the market for corporate control to stimulate efficiency in a 1992 context if the liberalised product and factor markets post-1992 are achieving the objective more precisely and effectively. If anything, the evidence suggests that an active market for the corporate control at European level could seriously detract from the very objectives of competition and efficiency embodied in the 1992 programme itself.

In the next section we shall consider how the Commission's enthusiasm for pan-European cooperation may have led to the construction of a misguided typology of industries for merger control purposes.

8.3 Sectoral analysis and merger control

The CEC (1989) report analyses merger activity in EC industries over the period 1982–87, comparing growth industries with other EC industries. Growth industries were classified as those in which domestic EC demand growth averaged at least 5 per cent a year over the period, and was heavily characterised by high technology industries including computers, electronics, telecommunications, chemicals and pharmaceuticals (p. 41).

According to CEC (1989),

> The number of mergers and acquisitions of majority holdings involving firms in the top 1,000 has risen significantly less quickly in growth sectors than in the rest of industry ... this is at first sight surprising in that in these industries mergers often produce substantial efficiency gains. A comparison of the size of European firms with that of their American and Japanese competitors ... reveals that the European market leaders are smaller (pp. 41–2).

There are a number of problems with this line of argument. Firstly no evidence is provided for the 'substantial efficiency gains' claimed for mergers in growth sectors. Indeed the evidence already cited by CEC (1989) above, and the evidence generally available, tends to conflict with this claim. Secondly there appears to be an implicit assumption that American and Japanese firms are often better performing than their European competitors because they are larger. A more reasonable claim would be that they are larger because they are better performing – success breeds size rather than vice versa. Thirdly, even if size was a contributory factor in strong industrial performance in these sectors, it certainly does not automatically follow that growth by merger is the route by which scale should be achieved. For example, internal expansion may be slower but is more likely to be a guarantor of success in the long run.

Despite this, CEC (1989) analyses industries by four main groups based on the assumption that merger activity should be encouraged in growth sectors; industries were assigned to the groups on the basis of whether or not merger was likely to lead to a reduction in competition and/or efficiency gains in a particular industry. The results are shown in table 8.3

The four groups identified above can be related to the corresponding four cases identified in table 8.1, group 1 being interpretable as case 1, and so on. In order to measure danger of reduction of competition, two indicators were used: demand growth[4] and the import penetration ratio.[5] The CEC (1989) report argued that *prima facie* there is less danger of reduction of competition if there is either strong demand growth *or* above average import penetration for a given industry.

The prospect of efficiency gains was assessed on the basis of two indicators intended to measure economies of scale and technology content on an industry-by-industry basis. Potential economies of scale were measured by estimates of cost gradients operating in a particular industry, that is the additional unit costs borne by firms operating at below 50 per cent of the optimal scale.[6] Technology content was measured by the ratio of R&D expenditure to output for each industry. Since the evidence discussed earlier suggested that mergers typically do not provide efficiency gains, the status of both these indicators merits closer examination.

Table 8.3. *Illustration of classification of industries for merger control purposes*

Group	Industry	Characteristics	Implications
1	Building materials Metal goods Paints and varnishes Furniture Paper goods Rubber goods Tobacco	• Declining or mature industries • Markets closed to international trade • Not technology-intensive or only slowly changing technologically • Economies of scale limited or acting as entry barriers	In these industries mergers offer little prospect of efficiency gains and present a danger of a reduction of competition
2	Steel Industrial and agricultural machinery Leather and leather goods Fur Clothing and textiles Sawn and processed wood and related products Pulp, paper and board Jewellery, toys, musical instruments	• Declining or mature industries • Fairly open to imports from inside and outside EC • In some industries, strong competition from low-wage countries • Economies of scale limited or already exploited • Not technology-intensive or with technology known throughout the world • Some industries highly fragmented (toys, furs)	Less danger of reduction of competition because of high import penetration and the fragmentation of some industries. But growth by merger is no longer an appropriate strategy for European firms. Instead, they should set out to specialise in top-of-the-range products, requiring modern and flexible production facilities

3	Advanced materials Chemicals/ pharmaceuticals Computers/ office automation Telecommunications Electronics Motor vehicles Aerospace Instruments	• Growth industries • Open to international trade • Strong competition from American and Japanese products • Large economies of scale • R&D very important, fast-changing technology	Less danger of monopolisation and prospects of substantial efficiency gains from mergers. In these industries, link-ups between European firms would allow them to internationalise their operations from a solid European base
4	Boilermaking Cables and heavy electrical plant Railway equipment Shipbuilding Some food industries (confectionery, chocolate, flour and pasta) Beer	• Mature industries • Little intra-Community trade and competition restricted by segmentation of public procurement markets or differences in standards and regulations • Not technology-intensive (food and drink industries) or only moderately so • Large economies of scale	In these industries the removal of barriers with the single market programme will lead to rationalisation and European-scale mergers. These may produce efficiency gains but there is also a danger of reduction of competition.

Source: CEC (1989) p. 32.

Table 8.4. *Products for which the cost slope at half minimum efficient technical size (METS) is superior or equal to 10 per cent*

NACE Code	Product	METS as percentage of production		Cost gradient at half METS
		UK	EC	
473	Books	n.a.	n.a.	20–36
241	Bricks	1	0.2	25
251	Dyes	> 100	n.a.	17–22
364	Aircraft	> 100	n.a.	20
251	Titanium oxide	63	50	8–16
242	Cement	10	1	6–16
251	Synthetic rubber	24	3.5	15
342	Electric motors	60	6	15
471	Kraft paper	11*	1.4*	13
251	Petrochemicals	23*	3*	12
26	Nylon	4*	1*	12
311	Cylinder block castings	3	0.3	10
311	Small cast-iron castings	0.7	0.1	10
438	Carpets	0.3	0.04	10
328	Diesel engines	> 100	n.a.	10

Note: * Probable underestimate
Source: CEC (1988) p. 112.

The earlier CEC report on the economies of 1992 (CEC, 1988) carried out an assessment of the prevalence of economies of scale drawing upon the same study by Pratten (1988) cited by CEC (1989). In fact, Pratten's study indicates that economies of scale are not a major issue in the substantial majority of industries in the Community. In 73 per cent of the cases studied, there was room in the EC for at least twenty plants all operating at minimum efficient technical size (METS). In these cases that would still leave room for at least two or three plants exploiting METS *within* larger EC national economics such as the UK, France and Germany. This hardly constitutes convincing grounds for arguing the case for cross-frontier mergers to promote efficiency, even if mergers were the preferred route to effective attainment of economies of scale.

However, CEC (1989) further muddies the waters by adopting a curious and limited interpretation of economies of scale. As can be seen from table 8.4, identifying industries as being characterised by economies of scale on the basis of cost gradients alone can give bizarre results. Table

8.4 is constructed from industries for which the cost gradient is at least 10 per cent from CEC (1988) as a source.

The highest cost gradients in table 8.4 are for books and bricks, neither of which are sectors known for massive economies of scale. There appears to be room for 100 brick manufacturers in the UK alone all exploiting METS. In fact, the median METS for these high cost-gradient industries was only 11 per cent of UK production and 1.4 per cent of EC (Kraft paper). When METS is looked at in these cases, the idea that cost gradient alone is a reliable indicator of economies of scale in European industry is simply untenable. Consequently, CEC's (1989) claims (pp. 29 and 64) that mergers could lead to potential efficiency gains in industries characterised by at least modest cost gradients (i.e., about 5 per cent) should be set aside as being unreliable and unjustified.

As to the second indicator, technological content, CEC (1989) p. 25 claims:

> there is an arguable case for saying that mergers can also be beneficial in high-technology industries. These industries are highly R&D intensive and because of indivisibilities in R&D up to certain thresholds firms require a sufficient scale of operation in order to undertake research programmes.[7]

However, the earlier (1988) CEC report did survey the empirical evidence in this area, and it is worth quoting their conclusions in some detail as an accurate summary of current research findings:

> Many empirical studies conclude that there are no economies of scale in the innovation process. The function of transforming research inputs into innovation outputs seems to be characterised by constant or even decreasing returns to scale ... [also] according to empirical studies the elasticity of R&D activities with respect to size of firms is less than unity ... it seems that research activities increase proportionately more than size, up to a certain threshold (which varies with the industry), but that large firms spend relatively less on research than small and medium-sized enterprises.
>
> The above two results (constant or decreasing returns to scale and elasticity of R&D with respect to size less than unity) mean that the efficiency with which research inputs are transformed into innovation output does not increase with size of firm ... Most of the empirical studies confirm this finding and show that, apart from the chemical industry, large size does not favour innovation (p. 113).

Therefore the 'arguable case' in CEC (1989) that scale economies in R&D means that mergers can be beneficial in the high technology industries is simply not supported by the available evidence cited in DG II's own research.

The CEC (1988) report goes on (p. 113) to cite a study undertaken by Geroski for that report which found that in the UK firms with fewer than

10,000 employees generated 56.1 per cent of innovations in the period 1945–83. Further, small firms seem to be playing a growing role in the innovation process with 43.2 per cent of innovations coming from firms with fewer than 1,000 employees in 1983 compared with 29.6 per cent in 1945. Small firms also contributed more in terms of innovation than large firms in the most innovative sectors – machinery, mechanical and electronic equipment, chemicals, electrical equipment and instruments (Geroski, 1987).

Even if mergers had no integration problems relative to internal expansion, there appears to be an arguable case for de-merger rather than merger in the EC high technology industries when considerations based on technology content are brought into play. Once it is recognised that evidence consistently points to merger being a clumsy, costly and inefficient route to increased size, there remains no reason to encourage merger activity on technology content grounds, despite CEC's (1989) arguments to the contrary.

In short, CEC's (1989) claims that there are industries in which merger activity may be at first sight beneficial (see p. 29 especially) are unjustified on the basis of evidence cited by both CEC reports. Instead there is no obvious case for encouraging merger activity on the grounds argued in the report. The report should be set aside as a largely unhelpful contribution to the policy debate on European merger policy. In the next section we shall consider the context in which the Commission's policy on European merger control has been developing in recent years and argue that CEC (1989) is representative of a Commission perspective that may have adverse implications for European competitiveness post-1992.

8.4 The CIM and CEM of European competitiveness

The CEC (1989) study was developed in the context of the basic question identified in the foreword – 'should European competition policy be strengthened or loosened in the context of achieving the internal market?' (p. 9).

Unfortunately the subsequent analysis continues a confusion of themes that was introduced in the White Paper on the completion of the internal market (CEC, 1985). The very first sentence of the White Paper embodies the tensions and conflicting agendas that have characterised the subsequent development of the programme and related economic analyses: 'unifying this market (of 320 million) presupposes that Member States will agree on the abolition of barriers of all kinds, harmonisation of rules, approximation of legislation and tax structures, strengthening of monetary cooperation and the necessary flanking measures to encourage European firms to work together' (CEC, 1985, para 1).

The sentence starts with the concept of a market (and by implication, competition and trade) and finishes with the picture of European firms finding ways to 'work together'. Working together and cooperation is interpreted loosely and widely in the White Paper, but does include joint projects, minority shareholdings and mergers (paras 133–44). The White Paper argues that cooperation between firms will 'strengthen the industrial and commercial fabric of the internal market' (para 133).

In principle, there may be no conflict between improving and reinforcing the working of the internal market through competition and trade, and encouraging mechanisms to help firms 'work together' (e.g., joint ventures and mergers). In practice, merger and joint ventures reduce the domain over which competition and trade operate and reduce the number of competitors in specific industries and/or product-markets. The inclusion of measures that *reduce* competition in a programme designed to eliminate non-tariff barriers and so *increase* competition appears inconsistent and even perverse on closer examination. In fact, the treatment of cooperative measures in the White Paper is symptomatic of the existence of two separate agendas that have underlain the White Paper and subsequent economic analysis undertaken by the Commission in this area. The first agenda is represented by the explicit objectives of the White Paper concerning the *internal* market and the elimination of non-tariff barriers to trade. The second and more general agenda is focused on improving Community productivity and trade performance with respect to the rest of the world – that is, competing in the *external* market.

While the two agendas may be mutually supportive in some cases, there are also circumstances in which they will be inconsistent. The problem is that the different agendas are never recognised as such, let alone reconciled; for example CEC's (1988) opening section is titled 'Dimensions and structure of the *internal* market' (italics added), but in fact most of this section is concerned with external trade and the EC's relations with the USA and Japan.

This ambiguity in agenda-setting permeates the published work of the Commission's Economic Directorate (DG II) since the publication of the White Paper, including CEC (1988). There is a genuine conflict between the explicit agenda set out in the White Paper of completing the *internal* market (CIM) and the parallel agenda of competing in the *external* market (CEM). The CIM agenda is really a devise for attainment of the CEM objective in the Commission's view as its informal discussion in various publications since the 1985 White Paper makes clear.

The fusion of agendas is used to legitimate a loose approach to merger control that bodes ill for a balanced and reasonable treatment of European mergers in a post-1992 context. For example, the empirical evidence that tends to find direct relationships between concentration and both price–cost margins and X-inefficiency is recognised by CEC (1988), but when this study looks at the possible relationship between competitive pressure and 'restructuring' (which includes mergers, joint ventures and bankruptcies), it recognises the direct effect of increased competitive pressure on restructuring, but ignores the possibility of a feedback effect in the opposite direction (p. 106). Since 'restructuring' tends to involve reduction in actual or potential competitors and a general softening of competitive pressure, such neglect is unjustified. In a similar vein CEC (1989) argues that for the majority of industries which do not pose efficiency opportunities from merger, this should 'not lead to the rejection of mergers which do not reduce competition, competition policy and industrial policy should be kept separate' (p. 29). This is consistent with Emerson *et al.*'s (1988) promotion of 'mergers and takeovers ... [which] create truly European companies which have no special links to a particular country and are thus able to escape from the "national champion" mentality' (pp. 173–4). In these cases the CEM agenda appears in the guise of industrial policy and the promotion of 'European champions'.

These arguments explicitly indicate a willingness to subvert CIM objectives to CEM objectives. Ironically, however, if the Commission's enthusiasm for stimulating cross-frontier mergers post-1992 is allowed full rein, all the evidence cited above suggests it could have profoundly deleterious consequences, not only for competition within the internal market, but also for Community competitiveness vis-à-vis the rest of the world. Compromising CIM will in turn impede CEM.

Similar problems appear in the Commission's treatment of joint ventures and other collaborative activity. As discussed in more detail in Kay (1991), the CIM/CEM dyad is also to be found in the Commission's treatment of industrial collaborative activity, and suffers from the same problems of interpretation. The White Paper sees 1992 as creating an environment favouring industrial cooperation (p. 34) and the formation of collaborative arrangements such as joint ventures (pp. 34–6), and a major section of the White Paper is devoted to this issue.

In fact, Kay (1991) surveys a number of studies and databases and draws the opposite conclusion; the direct effect of moving towards market completion is typically to *diminish* the frequency of industrial collaborative activity in general, and joint venture arrangements in particular. Joint venture activity tends to be a bureaucratic and costly form of economic organisation compared with fully internalised alternatives such as internal expansion and multinational enterprise. In high technology sectors particularly, joint ventures may be characterised by severe appropriability problems insofar as intangible assets such as intellectual property may be appropriated by partners.

Evidence suggests that firms tend to resort to joint ventures only when simpler or cheaper avenues of exploiting venture opportunities have been exhausted – for example, multinationals being forced into joint ventures with local firms by Third World governments as the price of market access (Kay, 1991). Therefore joint venture activities as strategies of last resort tend to be stimulated by trade barriers, and these same barriers may also help to provide insulating barriers with respect to appropriability problems – losing intellectual competitive advantage to a partner is likely to be more problematic if they are potential future competitors and very close rivals within a completed market.

Thus, where 1992 is successful, its direct effect should be to switch the emphasis in corporate strategies from cooperation to competition. Yet there is no acknowledgement in the Commission's reports on 1992 and corporate strategies that there is likely to be a 1992/industrial collaboration trade-off. The official perspective instead appears to be dictated by the White Paper's arguments (pp. 34–61) that non-tariff barriers to trade have typically *impeded* industrial collaborative activity that would otherwise have been undertaken. For example, CEC (1988) argues for industrial R&D cooperation within the completed market without recognising that their public good benefits of knowledge spillovers are also the innovating firms' appropriability problems and possible strategic own goals.

Industrial technological collaboration programmes like ESPRIT and BRITE are discussed in the White Paper as programmes supporting the development of the internal market, while CEC (1988 pp. 112–14) argues that market integration helps create the conditions for the rapid development of cross-frontier cooperation for R&D. The reality that 1992 will *raise* the price of technological cross-frontier collaboration within the EC is not recognised, a serious omission considering the political and economic significance of the EC technology cooperation programmes. However, as with mergers and acquisitions, the CEM objective underlies the Commission's strategy in this area; in discussing high technology industry, CEC (1988) argues 'concentration and cooperation at European level are ... often necessary (but not sufficient) conditions for the recovery of lost global market share' (p. 135). Again, in a report on the implications of CIM, CEM objectives subvert the analysis at the expense of a realistic appraisal of the likely effects of 1992 and its policy implications.

8.5 The EC's 1990 Merger Regulation

The growth in importance of European merger and acquisition was not adequately anticipated in the Treaty of Rome, and its articles 85 and 86 provided an incomplete and unsatisfactory basis for dealing with this phenomenon. The 1990 Merger Regulation was designed to give the European Commission the direct authority directly to control or prevent EC mergers that threaten competition.

A merger is now deemed to fall within the competence of the EC authorities, if the combined worldwide turnover of the combined companies is ECU 5 billion or more, and the EC turnover of each of at least two of the companies is ECU 250 million or more, though a merger will be exempt from Brussels jurisdiction if each company has more than two-thirds of its EC turnover in one country. It is expected that will result in 50–100 mergers a year for the EC authorities to vet.

The question which the Commission has to decide is whether the merger is 'compatible with the common market'. It must decide whether the merger creates or strengthens a dominant position in the EC. The question and criteria to help judge it are all related to the question of *competition*. The idea of an 'efficiency defence' to trade off against any anti-competitive effects of mergers was not written into the regulation, despite hard lobbying from some quarters. Although the regulation does recognise that account should be taken of technical and economic progress, this is not allowed to detract from the principle of competition as the yardstick by which the merger should be judged.

The mergers falling within the competence of the Merger Regulation are a subset of all EC-related merger and acquisition activity in the EC and amounted to fifty-four deals in the first year of operation from September 1990. Of these, virtually all were approved without change, except three which were approved after modification of the terms and one (France's Aerospatial and Italy's Aleria's plans to share in the acquisition of De Havilland) which was blocked. The Commission ruled that the new company would have achieved domination of 67 per cent of the EC market for commuter aircraft.

It is ironic that EC competition policy has been attacked by lobbyists for not entertaining an 'efficiency defence'. As CEC's own survey (1989) of the empirical evidence indicates, there are stronger grounds in general for putting forward an efficiency *objection* to mergers. The fact that only one European merger has been blocked in the first year of the new merger policy suggests that competition policy in this area is too permissive and tolerant.

8.6 Conclusions

The European Commission's analysis of trends towards industrial concentration as represented by the report of the economics Directorate are highly problematic. Contrary to these arguments, there is no sound *prima facie* case for encouraging cross-frontier mergers in a wide range of industrial sectors. The resulting analysis of the efficiency implications of merger is unsound and leads to policy conclusions that may be to the detriment of European competition and competitiveness.

If there is a root cause for these problems it appears to be the argument that consolidation and amalgamation, whether through merger or joint venture, may be necessary to achieve European competitiveness in a global context. There is no general case for such arguments. A further problem is that 1992 policy development has been characterised by a fusion of agendas on the part of the Commission in which completion of the internal market is frequently analysed in terms more appropriate to competing with other trading blocs in the external market. The result has been detrimental to the analysis of the roots of European competitiveness and the policy proposals on which this builds.

Notes

1 Henceforth 'CEC' and 'Commission' will be used to represent the Commission of the European Communities.
2 The CEC (1989) study concentrates on horizontal mergers while some of the empirical evidence cited here covers mergers in general. Horizontal mergers tend to bring policy issues into sharper focus because of the general expectation that they may generate stronger efficiency *and* monopoly effects compared with mergers between less closely related partners.
3 Learning curve effects and scope economics (economies from products sharing resources) may reinforce scale economies in this basic model (CEC, 1989 p. 17).
4 Domestic demand is calculated for EUR (D + DK + F + I + IRL + NL + B/L + UK) as production plus imports minus exports in real terms over the period 1980–85.
5 Import penetration was defined as the proportion of domestic demand supplied by imports for EUR 9.
6 The data were mainly drawn from a survey of research by Pratten (1988).
7 From Scherer (1980) and Kamien and Schwartz (1982).

References

CEC, 1985. *Completing the Internal Market: White Paper from the Commission to the European Council*, Luxembourg.

1988. 'Economics of 1992', *European Economy*, 35.

1989. 'Horizontal mergers and competition policy in the European community', *European Economy*, 40.

Coley, S. and Reinton, S., 1980. 'The Hunt for Value', *The McKinsey Quarterly*, Spring.

Cowling, K. *et al.*, 1980. *Mergers and Economic Performance*, Cambridge: Cambridge University Press.

Emerson, M. *et al.*, 1988. *The Economics of 1992*, Oxford: Oxford University Press.

Geroski, P., 1987. *Competition and Innovation*, Report prepared for the CEC (Brussels).

Hughes, A., 1989. 'The impact of merger: a survey of empirical evidence for the UK', in J. A. Fairburn and J. A. Kay (eds.), *Mergers and Mergers Policy*, Oxford: Oxford University Press, pp. 30–98.

Kamien, M. I. and Schwartz, N. L., 1982. *Market Structure and Innovation*, Cambridge: Cambridge University Press.

Kay, N., 1991. 'Industrial collaborative activity and the completion of the internal market', *Journal of Common Market Studies*, 29, 347–62.

Meeks, G., 1977. *Disappointing Marriage: A Study of the Gains from Merger*, Cambridge: Cambridge University Press.

Mueller, D., 1980. *The Determinants and Effects of Mergers: An International Comparison*, Cambridge, MA: Oelgeschlager, Gum and Marin.

1988. 'The corporate life cycle', in S. Thompson and M. Wright (eds.), *Internal Organisation, Efficiency and Profit*, Oxford: Philip Allan, pp. 38–64.

Pratten, C., 1988. 'A survey of the economies of scale', in *Research on the Cost of non-Europe*, vol. II, ch. 2, EC Commission (Brussels).

Scherer, F., 1980. *Industrial Market Structure and Economic Performance*, Chicago: Rand McNally.

Thompson, S., 1989. 'Agency costs of internal organization', in S. Thompson and M. Wright (eds.), *Internal Organisation, Efficiency and Profit*, Oxford: Philip Allan, pp. 65–85.

Williamson, O. E., 1968. 'Economies as an antitrust defence: the welfare trade-offs', *American Economic Review*, 58, 18–36.

9 Growth, structural change and real convergence in the EC

CHRISTINE OUGHTON

9.1 Introduction

The purpose of this chapter is to consider the prospects for prosperity and the convergence of economic performance in the European Community (EC). The question of real and nominal convergence has been central to the EC since its formation but has been reiterated recently in both the discussion on 1992 and the gains from the completion of the internal market, and the debate on European Monetary Union. A key question surrounds the distribution of the gains. In order for there to be real convergence of per capita incomes across member states, the benefits of the internal market in terms of higher growth and higher productivity must be positively weighted towards the less prosperous countries (EUR 4: Greece, Ireland, Portugal and Spain).[1] This paper is concerned with the theoretical and empirical conditions that must be met in order to guarantee the convergence of real per capita incomes.

The chapter is structured as follows. Section 9.2 outlines the recent historical record on economic performance and the convergence of real per capita incomes across member countries. Section 9.3 provides a theoretical discussion of the necessary conditions for the convergence to equilibrium characterised by the equality of factor returns across countries. In the light of these conditions the following section considers the empirical prospects for growth and convergence in the EC. It is shown that in respect of two of the four poorer countries of the Community, divergence of per capita incomes away from the EC average is the most likely outcome in the next few years.

9.2 Real convergence in the EC: the historical record

The convergence of economic performance within the EC covers a variety of possible variables. In the extreme it is possible to claim that the objectives of the Community are governed by a desire to see convergence of all nominal and real variables. Recent discussions on European Monetary Union have emphasised the necessity of achieving uniform and low rates of inflation and budgetary deficits, and low exchange rate variation (narrow bands), prior to the adoption of a single currency. The convergence and stability of price variables, which is an essential prerequisite for stable exchange rates, is normally termed nominal convergence. By contrast, the convergence of per capita incomes, that would be attained by the existence of a positive growth rate differential for the EUR 4 countries, is termed real convergence.[2] There is general recognition that the convergence of both real and nominal variables is inextricably mixed. This is necessarily the case since the constraints imposed by a single currency limit the scope for variation in growth rates across member states. Hence, despite the recent emphasis on nominal variables within the context of monetary union, real convergence is a parallel requisite that lies at the heart of community policy and remains an important objective of the Single European Act. Indeed the convergence of per capita incomes has always been a fundamental objective of the community and numerous statements of this can be found in EC documentation, for example,

> The convergence of GDP per capital has been a major aim of Community policies since the very inception of the EEC. The accession in the 1980s of relatively less-prosperous countries has enhanced the importance and the necessity of greater real convergence.[3]

Recent progress on nominal convergence and monetary union has only served to highlight the necessity for real convergence.

Under the Single European Act the main benefit of the completion of the internal market is higher productivity growth brought about by cheaper inputs, economies of scale, reductions in monopoly power and increased competition. These factors should combine to produce an increase in both the rate and the dynamism of investment and hence result in increased efficiency and higher growth. In order to achieve real convergence it is essential that these benefits must fall in larger part on the less prosperous economies, that is, poorer member states must grow more quickly than richer countries to effect the catching-up process. Ideally real convergence would be brought about by market forces: higher profitability in the poorer countries will induce investment and increase the rate of growth. At the same time within an individual country investment will be attracted into the most profitable sectors inducing structural change. For the poorer countries such change will be associated with the transfer of resources from agriculture to manufacturing industry.

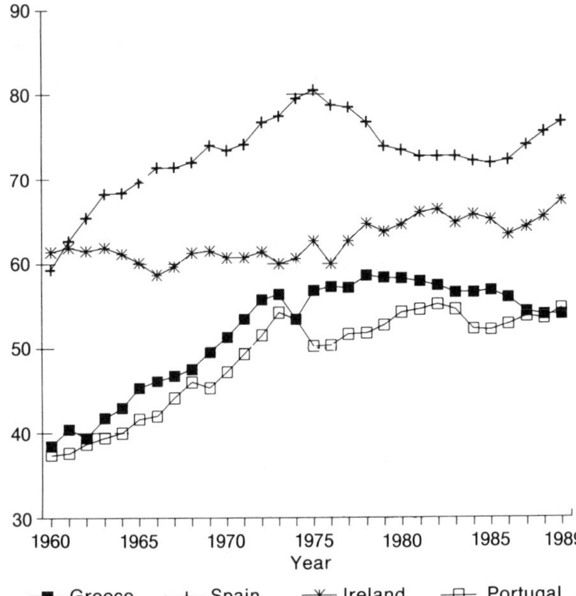

Figure 9.1 Relative per capita GDP in the least favoured countries (EUR 12 = 100).

The difficulty with such a process of growth is that raising efficiency requires structural adjustments (that are likely to be more acute in the EUR 4 countries) which in themselves can result in unemployment and slow growth. In order to limit the short-term impact of structural adjustment the EC devotes considerable resources to its structural funds.

The empirical record on real convergence is indicated in figure 9.1 which presents data on real per capita incomes in the EUR 4 countries relative to all EC countries (EUR 12) over the period 1960–1989. It can be seen that in Greece and Portugal per capita incomes are roughly half the average community level, while in Ireland and Spain the figures are around 66 and 75 per cent respectively. During the period 1960–1973/4 there was a continuous improvement in the relative positions of Spain, Greece and Portugal, while the period 1976–1986 saw a reversal of this process for Spain and Greece and a significant reduction in the pace of convergence in Portugal. In Ireland there was little evidence of catch-up during the 1960s and 1970s but since 1975 there has been a marginal improvement. Part of the explanation of Ireland's poor record on catch-up can be found in the relatively high proportion of employment in services and agriculture which tends to act as a drag on growth. With the exception of Ireland, the picture that emerges is that restructuring and

Table 9.1. *Growth differential with EUR 12*

	Greece	Spain	Ireland	Portugal	EUR 4
Historical Record					
1961–73	3.1	2.1	−0.2	2.9	2.3
1974–79	0.6	−0.9	1.0	−0.5	−0.6
1980–87	−1.0	0.0	0.0	0.0	−0.1
1988–92[a]	−1.0	1.4	0.3	0.7	1.0
Growth Differential Required for Reducing the Prosperity Gap to 90 per cent					
1992	10.6	3.9	7.1	10.8	5.6
1997	5.2	1.9	3.5	5.3	2.8
2002	3.4	1.3	2.3	3.5	1.8
2007	2.5	1.0	1.7	2.6	1.4

Note: [a] Commission Services Forecast.
Source: *European Economy*, November 1988, p. 120.

convergence has occurred most successfully in periods of high growth[4] in the Community as a whole. During periods of low growth there is evidence of economic divergence between the richest and poorest countries (EUR 8 and EUR 4).

Table 9.1 shows the differential between EUR 4 and EUR 12 growth rates since 1960. It can be seen that after a period of catch-up during 1961–73 the latter part of the 1970s and early 1980s saw the less prosperous countries fall behind. For the period 1988–92 the EC forecast a return to convergence but these forecasts were made before the Gulf crisis and the onset of the subsequent slowdown in growth. More recent analysis[5] suggests that during 1991 the process of convergence slowed considerably, so that, real per capita incomes remained constant in Spain, Ireland and Portugal and declined in Greece. The second half of the table presents estimates of the growth differential required to reduce the gap between EUR 4 and EUR 12 to 90 per cent. To achieve this objective by the turn of the century would require a relative growth performance for EUR 4 broadly in line with that experienced by these countries during the golden age of economic growth, 1961–73.

One of the main factors underlying productivity and growth differentials between the less prosperous economies and the rest of the EC is differences in the structure of industry across the two sets of countries. Table 9.2 sets out sectoral shares of employment in EUR 4 and EUR 12 countries.

Countries with a high proportion of employment in agriculture exhibit lower levels of productivity compared with more industrialised economies. In order to raise productivity, resources must be shifted out of the

Table 9.2. *Sectoral shares in employment*

	Agriculture		Industry		Services	
Spain	28.5	15.6	36.0	31.0	35.5	53.4
Greece	38.8	27.2	23.8	26.8	37.4	46.0
Portugal	32.8	21.5	32.7	33.5	34.5	45.0
Ireland	26.9	15.6	29.6	28.0	43.5	56.4
EUR 12	13.7	8.1	40.8	32.5	45.6	59.4

Source: *European Economy*, November 1988, p. 108.

agricultural sector towards industry. Indeed, changes in the structure of industry during economic development have been shown to follow a well established pattern (Rowthorn and Wells (1987)), see figure 9.2. Initially the structure of employment is heavily weighted towards the agricultural sector. With the commencement of industrialisation resources are shifted out of agriculture towards industry and services. During this phase of industrialisation productivity growth is high and the share of employment in industry increases rapidly. As development continues the share of agricultural employment continues to decline until it stabilises at a very low level. At this point, which Rowthorn has defined as the point of economic maturity, any further expansion of the service sector takes place at the expense of industry i.e., further development is charactierised by deindustrialisation. Rowthorn and Wells (1987) have argued that deindustrialisation is a symptom of economic development that may be associated with both a successful (highly efficient) and an unsuccessful industrial sector; that is, a decline in employment in industry may reflect low industrial profitability and investment and low productivity growth, or high investment and productivity growth such that increases in output can be achieved with fewer workers. Hence, deindustrialisation may be associated with either the economic failure, or the economic efficiency, of the industrial sector. A further possibility is that deindustrialisation arises as a result of changes in trade specialisation. In fact, patterns of trade specialisation are associated with persistent differences in employment structures. This is consistent with the finding that trade among the advanced European economies (EUR 8) (which share similar industrial structures, in that, the share of agriculture tends to be very small) tends to be intra-industry trade, whereas trade among the advanced and less prosperous (EUR 4) countries tends to be inter-industry trade (Schwalbach, 1989).

Given the diversity of industrial structures in the EC, real convergence

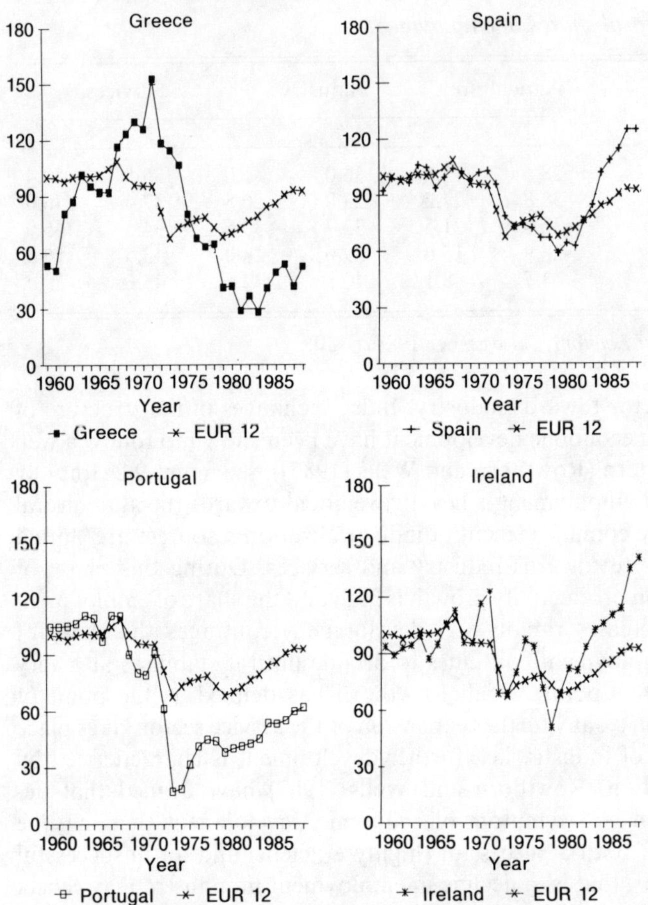

Figure 9.2 Profitability of fixed capital by country (indicers 1961–73 = 100).

of per capita incomes requires a reduction in the share of agricultural employment in the less prosperous countries. If this is to be achieved without generating unemployment, investment in the industrial sectors of these economies must be high. It is this transfer of resources from agriculture to industry that provides the mechanism for the catching-up process.

In view of the fact that the industrial sectors of the EUR 4 countries will not enjoy the benefit of protection from tariff and non-tariff barriers to trade, and given that the removal of capital controls will significantly increase the mobility of capital, development of the industrialised sectors of the EUR 4 countries must be secured on the basis of competitive criteria (notwithstanding aid from EC structural funds) in the context of a

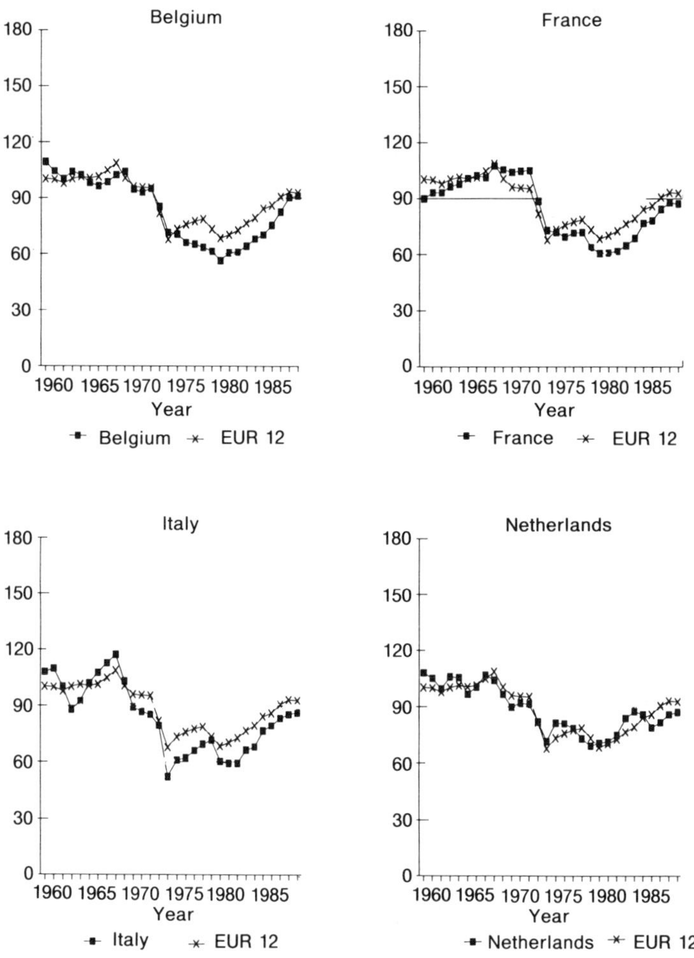

Figure 9.2 (*continued*).

growing European economy. Despite the fact that this is implicit in EC documentation on the gains from 1992 and convergence, there has been little formal theoretical analysis of either (i) the model of dynamic competition underlying the EC view or (ii) the necessary conditions to ensure convergence. In the following section we outline a theoretical treatment of the analysis of growth, structural change and the conditions for convergence based on classical competitive models of dynamic adjustment. Section 4 then considers the empirical evidence on convergence conditions in the EC.

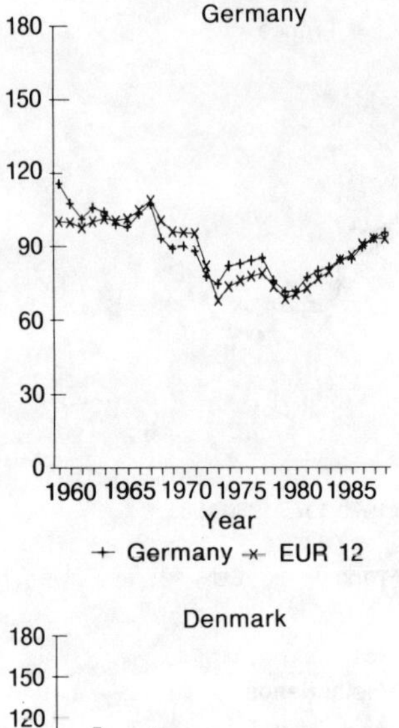

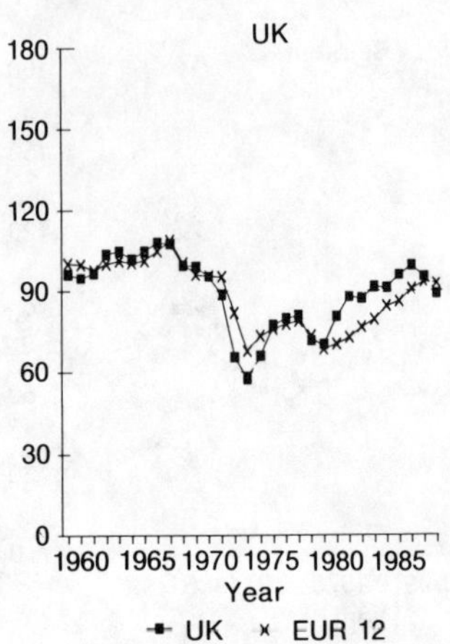

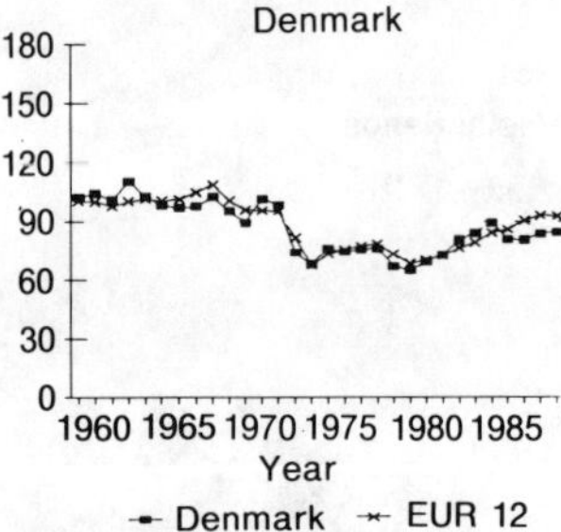

Figure 9.2 (*continued*).

9.3 Theoretical analysis of real convergence

Within the theoretical and empirical literature on real convergence published by the Community, emphasis has been placed on the catching-up process. However, the precise conditions/mechanisms for bringing this about are not normally discussed beyond pointing out the need to raise the level and efficiency of investment. Moreover, little attention has been paid to the possibility that trade liberalisation and the removal of capital controls in the EC may actually slow down convergence. To some extent the failure to be precise on these theoretical issues reflects the malaise of standard neoclassical theory which lacks an adequate theoretical formalisation of the adjustment from short-run to long-run equilibrium. However, recent work on the formalisation of classical theory has made a substantial contribution to our understanding of the process of convergence to equilibrium characterised by an equalisation of the rate of profit across industries. Although this analysis has been developed in the context of growth and structural change within and across industries in a single economy, it can also be applied to competition within industries across economies when there is free trade and free mobility of capital and labour.

The classical theory[6] of competition rests on the distinction between market prices and natural prices. Market prices are determined by the interaction of supply and demand. As Smith notes: 'The market price of every particular commodity is regulated by the proportion between the quantity which is actually brought to market, and ... effectual demand' (Smith, 1981 p. 73). By contrast, natural prices are long-run equilibrium prices which represent the sum of natural or average cost of all factors, of production (i.e., stock (capital), labour and land; the natural price of a commodity 'is the central price, to which the prices of all commodities are continually gravitating' (Smith, 1981 p. 75).

Market prices tend to converge towards natural prices by virtue of the mobility of factors of production, most notably, capital and labour. Capital and labour flow into (out of) industries with above (below) average profit rates and wage rates. Capital flows act on the supply side of the economy and bring about the continual gravitation of market prices towards natural prices (see Smith, 1981 p. 77). Given the historical nature of the classical analysis it is apparent that the adjustment process is not instantaneous and that market prices may remain above natural prices for considerable periods of time. Smith, Ricardo and Marx came to different views about the extent of the disruption associated with the competitive process. Smith placed great emphasis on the inhibiting effects of sources of market power, such as secrets of production, trade unions, collusion, legal restrictions and monopoly. According to Smith these factors tend to hold market price above the natural price thus inhibiting the competitive process and imposing welfare losses on society. However, it is important to note that even in the absence of these factors market prices would still differ from natural prices because of the introduction of new products and changes in tastes and preferences. This point was emphasised by Ricardo who argues that, shifts in supply and demand interact so that

> In the ordinary course of events, there is no commodity which continues for any length of time to be supplied precisely in that degree of abundance, which the wants and wishes of mankind require, and therefore there is none which is not subject to accidental and temporary variations in price ... With the rise or fall of price, profits are elevated above, or depressed below their general level, and capital is either encouraged to enter into, or is warned to depart from the particular employment in which the variation has taken place (in Sraffa, 1981 p. 88).

One of the most important differences between Marx's analysis and the earlier work of Smith and Ricardo is that Marx provided a more comprehensive analysis of welfare losses and crises. Marx's analysis criticised Smith for failing to recognise that the decline of industries with below average profitability could have macroeconomic implications. Given the existence of vertical linkages between industries, a fall in output in any one industry will result in reductions in demand for intermediate products. As a result the dynamic process of competition may result in a crisis of disproportionality between sectors or the spread of the decline of a particular industry in a recession of general magnitude. Both types of crisis reduce the rate of investment and growth. This distinction between Smith and Marx is the significance for the main theme of this chapter, namely the possibility of real convergence in the EC. Plainly, if increased capital mobility and freer trade result in an increase in the rate of international disinvestment from countries with below average profitability then both economic growth and the catching-up process for these countries will diminish.

Despite this difference relating to the possibility of slow growth and recession, Marx's analysis of the competitive process employs the same cross-dual adjustment mechanism: market prices are determined by supply and demand and positive (negative) deviations of industry profit rates from the average rate attracts resources into (out of) those industries. This process tends to drive market prices into equality with natural prices and results in an equalisation of profit rates across industries.

9.3.1 Dynamic competition and the conditions for real convergence

The classical model of competition discussed above describes a cross-dual process whereby price and profit signals act on the supply side of the economy to bring about movements of capital and labour which engender the convergence of actual prices and profit rates to their natural counterparts. The main difference between the classical and neoclassical model of competition is that the latter is quintessentially static in nature in so far as it lacks a convincing account[7] of the adjustment process or the stability of equilibrium.

In an attempt to extend the classical theory, a number of economists have modelled the cross-dual process in order to determine the necessary conditions for the convergence of both market prices to natural prices and actual profit and wage rates to their natural rates.

A number of early papers by Nikaido (1978; 1983; 1985) cast doubt over the stability of the classical system by showing that industry profit rates do not always converge to a uniform equilibrium rate. However,

Flaschel and Semmler (1987) have criticised Nikaido's work on the basis that it gives insufficient attention to the interaction of price adjustments and real quantity adjustments. As a result it fails to capture the true nature of the cross-dual process between prices and quantities that is central to the classical model (see Flaschel and Semmler (1987) and Dumenil and Levy (1985)).

Steedman (1984) has also expressed doubts concerning the stability of the cross-dual. Steedman models the classical process of competition within a Sraffian (Sraffa, 1960) framework and shows that deviations of market prices and profit rates from their natural counterparts may be of opposite signs if the prices of intermediate inputs differ from their natural prices to an even greater extent than final product prices. That is, if an industry whose product price lies above the natural price purchases inputs at a price even further above the corresponding natural price then the profit rate of the purchasing industry may be below the natural rate and resources will not be attracted into that industry, despite the fact that the industry faces excess demand. Under these circumstances the natural price and profit rate system may fail to act as a centre of gravity. However, it is important to note that stability is ensured whenever Steedman's special case does not hold and that even under Steedman's special case stability is not ruled out if the model is extended to take specific account of stocks, fixed capital, investment lags, beliefs and expectations.

Following the classical tradition Flaschel and Semmler (1987) have provided a significant contribution to the formalisation of the necessary conditions for convergence. The authors adopt a Sraffian-type schema involving joint production and formalise the cross-dual process by incorporating demand and supply-side effects. The demand side of the model determines market prices by relating the growth rate of prices to excess demand for all industries. Price in any industry increases (decreases) whenever excess demand is positive (negative) – this is termed the *law of demand.* The supply side of the model relates the industry rate of growth to the extent of industry excess profitability. Hence, the *law of profitability* is modelled by setting the rate of growth of output of each industry as a sign-preserving proportional function of the deviation of industry profit rates from the equilibrium rate. It is shown (using Liapunov functions) that such a system will be locally stable.

Flaschel and Semmler also consider the conditions for global stability of the classical system. If the law of profitability is modified so that movements of capital and associated changes in outputs occur in response to the sign of change of extra profits then the system is also globally stable. It is important to note that both local and global stability depend crucially on the role of comparative profitability: as the authors point out 'the cross-dual process is stabilized through the "law of profitability" and the sensitivity of producers to profit changes' (Flaschel and Semmler, 1987 p. 33). This condition for global stability provides a useful rule for assessing whether or not an economic system exhibts the necessary conditions for the convergence of prices, profit rates and per capita incomes to their natural rates.

It is important to note that within formalisations of the classical approach the distribution of income is determined exogenously: one distributive variable, either the wage rate or the rate of profit, is determined outside the price/production schema. This is in contrast to neoclassical models where equilibrium relationships between factor prices and their marginal (value) products are determined endogenously. If the uniform wage rate across industries is given historically (exogenously) by social convention then convergence towards equilibrium is brought about by capital flows in response to profit signals. The alternative approach would be to assume an exogenously given uniform rate of profit and let the wage rate vary. In this case convergence to equilibrium would be brought about by labour mobility in response to deviations of industry wage rates from the natural wage rate. The standard approach within formalisations of the classical model was to treat the wage rate as exogenous and allow profit rates and capital movements to form the basis of the cross-dual. Given that capital mobility within the EC exceeds labour mobility it seems appropriate to follow this tradition.

It is interesting to note that given the exogeneity of the wage rate in the classical model it is possible that the *long-run* value of this variable be determined by a bargaining process whose outcome reflects the relative strengths of workers and employers. The clearest statement of this view can be found in Smith (1981):[8]

> What are the wages of labour depends every where upon the contract usually made between those two parties, whose interests are by no means the same. The workmen desire to get as much, the masters to give as little as possible. The former are disposed to combine in order to raise, the latter in order to lower the wages of labour. It is not, however, difficult to foresee which of the two parties must, upon all ordinary occasions, have the advantage in the dispute, and force the other into a compliance with their terms. The masters, being fewer in number, can combine much more easily; and the law, besides, authorises, or at least does not prohibit their combinations, while it prohibits those of the workmen . . . [Moreover] In all such disputes the masters can hold out much longer . . . Many workmen could not subsist a week, few could subsist a month, and scarce any a year without employment. In the long-run the workman may be as necessary to his master as his master is to himself; but the necessity is not so immediate (Smith, 1981 pp. 83–4).

It is clear that Smith viewed the determination of wage rates as the outcome of the interplay between the relative strengths of workers and employers. Hence, the wage rate is determined by bargaining power and by past norms and standards for wage payments. Smith argued that in the long run the movement of employees between different industries would tend to bring about the convergence of wage rates towards the natural rate. Hence, industry wage rates are continually tending to equality, once non-pecuniary benefits have been accounted for. For uniform technology across countries this implies an equalisation of unit wage costs as wage earners leave low wage sectors/countries and transfer to high wage sectors/countries. However, given the existence of older technology and lower productivity in the less prosperous regions the movement of workers out of these economies and into the more prosperous economies is unlikely (quite apart from cultural and linguistic problems) to contribute to an equalisation of unit labour costs without the transfer of technology.

To summarise, it can be seen that the key to nominal and real convergence is a positive profit rate differential for the less prosperous countries compared with the advanced economies. This would stimulate investment and raise productivity, thus lowering unit labour costs.

9.4 Empirical conditions for convergence

The theoretical discussion in the previous section has argued that a necessary condition for real economic convergence is that profit rates in the less prosperous countries are higher than those in the more advanced economies. In a dynamic context the condition for global stability is that the differential between EUR 4 and EUR 8 profitability is positive and increasing. Under these conditions, and given the free mobility of capital, investment will be attracted out of the advanced economies towards the less prosperous countries. However, this represents a necessary rather than a sufficient condition, since investment patterns may be disturbed by the monopolisation of industries and/or R&D technology.

Data on the profitability of fixed capital for all member countries are presented in figure 9.3. These data are expressed in index form for each country with the period 1961–73 set as the base (= 100). Although the data are not strictly comparable across countries, the change in the differential between each country's profit rate and the average profit rate (EUR 12) provides a good indication of the relative movements in the profitability of member countries and corresponds to the global stability condition outlined above.

For the advanced economies it can be seen that the profit rate differentials

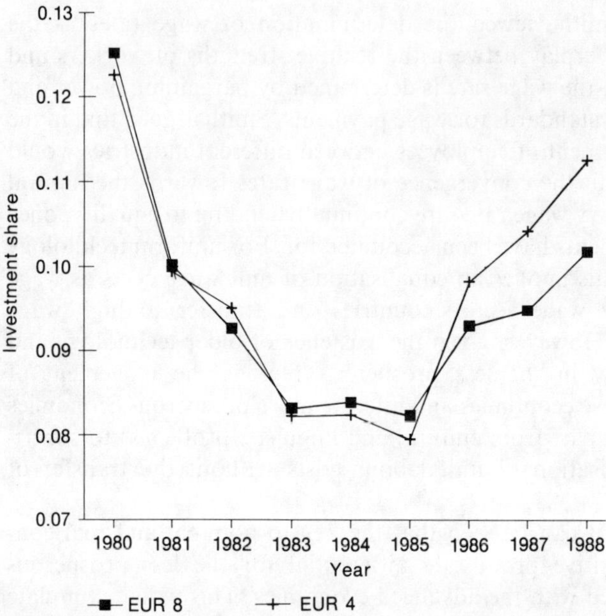

Figure 9.3 Investment shares in GDP, EUR 8 and EUR 4; current prices.

are small and fairly uniform over time. This can be compared with the picture for the EUR 4 countries where profit rate differentials are significantly larger and show marked changes over time. In Spain it can be seen that profitability closely tracks average profitability for EUR 12 until 1975 when the profit rate differential increases and becomes negative until 1981–81. This matches the divergence of relative real per capita income that took place between Spain and the advanced economies during this period. Post-1984, the profit rate differential between Spain and the EUR 12 average becomes increasingly positive. During this period there is increasing convergence of Spain's per capita income level towards the European average.

In the Republic of Ireland the profit rate differential follows a cyclical pattern until 1981 when it becomes increasingly positive. Relating this movement to changes in relative per capita income it can be seen that there is no evidence of trend convergence for Ireland until 1976. Post-1985 there is a significant increase in convergence that coincides with a steep increase in the profit rate differential for Ireland vis-à-vis EUR 12.

In Greece the profit rate differential is positive and fluctuates in a cyclical manner until 1975 when an increasingly negative profit rate differential opens up. The existence of the negative profit rate differential coincides with a period of divergence in per capita income in Greece relative to EUR 8. A similar pattern is discernible in Portugal although here the decline in profitability begins slightly earlier.

9.4.1 EC forecasts and prospects for convergence

Prior to the Gulf crisis EC medium-term forecasts to 1992 indicated that the four least favoured countries were expected to grow at a marginally (about one percentage point) faster rate than the average. These forecasts were based on an expected increase of 25 per cent in the investment share. Moreover, it is apparent that, when relative price effects are taken into account, there is no significant improvement in the rate of investment in EUR 4 countries compared with EUR 8 countries. Net investment shares in current price GDP are presented in figure 9.3, where it can be seen that the last three years has seen the emergence of a positive differential between the rate of investment in EUR 4 and EUR 8 countries. However, the investment share measured in current prices can be a misleading indicator of the proportion of a country's real output devoted to investment since it is unadjusted for changes in the relative price of capital to output. In a dynamic setting the rate of growth in the nominal investment share is given by:

$$\frac{i}{Y} = \frac{\bar{I}}{Y} + \frac{p_k}{p_y} \tag{9.1}$$

Given that changes in the relative price of capital do not contribute to greater productivity it is apparent that the real investment share is a better guide to future changes in efficiency occasioned by investment in fixed assets. Figures for the real gross investment share are illustrated in figure 9.4. It can be seen that for the period 1980–85 real investment shares were falling for both the EUR 8 and EUR 4 countries. Real investment shares exhibit a recovery over the period in both sets of countries but there is no evidence of a sustained faster rate of investment in the EUR 4 countries. The difference between rates of change in investment shares in real and nominal terms between the two sets of countries arises because the EUR 4 countries, which are typically not capital-goods producers, have experienced an adverse relative price effect of output to capital employed.

In terms of raising productivity it is not just the level of real investment that matters but the efficiency of investment. Ideally, the efficiency of investment would be captured by capital productivity as measured by the real output–capital ratio. This measure may be proxied by the change in real output divided by real investment – what the EC refers to as the marginal efficiency of capital (MEC). This measure is graphed in figure

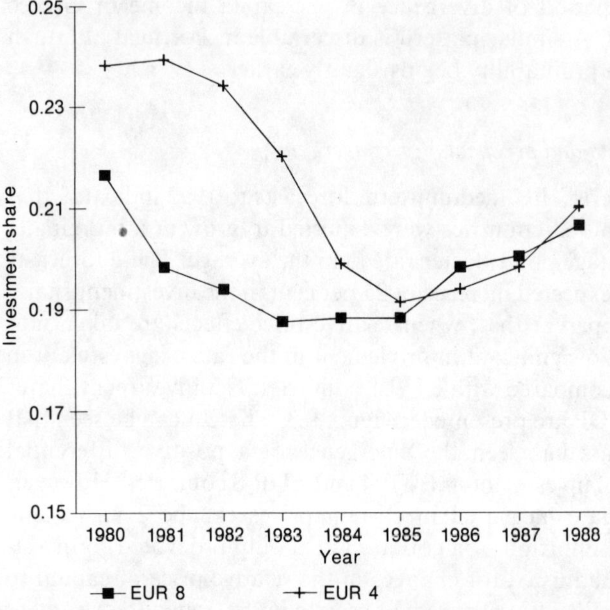

Figure 9.4 Real investment shares in GDP, EUR 8 and EUR 4.

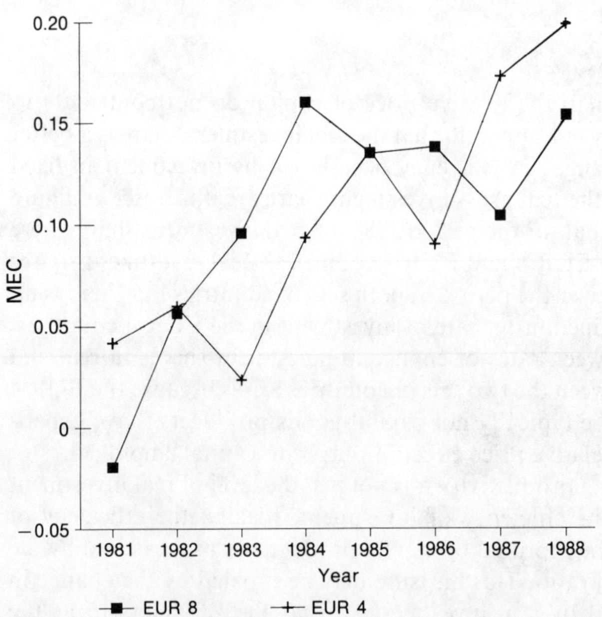

Figure 9.5 Marginal efficiency of capital – change in real GDP/real investment.

9.5 for EUR 4 and EUR 8 countries. It should be noted that the level of capital productivity is significantly higher in EUR 8 countries compared with EUR 4 countries; as a result it is easier to effect output growth via investment in EUR 4 countries. Over the 1980s it can be seen that the MEC was higher in EUR 8 countries until 1987 when there was a marked improvement in the MEC in EUR 4.

To conclude this section it can be seen that while the necessary conditions for convergence are met in the case of Spain and Ireland this is not the case for Greece and Portugal. As a result it is not surprising to see that in recent years convergence has resumed in Ireland and Spain but has not done so in Greece and Portugal. Of all the EC countries the last two have the largest proportions of their employment concentrated in the agricultural sector (see table 9.2) and hence significant investment in industry is required to improve relative levels of per capita income. Given the current state of profit rate differentials and levels of investment this seems unlikely to occur.

9.5 Conclusion

The discussion around the creation of a single market and increased capital and labour mobility has laid emphasis on the importance of the catching-up process. This paper has used the classical theory of competition and dynamic adjustment to outline the necessary conditions for convergence.

The historical record on the convergence of real per capita incomes in EUR 4 countries towards EUR 12 is mixed. Significant catching-up by Spain and Portugal was achieved during the long postwar boom (1961–73), but since 1973 these economies have tended to diverge from EC norms for per capita income. While it is clear that restructuring and catch-up are more readily achieved during periods of high and sustained growth in the EC as a whole it is also apparent that the most successful period of catch-up occurred when Spain, Greece and Portugal were not members of the EC. During this time these countries followed protectionist policies and the mobility of capital was limited.

As economic and monetary union progresses the danger facing the EUR 4 countries is that they do not receive a disproportionately large share of the gains. Given the existing pattern of profit rate differentials this seems a distinct possibility in the case of the two poorest countries: Greece and Portugal. These economies therefore face a significant chance of being left behind. In recognition of this possibility the EC has recently doubled the size of the funds designed for restructuring. These now represent 3.5 per cent of GDP in Portugal and 2.9 per cent of GDP in Greece. However, given that investment shares in GDP in Greece and Portugal tend to lag behind both the EUR 8 and EUR 4 averages it seems unlikely that significant progress on convergence will be made in these economies in the medium term.

Notes

I am grateful to fellow participants of the seminar on European Competitiveness held at WZB Berlin in June 1991 for useful comments and suggestions. The usual disclaimer applies.

1 Throughout this chapter EUR 4 refers to Greece, Ireland, Portugal and Spain, while EUR 8 refers to the more advanced economies: Belgium, Germany, Denmark, France, Italy, The Netherlands, Luxembourg and the UK. Note that in the case of Germany most data relate to western Germany (formally the FRG).

2 In a recent paper Barro and Martin (1991) argued that real convergence can be captured by two concepts: (i) the rate of convergence i.e., the rate at which per capita income converges towards the average or steady-state per capita income level and (ii) the change in the cross-country dispersion of per capita income.

3 *European Economy*, November 1988, p. 117.

4 For an extended discussion of this point see Rowthorn (forthcoming).

5 *European Economy*, December 1991, p. 13.

6 In focusing on a comparison between classical analysis and neoclassical analysis a number of important differences between the theories of Smith, Ricardo and Marx have been obscured for the sake of clarity of exposition and brevity. This omission is regrettable but a detailed comparative study of the classics lies beyond the scope of this chapter.

7 That is, an account that, in Hahn's (1987) words, 'does without' the auctioneer.

8 I am grateful to Fiona Carmichael for drawing my attention to the role of bargaining and power in Smith's analysis of wage determination. See Carmichael (1989) for a fuller treatment of this topic. A similar view can be found in Marx (1975), see especially, pp. 71–9.

References

Barro, R. J. and Sala-i-Martin, X., 1991. 'Convergence across states and regions', *Brookings Papers on Economic Activity*, 1:1991, 107–82.

Carmichael, F., 1989. 'The legislative role of the government and union bargaining', University of East Anglia, mimeo.

Commission of the European Communities, 1988. *European Economy*, November.

1991. *European Economy*, December.

Dumenil, G. and Levy, D., 1985. 'The classicals and neoclassicals: a rejoiner to Frank Hahn', *Cambridge Journal of Economics*, 9, 327–45.

Flaschel, P. and Semmler, W., 1987. 'Classical and neoclassical competitive adjustment processes', *The Manchester School*, 55, 13–37.

Hahn, F., 1987. 'Information, dynamics and Equilibrium', *Scottish Journal of Political Economy*, 33, 321–34.

Marx, K., 1975. *Wages, Price and Profit*, Foreign Languages Press, Peking.
Nikaido, H., 1978. 'Refutation of dynamic equalization of profit rates in Marx's schema of reproduction', University of Southern California, mimeo.
1983. 'Marx on competition', *Zeitschrift für Nationalokonomie*, 43, 337–62.
1985. 'Dynamics of growth and capital mobility in Marx's schema of reproduction', *Zeitschrift für Nationalokonomie*, 45, 197–218.
Rowthorn, R. E. (forthcoming). 'Notes on the falling rate of profit' in M. Landesmann and R. E. Rowthorn, (eds.), *The Structural Dynamics of Market Economies*, Oxford: Oxford University Press.
Rowthorn, R. E. and Wells, J., 1987. *De-industrialisation and Foreign Trade*, Cambridge: Cambridge University Press.
Schwalbach, J., 1989. 'Structural difference and the convergence to a European internal market', Berlin, mimeo.
Smith, A., 1981. *An Inquiry into the Nature and Causes of the Wealth of Nations*, Vol. I, edited by R. Campbell, and A. Skinner, Library Classics Edition, Indianapolis, Liberty Press.
Sraffa, P., 1960. *Production of Commodities by Means of Commodities: Prelude to a Critique of Economic Theory*, Cambridge: Cambridge University Press.
1981 (ed.) *On the Principles of Political Economy and Taxation*, Vol. I of the Collected Works of David Ricardo. Cambridge: Cambridge University Press.
Steedman, I., 1984. 'Natural prices, differential profit rates and the classical competitive process', *The Manchester School*, 52, 123–40.

10 Public services and competitiveness

HUGH MOSLEY AND GÜNTHER SCHMID

10.1 Introduction

In a world of increasing interdependency and liberalisation of markets there is naturally a growing concern about the competitiveness and performance of enterprises and national economies. The expansion of the public sector and in particular public services is a prominent candidate among the many possible reasons why competitiveness may deteriorate. The dominant view is that the evolutionary process from the 'night watchman' to the welfare state has gone too far. For example, it is argued:

that too many public services are provided due to the lack of cost-consciousness among consumers;

that the vested interests of public bureaucracies and the lack of economic incentives for public employees (who do not have to fear unemployment) impede productivity growth;

that public services displace private services;

that the costs of financing public services crowd out private investment.

This list is certainly not exhaustive, yet it leads to the crucial question: Are states with larger public sectors and a high level of public services at a competitive disadvantage? A survey of this relatively neglected theme in comparative research seems to be extremely interesting, especially in view of the large public service sector in European Community states. Given the breadth and complexity of the issue, our aim in this chapter can only be to present an overview of principal issues and to survey available data and evidence on the role of public services in competitiveness, identifying gaps in existing knowledge and research needs.

Section 2 discusses the issue of the relationship between government or public services and competitiveness in terms of the relevant literature. Section 3 presents descriptive evidence (expenditure and employment data) on patterns of public sector activity in OECD countries, with particular reference to their possible contributions to competitiveness.

Section 4 surveys the results of cross-national econometric studies on the relationship between the public sector and economic performance. While a number of earlier studies in a cross-section framework pointed to a negative relationship between the size of the public sector and economic performance, several recent contributions to the literature on comparative public policy have found evidence that the public sector may actually contribute to economic performance.

In our concluding section 5 we suggest that further cross-national policy research requires a more differentiated analysis based on the hypothesis that it is not the size of public services as such but their composition, institutional tradition, and effective linkage to enterprises that determine their impact on competitiveness and performance.

10.2 Public services and economic performance: an overview of the literature

10.2.1 Market efficiency and market failure

Analysis of the relationship between the public sector or public services and competitiveness is still dominated by the market paradigm of classical and neoclassical economics. Market organisation of the provision of goods and services is assumed to be inherently more efficient, and hence preferable, unless special circumstances justify public intervention. In this perspective the relationship between the state (or public services) and competitiveness is in principle little changed since Adam Smith's critique of mercantilist (i.e., statist) policies in *The Wealth of Nations*: public regulation and public provision of goods and services are regarded as a threat to the efficient functioning of markets. In the 1980s we have witnessed a renaissance of these views in the policy domain under the banner of 'privatisation' and 'deregulation', especially in the United Kingdom and the United States. The collapse of the centrally planned economies in Eastern Europe has given new impetus to these neo-liberal policy prescriptions.

Within a neoclassical framework the limitations of the market model and hence the scope for public sector activity are usually analysed in terms of theories of 'market failure' in public finance and public sector economics literature. Market failure is associated with circumstances such as natural monopoly, public goods, externalities and so forth, in which the model of perfect competition is deemed inapplicable and hence public sector intervention justified (Bator, 1958; Musgrave and Musgrave, 1968; Stiglitz, 1986). More recently neo-liberal theorists have sought to raise the threshold at which public intervention is justified by emphasising the corresponding problem of 'government failure', i.e., that government provision may involve equal or greater inefficiencies so that market failure alone is not a sufficient condition to justify public intervention (Wolf, 1987; 1988).

10.2.2 The disjunction of theory and practice

Although these textbook distinctions in normative economics are widely recognised, their application to particular cases entails judgements as to facts and values that make them inherently controversial. They are, furthermore, a poor predictor of actual developments in historical capitalist regimes. During the postwar era OECD countries have experienced both a broad advance of the welfare state and the mixed economy and, since the late 1970s, a resurgence of laissez-faire principles and market-oriented policies (privatisation, deregulation, etc.). There has been, moreover, a great variety of responses in different countries both during the initial phase of expansion and in the subsequent period of retrenchment. Where the line between the public and private sectors is drawn thus appears to be to a large extent a function of national traditions, circumstances, and goals and certainly cannot be determined a priori (Hirschman, 1982).

Despite the bias in economic theory in favour of market-oriented solutions and the current popularity of the neo-liberal model, there is no simple correlation between the size of the public sector and economic performance. Indeed economies with complex institutional structures and large public sectors (e.g., Germany) or activist governments and small public sectors (e.g., Japan) have frequently been remarkably successful. Instead of prescription, there is a need for more sophisticated comparative analysis of the role of the public sector and public services in economic performance and trends in their size and composition.

There is a large body of literature on the growth of the public sector expenditures and employment, which provides an invaluable source of data and information on public sector expenditures and – to a lesser extent – employment, which can be utilised in analysing patterns and identifying trends in public service activities.[1] The focus of the government growth literature is largely on the determinants of government size and composition (i.e., government spending or employment is the dependent variable) and not on the impacts of government, and in particular public services, on economic competitiveness and performance. However, this body of literature also includes a number of cross-national econometric studies in the government growth literature that do address the issue of the relationship between government spending and economic performance (see section 4 below).[2]

10.2.3 Institutions, the state and competitiveness

The importance of social and institutional factors for economic competitiveness and performance has already been documented in research on comparative work organisation, industrial relations and corporatism.[3] More recent literature has provided further evidence and insights into the role of education and training, labour market policies, financial systems and other institutional factors in competitiveness.[4] Although neglected in the market-oriented paradigm of mainstream economics, recent comparative and policy-oriented literature evinces a growing awareness that the public sector, and in particular public services, may be an important institutional condition of competitiveness. This is the case not only in the trivial sense of the classical public functions (e.g., defence, foreign affairs, internal security, administration of justice), which are a prerequisite for the functioning of markets (or any form of complex social organisation), but also especially in innovative, high-skilled, high value-added forms of production.[5] The latter are characterised *inter alia* by (i) greatly increased requirements for intangible and frequently indirect service inputs ('dematerialisation of production' – e.g., technology, skilled-labour, marketing, engineering, and financial services), (ii) health care, social security, environmental protection and other compensatory functions and (iii) qualitatively enhanced traditional services such as transportation and communication. In this perspective there is – in contrast to the strong tendency to identify public services with consumption and redistribution[6] – reason to think that, far from being merely a drag on economic performance, efficient and effective public services can be an important institutional source of 'comparative advantage' in developed market economies. This perspective on public services and competitiveness is related to the broader discussion of the implications of the growth of the service sector in modern societies, of which the public sector is a major, and in some countries even the dominant, component.[7]

Much recent literature on international competitiveness has stressed in particular the role of government in fostering comparative advantage. In traditional trade theory nations are deemed to maximise efficiency and competitiveness by specialising in those products in which their existing comparative advantage is greatest, which will be best achieved by relying on market mechanisms and not by government intervention. It assumes that all countries have access to the same technology and differ only in their factor endowments in labour, capital and natural resources. This viewpoint has been criticised not only for ignoring imperfect competition but, more fundamentally, for its essentially static conception of competitiveness and efficiency. In a dynamic view of competitiveness and efficiency the assumption that technology as well as physical and human capital endowments are fixed is abandoned. Comparative advantage is not merely revealed in trade statistics but can be 'created', i.e., government policies may play an essential role in maintaining or increasing a nation's standing in high-wage high value-added production (Cohen and Zysman, 1987; Porter, 1990; Zysman 1983).[8] Japan is the most frequently cited example for such a growth oriented and dynamic model with a strong role for the state as a protector and promoter of key domestic industries through a strategy of industrial targeting. The distinctiveness of the Japanese model lies of course not only in the role of the state but also *inter alia* in the complex relationships between firms that are said to facilitate longer-term growth and innovation-oriented strategies and reduce foreign penetration of the Japanese domestic market (Johnson, 1982; Johnson *et al.*, 1989).

The actual role played by government and public services depends not only on national strategies but also on national institutions and traditions as well as on the particular national circumstances. In addition to statist models such as found in Japan and France, there are also negotiated or corporatist models such as found, for example, in Sweden, Austria and, in weaker form, in Germany. The Anglo-Saxon model (e.g. the USA and the UK), which is not evidently the most successful, perhaps best approximates the laissez-faire model of economic textbooks (Zysman, 1983; Katzenstein, 1985).

10.2.4 Macro- and micro-competitiveness

This distinction between static and dynamic efficiency also implies a fundamental distinction between micro or enterprise-level competitiveness and efficiency, and macro-competitiveness and efficiency, which is of special relevance to our concern with the relationship between public services and economic performance. Micro-competitiveness or efficiency (competitive advantage) is a characteristic of enterprises; it can be defined as the firm's ability to sell its products in internationally contested markets. The competitiveness of enterprises is based on the relative price and quality of their products in comparison with those of foreign competitors. For enterprises, low costs, including cheap labour, may provide a competitive advantage because *ceteris paribus* they enhance price competitiveness. However, for a national economy competitiveness and efficiency (comparative advantage) must be understood differently. It would be mistaken to regard a nation (or transnational economy) as being competitive in the appropriate macro-competitive or societal sense if it competes on the basis of cheap labour and hence permanently lower wages and working conditions for its labour force. It would be more accurate to say that such a nation (or transnational economy such as the European Community) is incapable of providing higher incomes for its citizens because it is not competitive enough. The competitiveness of a national economy thus refers to its ability to achieve high factor incomes when exposed to international market forces. The goal is not merely to balance trade but to do so at high wage levels on the basis of superior productivity, qualitative excellence, and innovation, in which public policies and public services may play an important role (Pfaller *et al.*, 1989).[9]

Within the European Community framework, the distinction between micro-efficiency and macro-efficiency has to be extended to a third level: the competitiveness and performance of the EC economy as a whole, which is not identical with optimum (partial, perhaps beggar-thy-neighbour) national policies. Indeed, the realisation of a common internal market is placing increasing restrictions on national policies (e.g., state aids to industry or preferential treatment of 'national champions' in public procurement) and leading to increased efforts at coordination *inter alia* of industrial policy from an EC perspective.[10]

Within the public sector, we wish to give particular attention to the 'visible hand' where it takes the form of direct provision of services. There are many forms of public sector intervention and the choice of instruments is not addressed by an analysis in terms of the conditions of market failure. This specific mix is, however, of great importance for public policy; in particular we need to know more about the specific benefits (justification and limitations) of the direct public provision of services in contrast, for example, to regulation, transfers or subsidies.

10.3 The public sector and public services: evidence

10.3.1 Public service expenditures

OECD estimates of general government expenditure in OECD countries represent a crude indicator of the level of and trends in public sector activity. The variation in the level of government outlays as a percentage of GNP/GDP within the OECD is impressive, ranging from a high of 59.3 per cent in Sweden to a low of 32.9 per cent in Japan; within the European Community The Netherlands is the highest (57.9 per cent) and Spain (41.8 per cent) the lowest (see table 10.1). Between 1967 and 1986, total outlays of government as a percentage of GDP increased from 36.4 to 48.3 in the EEC and from 31.5 to 40.2 in the OECD (OECD, 1988a). Since the beginning of the 1980s, however, this development seems to have come to a halt; in some countries there are even signs of a reversal of this long-term trend.

Table 10.1. *Structure of general government outlays*[a] *(percentage of GNP/GDP)*

	United States		Japan		Germany		France		United Kingdom	
	1987	Change 79–87	1988	Change 79–88	1987	Change 79–87	1986	Change 79–86	1986	Change 79–86
Total expenditure	36.9	5.2	32.9	1.3	46.9	−0.7	51.6	6.6	45.5	2.8
Traditional domain										
Public goods[b]	9.7	2.0	..	..	7.9	0.0	7.8	0.8	8.9	0.6
The welfare state										
Merit goods[c]	6.0	−0.2	11.4	0.0	12.2	−0.5	13.4	−0.7	12.1	0.0
Income maintenance[d]	7.9	0.3	7.9	1.6	16.4	−0.5	23.9	7.0	13.2	2.7
The mixed economy										
Economic services[e]	5.7	1.1	4.9	−1.1	4.7	−0.7	3.6	0.1	4.3	−0.5
Public debt interest	5.0	2.2	4.3	1.7	2.8	1.1	2.9	1.5	4.5	0.1
Balancing item[f]	2.2	−0.6	3.6	−0.9	3.0	0.0	0.0	−2.1	2.6	−0.1
Net lending	−3.7	−3.9	2.1	6.8	−1.9	0.7	−2.7	−1.9	−2.8	0.5

	Australia		Austria		Denmark		Finland	
	1987	Change 79–87	1987	Change 81–87	1988	Change 79–88	1988	Change 79–88
Total expenditure	36.4	3.0	52.8	2.5	57.6	4.4	40.2	3.5
Traditional domain								
Public goods	6.7	0.3	5.3	0.0	8.2	0.4	4.6	0.3
The welfare state								
Merit goods	12.1	0.6	10.1	0.6	13.8	−1.5	10.9	1.0
Income maintenance	7.3	0.2	20.3	1.7	15.4	0.7	11.6	3.0
The mixed economy								
Economic services	5.1	−0.5	7.2	−0.9	5.7	−0.3	6.1	−2.9
Public debt interest	4.0	1.9	3.9	1.1	8.3	4.8	1.6	0.7
Balancing item[f]	1.2	0.6	5.9	0.0	6.1	0.3	5.4	1.4
Net lending	0.5	1.9	−4.3	−2.5	2.5	4.2	1.4	1.0

Table 10.1. (*cont.*)

	Netherlands[g]		Norway		Sweden	
	1988	Change 79–88	1988	Change 81–88	1987	Change 81–87
Total expenditure	57.9	2.7	53.5	5.6	59.3	−4.9
Traditional domain						
Public goods	13.7	−0.8	7.2	0.8	6.7	2.8
The welfare state						
Merit goods	13.0	−1.2	16.5	1.4	14.7	−0.7
Income maintenance	19.1	0.5	15.6	3.3	17.2	0.5
The mixed economy						
Economic services	3.7	1.1	9.4	−0.9	7.7	−5.3
Public debt interest	6.9	2.7	3.9	0.6	6.5	1.1
Balancing item[f]	2.1	1.0	0.8	0.4	6.5	−3.3
Net lending	−5.0	−1.3	2.5	−2.2	4.2	9.5

Notes: [a]fiscal year beginning 1 July; [b]defence and general public services; includes latter outlays not allocated by function; [c]education, health, housing and other; [d]pensions, sickness benefits, family allowances, unemployment compensation and other; [e]capital transactions, subsidies and other; [f]the data coverage of the different items are not entirely consistent, which explains the presence of this item; [g]for The Netherlands General Public Services equal public consumption and investment less subcategories relating to defence and education. Total Income Maintenance equals social assistance grants plus social security benefits excluding spending on the health cost insurance. Housing and other includes subsidies to private owners of rental accommodation and contributions to owner occupiers.

Source: Oxley *et al.* (1990) (totals may not add due to rounding).

Not only the level but also the composition of government spending varies considerably among countries. Table 10.1 presents cross-sectional estimates of government spending in the mid-1980s disaggregated by functional categories and grouped into three broad areas: traditional public functions (defence, general administration); the welfare state, including both merit goods (education, health, etc.) and income maintenance; and the 'mixed economy', i.e., 'economic services'.[11] There is a clear preponderance of the social expenditures of the welfare state for both merit goods and income maintenance, which together range from 13.9 per cent (USA) to 37.3 per cent (France) of GDP, whereas public 'economic services', including public business services, range from 3.6 per cent (France) to 9.4 per cent (Norway) in OECD countries in the late 1980s. The reported differences in the level and composition of public spending reflect in part different national priorities (e.g., relative weight of welfare state and military spending) but also, importantly, national differences in the public/private mix in financing health care, pensions, etc. – only public expenditures are reported. There are, moreover, large cross-national differences in the relative importance of services (e.g., merit goods) and transfer payments (cash benefits) or subsidies, especially in the area of the welfare state.[12] France (23.9 per cent) turns out to be the largest spender on transfer payments (due, probably, to extensive early retirement programmes), followed by Austria (20.3 per cent) and The Netherlands (19.1 per cent), whereas Norway (16.5 per cent) and Sweden (14.7 per cent) lead the 'services league'.

As discussed above, the traditional domain of pure public goods is of only indirect relevance for our concern with the contribution of public services to economic competitiveness and performance, and primary attention among public services should accordingly be given to analysis of the merit and mixed goods of the 'welfare state' and 'mixed economy'. Analogous to the distinction between consumer and producer services in the extensive literature on the growth of the private service sector, we think it fruitful to identify not only public economic services but also other indirectly productive public services for education, training, research and development, infrastructure, etc.[13] Moreover, even transfers and social programmes such as those for retirement, unemployment benefits or labour market services may also entail efficiency gains for enterprises and the performance of national economies (see below).

Social services

The welfare state including merit goods and transfer payments to individuals represents by far the largest single component of public sector activity. Good comparative data are available on the welfare state, and its major programme areas (health care, education, income maintenance) have been extensively studied (e.g. OECD, 1988b; 1990a).[14] The relationship between welfare state services and competitiveness in European policy discussions is usually narrowly focused on supposed competitive cost disadvantages for enterprises. It is argued (1) that the welfare state imposes major costs on firms (non-wage labour costs);[15] (2) that if labour costs in a country rise above those of its competitors, there will be a deterioration in the trade balance and a loss of employment in the short run as high-cost producers are displaced by low-cost producers; (3) that in the long run firms will either relocate their operations or shift future investments outside such high labour-cost countries.

This pessimistic view of the impact of the welfare state in international competitiveness and the downward pressure on levels of social protection that it implies ('social competition') is open to criticism on a number of points:[16]

(1) Differences in welfare state benefits and services do not necessarily reflect differences in firms' labour costs. This is due not only to national differences in the mode of financing (e.g., general taxation or contributions and the relative share of the latter borne by employers) but more generally because more generous social benefits may reflect merely the allocation of a larger share of total labour costs to indirect compensation in the form of social security or other social services.[17] Finally, public programmes may merely replace private programmes, eventually with actual efficiency gains (see below).

(2) An excessive emphasis is placed on labour costs as a factor in (static) competitiveness, whereas competitiveness depends not directly on (indirect and direct) wages but on productivity-adjusted compensation. As Pfaller has observed, a key question is the extent to which the prevailing levels of labour productivity in a country are able to sustain higher levels of wages and welfare state in the most advanced economies of the European Community.

(3) Productivity and competitiveness, as well as locational decisions, are the complicated result of innumerable factors such as infrastructure, qualifications of the labour force, industrial relations climate, proximity to customers and suppliers, research and education centres, political stability, etc. In this perspective 'social competition' takes on a broader meaning in which the welfare state may play a potentially positive role. Nevertheless, even in successful 'dynamic competitiveness' there will be losses as well as gains at the firm and industry levels (e.g., steel, textiles and footwear). This process is, however, not necessarily a threat to levels of employment, wages and social protection as long as they are replaced by new products and new markets in

a stream of innovation. A highly developed welfare state may be an integral part of this more complex productivity constellation, both as a provider of services and as an employer.

In contrast to public 'economic services' (discussed below) the direct beneficiaries or 'users' of public social services and social security programmes are, in most instances, not firms but individuals. Nevertheless, it would be erroneous to regard such programmes as representing merely public consumption or redistribution. The greater part of such expenditures, i.e., for education, health, labour-market services (training, placement, information services, etc.) and social security programmes, are closely linked functionally to the labour market and production. It is generally recognised that this is the case for education and training systems. Other types of social services also represent an important 'social wage' component in all developed countries, supplying services which, in the absence of public programmes, have to be directly purchased by firms in the form of employee benefits. This is reflected in the fact that health and social security benefits are usually financed through wage-related contributions, a substantial share of which is borne by the employer.

Public provision of these services is relevant not only to equity considerations but to efficiency and competitiveness. This point can be illustrated by the example of public health insurance, or the lack of it, in the United States. While the United States had the highest total health care expenditures (11.2 per cent of GDP) of any OECD nation in 1987 (mean = 7.3 per cent), the most recent year for which data are available, it is one of the lowest ranking countries in infant mortality, a widely used index of the quality of health care, and below average in life expectancy (OECD, 1990a).[18] These aggregate statistics on the costs of health care have important implications for competitiveness. Although the lack of a public health insurance system in the USA means that public (welfare state) health expenditures are relatively low (4.6 per cent of GDP in 1987), the health costs of American workers are in fact largely borne by voluntary or negotiated employer-financed company health care programmes, which currently insure an estimated 136 million workers and dependants.

By most accounts this health care system has the distinction of being not only inequitable (e.g., *c.* 30 million uninsured persons) but also patently inefficient. This can be illustrated by comparison with the Canadian public health insurance system, which provides universal coverage based on need and is frequently cited as an alternative model in US policy discussions. In 1987 Canadian health costs amounted to only 8.6 per cent of GDP in comparison to 11.2 per cent in the USA in 1987; this is equivalent to $1,483 per capita in Canada in contrast to the 38 per cent higher per capita costs in the USA ($2,051). At the firm level the variation in costs both within and between countries is even greater. Thus in the US motor industry, which has become a principal proponent of public health insurance, the cost of health care services – in a private health care system which is one of the industry's major suppliers – are said to be much higher in the USA than Canada. According to industry statistics cited by Chrysler's chairman Lee Iacocca, a major critic of the US health care system, the company's health care costs *c.* $700 per vehicle in the US average but only $233 in Canada.[19]

What explains this cost difference? The following factors seem to be most important:

(1) A unified national health insurance programme exhibits important economies of scale in contrast to the fragmented and competitive public (Medicare, Medicaid), private, and employer-based US system. For example, an estimated 15 to 20 per cent of US health care expenditures are for administrative costs compared with 2–3 per cent in Canada.[20] Moreover, in contrast to competitive private carriers, there are no sales costs or profit mark-ups.

(2) As the sole purchaser of health care services the government is better able to constrain costs than in the fragmented and competitive US system by negotiating doctors' and hospital fees, limiting the availability of certain kinds of health care providers, services, and high technology medical equipment. Doctors and dentists not only earn less than in the entrepreneurial US system but their numbers are also limited (on the theory that medical services are supply driven);[21] hospital occupancy rates and the utilisation of specialised high-tech equipment are higher.

(3) For individual firms the decentralised and fragmented US system of employer-based health care not only makes health care on average more expensive but also results in competitive distortions in the form of wide variations in health care costs even within the same industry. This is because health care costs depend not only on the generosity of the actual plan negotiated but also on characteristics of the individual firm's workforce such as age structure and ratio of active workers to retirees (retired workers are usually eligible for company health insurance benefits until they become eligible for public Medicare at age 65). Firms in mature or declining industries or those that have reduced their workforces through early retirement schemes can be especially hard hit – this is presumably one reason why national health insurance is popular even among motor industry executives. Conversely start-up firms with a young workforce and no retirees have a competitive advantage (e.g., Japanese transplants in the USA). Because corporate health plans usually commit the company to supply certain

services their actual costs to the company are in part unpredictable, depending on the rise in costs for such services. Finally, the reliance on employer-based health programmes means that the firms become the locus of conflicts over health care costs: efforts of US companies to cut back health care costs have been an important factor in many industrial conflicts in recent years.[22]

Economic services

The heterogeneous economic activities of the state grouped under the category of the mixed economy have been relatively neglected in comparative research. The data reported in table 10.1 give some indication of the approximate level of general government expenditures for 'economic services' in GDP.[23] Welfare state expenditures are far greater in every country, with economic services exceeding traditional public goods only in Italy and Japan. Japan, with relatively low expenditures for merit goods and especially income maintenance, devotes the highest proportion of public spending to economic services. It should be noted, however, that data on general government expenditure for economic services[24] greatly underestimate the actual government role because OECD data on general government spending exclude by definition market activities of government including the entire public enterprise sector. Moreover, such highly aggregated data are, however, not very helpful in identifying the purposes for such expenditures. We know from descriptive accounts that states undertake a wide range of direct activities in support of economic development. Excluding such essentially regulatory activities as investment, trade and competition policies, these activities appear to fall into five principal categories:

(1) Infrastructure activities (transport, communication, and public utilities) and other diverse public enterprises;
(2) Research and development;
(3) Business services (i.e. innovation and technology diffusion, business advisory services, including in particular special programmes for small and medium-sized enterprises);
(4) Sectoral programmes;
(5) Regional development.[25]

Infrastructure activities and other public enterprises certainly constitute the largest component of public sector economic activities. For example, the public enterprise sector is estimated to have accounted for *c*. 10.5 per cent of all employees, 12.5 per cent of value added, and 19 per cent of gross capital formation in the market sector in the European Community in 1987. The importance of this sector varies considerably within the European Community with public enterprises accounting for *c*. 20 per

Table 10.2. *State aid to industry, average 1981–1986*

	Lux	I	Irl	F	D	B	UK	NL	DK	GR	EWG 10
Percentage of public expenditures	19	15	12	11	10	10	5	4	3	–	–
Percentage of GDP	6.0	5.7	5.3	2.7	2.5	4.1	1.8	1.5	1.3	2.5	3.0
Percentage of value added in manufacturing	7.3	16.7	12.9	4.9	3.0	6.4	3.8	4.1	2.6	12.9	6.2

Source: Commission of the European Communities (1989).

cent of GDP in both France and Italy in 1987 but markedly lower percentages in Germany (11.8), Belgium (11), The Netherlands (8.3), Denmark (11), and the UK (11). Public enterprises are concentrated above all in energy distribution (70 per cent of employment), transportation and communications, and finance (60 and 30 per cent respectively). The share of public enterprises in industrial production is by contrast estimated to be no more than 7 per cent – with stronger concentrations in the steel, motor, aerospace and chemical industries (CEEP, 1987). As noted above, most of these activities represent mixed goods, which as market activities are excluded from data on general government expenditure reported in tables 10.1 and 10.2, except for subsidies or other transfers from general government funds.

The quality and cost of such public utilities may have an important impact on the competitiveness of firms or industries for which they are a particularly significant factor. Nevertheless, while public infrastructure at international standards – at least in the sense of business services (e.g., transport and communication) – may be a necessary condition for international competitiveness (this is particularly evident in extreme situations such as eastern Germany where the lack of a modern infrastructure represents a severe obstacle to economic development) they probably play only a limited role as a factor in comparative advantage between the most developed market economies.[26]

In many countries public enterprises, like public procurement, have also been key instruments of national industrial policies not only in the field of regional development but in efforts to promote 'national champions' in international competition, although the liberalisation of public procurement and increased restrictions on state aids to public enterprises in the context of the internal market programme may increasingly restrain such practices.[27]

Research and development is a major and relatively well documented area of government activity in support of economic development. In addition to a major role in basic research through universities and research institutions, governments are also main actors in financing industrial research and development. According to recent OECD estimates the share of publicly financed R&D expenditure in manufacturing varies from a high of 33.3 per cent in the USA in 1985 to a low of 1.4 per cent in Japan with other major OECD countries occupying a range of intermediate positions (Germany 12.5, France 24.0, UK 24.2, Italy 17.3 and Canada 9.3 per cent). There is, moreover, a great deal of variation in the sectoral allocation of such support with US expenditures concentrated for example in the defence-related aerospace, electronics and computer industries (OECD, 1989b p. 68). Support for industrial R&D takes a variety of forms, the most important of which are grants, tax concessions and financing related to public military and other procurement; data for the EC indicate that procurement-related R&D support is substantially greater than that funded by direct state aids (see below). Although, as the above data suggest, there is no obvious relationship at the macro level between levels of government-funded industrial R&D and competitiveness, government activities clearly play a major role in industry-related research and development and an even greater role in basic research.[28]

International data on *sectoral and regional policies* and on business services are not readily available. However some indication of the magnitude and character of such programmes is available from recent data on 'state aids' within the European Community compiled by the European Commission, which provides more detailed information on patterns of government support for domestic industries. State aids are defined as subsidies and other special financial benefits to specific firms and industries including capital transfers, special tax rebates and deductions and capital transactions.[29] State aids are of course by definition subsidies and not real transfers, although they are in many instances targeted on the provision of specific types of services, especially in the case of so-called horizontal subsidies.

Table 10.2 shows marked cross-national differences in average annual state aids from 1981 to 1986 as a percentage of both public expenditure and GDP; The UK, The Netherlands and Denmark exhibit a markedly lower level of such expenditure and, among the large states, Italy displays a significantly higher level of this form of public support for national industry. In all countries state aids are particularly concentrated in manufacturing, which might be indicative of a pattern of state promotion of international competitiveness. However, as table 10.3 on state aids by sector and purpose shows, the bulk of such public support in all countries

Table 10.3. *State aids by sector and purpose; industry/services (percentage figures), average 1981–1986*

	B	DK	D	GR	F	IRL	I	LUX	NL	UK
Horizontal goals	14	19	13	55	20	13	16	3	26	17
R&D	3	8	7	6	1	1	1	–	5	6
Environment	–	1	0	–	–	–	–	–	1	–
SME	3	–	2	3	–	2	3	1	13	1
Trade/Export	2	6	1	46	12	10	4	–	2	8
Energy Saving	–	3	1	–	–	–	1	–	2	–
Investment, general	3	–	1	–	6	–	1	2	3	1
Other	3	–	1	–	–	–	6	–	–	–
Individual Sectors	15	15	5	14	20	18	18	27	16	18
Steel	11	1	2	–	9	3	9	27	2	7
Ship Building	2	14	1	–	3	1	1	–	3	5
Other Crisis Sectors	2	–	–	–	4	5	–	–	7	5
Other Growth Sectors	–	–	1	–	2	–	10	–	1	0
Other Sectors	–	–	1	14	2	9	–	–	3	–
Regional Aid	5	1	18	17	3	21	20	5	8	15
State Aids under EC Directives	67	64	64	13	56	48	44	65	52	51
Agriculture	4	29	7	–	17	23	10	9	21	10
Fishing	–	1	–	–	–	2	–	–	–	1
Transport	35	34	31	13	26	12	34	56	30	14
Coal	28	–	26	–	13	–	–	–	–	19
Total	100	100	100	100	100	100	100	100	100	100

Source: Commission of the European Communities, (1990).

is devoted either to 'defensive' measures in declining industries undergoing adjustment (steel, coal, shipbuilding, agriculture) or to regional aid. Only assistance for the so-called 'horizontal' policies (R&D, programmes for small and medium-sized enterprises, trade/export assistance, etc.) appear to represent potential contributions to 'dynamic' competitiveness.[30] Leaving aside Luxembourg and the special cases of Greece and Ireland, a maximum of *c*. 15–20 per cent of expenditure for state aids goes for such modernising developmental purposes with The Netherlands devoting 26 per cent of its (lower) expenditure for such purposes.[31] It should be noted that the reported data on state aids include only a small fraction of public support for research and development since R&D in connection with public procurement including military-related R&D is not included. Moreover, research and development performed within public or quasi-public research institutions is excluded, since only state financial aids but not state support for industry in the form of direct provision of 'research' services are included. These two categories of R&D are estimated to account for more than ten times the financial volume of reported state aid for R&D in France and the UK (Commission, 1989 p. 32).

10.3.2 Public service employment

Expenditure data alone fail to capture the distinction between public provision in the form of public services and public financing and regulation. For example, within the European Community the merit good of health care is organised according to two quite distinct patterns: either as a public service in which health care services are primarily provided by public employees in public agencies without charge (e.g., the UK) or as social insurance, in which public financing and regulation of health care is combined with a primary reliance on the provision of health services by physicians in private practice or, at least in part, private hospitals (e.g., Germany). Expenditure data will reflect only levels of public financing but not the relative importance of services provided by government within a given functional area or in public sector activities as a whole.[32]

There seems to have been little or no effort to compare public services as a specific component of public sector activities. Given the limitations of expenditure data and the lack of data on the economic value of the services provided,[33] a public service employment perspective appears to us to offer the best approach for comparing and analysing the level and composition of service-intensive public sector activities across nations and functional areas. Although public employment has been much less studied than has public expenditure, there is a small body of comparative literature on trends in public employment (OECD, 1982; Rose, 1985; ILO, 1990).

While most existing studies focus on public sector employment in isolation, we think that a policy-oriented and comparative analysis must encompass service employment as a whole, both public and private. Only in this way is it possible to compare public sector service activities across nations with different mixes of public and private responsibility and to track structural shifts, which may be manifest primarily in a shifting division of labour between the public and private sectors, either overall or within a given functional category, and not necessarily in a decline in public sector employment.

The international data sources on service employment that would make possible a distinction between public and private employment by functional activities are – given the importance of the issue – surprisingly limited. There are two potential sources of comparative data on public

Table 10.4. *Employment by sector, 1985 (by percentage)*

	AUL	BEL	CAN	DK	FIN	FRA	FRG	ITA	NTH	NOR	SWE	SWZ	UK	USA
Agriculture	6	4	5	7	13	8	6	11	5	7	5	6	2	3
Industries	27	31	25	24	34	34	42	40	29	29	30	39	33	28
private	*84*	–	*96*	*99*	*84*	*94*	*98*	*98*	*87*	*91*	*94*	*97*	*89*	*97*
public	*16*	–	*4*	*2*	*16*	*6*	*2*	*2*	*13*	*9*	*6*	*3*	*11*	*3*
Services	66	66	70	69	53	58	53	49	65	64	65	54	65	69
private	*64*	*62*	*76*	*46*	*55*	*58*	*66*	*59*	*74*	*51*	*44*	*73*	*66*	*80*
public	*36*	*38*	*24*	*54*	*45*	*42*	*34*	*41*	*26*	*49*	*56*	*27*	*34*	*20*
Total	100	100	100	100	100	100	100	100	100	100	100	100	100	100

Source: WEEP project data files.

employment, both of which are subject to severe limitations. First, GNP accounts data on government service employment compiled by the OECD in its 'National Accounts' series, which provides aggregate data by country on government employment, i.e., 'producers of government services'. These data suffer from the same limitation of national account expenditure data discussed above: they are based on a narrow definition of government as 'general government', excluding all marketed services such as the post office, railways, etc. and of course public enterprise employment. The preferable alternative appears to be to use the more comprehensive and standardised data on the distribution of public and private service employment available from national labour force statistics, which as a rule define public employment in terms of ownership, rather than whether the service is marketed, thus providing broader and more differentiated data on public service employment.[34] This research strategy can also build on earlier international comparative work done on the service sector at the Science Centre Berlin (WZB) in the Welfare State Entry Exit Project (WEEP) during the mid-1980s, which collected and retabulated national labour force survey data on public and private service employment in a standardised format for sixteen OECD countries in 1975, 1980 and 1985.[35]

The growth of the service sector and service sector employment is one of the most frequently commented trends in 'post-modern' societies. As data on the public/private composition of service employment reported in table 10.4 illustrate, public service employment is an important component of total service employment in all countries. Even more striking, however, is the variation in the share of public service employment in total service employment. On the one hand, there is what may be termed the Scandinavian model with a high level of public employment in service

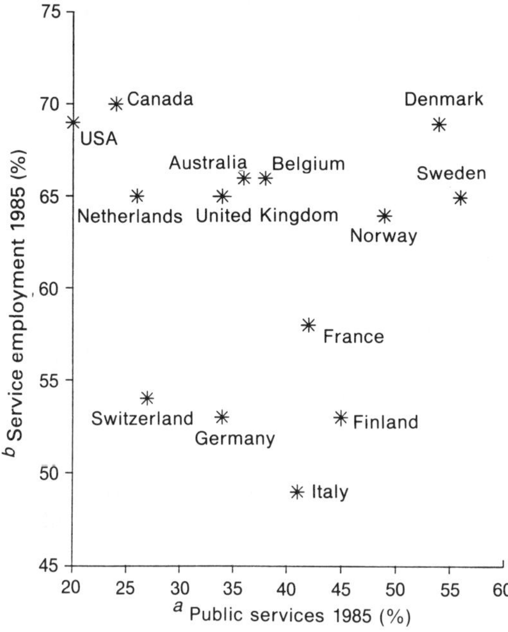

Figure 10.1 Service employment and pubic services, 1985 – [a]public service employment/total services employment × 100; [b]total service employment/total employment × 100.
Source: as table 10.4 © Social Sciences Centre Berlin/LMP.

employment (exceeding 50 per cent in Sweden and Denmark and at 49 per cent in Norway) and, on the other hand, an American model in which there is a heavy predominance of private service employment in the USA and Canada but also in Switzerland and in The Netherlands.[36] Other countries typified by France, Belgium, Germany and the UK occupy intermediate positions in what might be called a continental model. Interesting too is the fact that there is no evident relationship between the relative size of public service employment and the size of the service sector in total employment (figure 10.1).

10.4 The public sector and economic performance: cross-national studies

Although the primary focus of the existing large body of literature on government growth is on the determinants of changes in public sector expenditures and employment,[37] increasing attention has recently been given to quantitative cross-national analyses of the overall impact of government activities (usually defined in terms of governmental expenditures) on economic performance.[38]

The purpose of this section is briefly to survey recent research on comparative public policy dealing with this topic and to make suggestions for further research.

A number of earlier comparative studies in a cross-section framework pointed towards a negative relationship between the size of the public sector and economic performance. For example, in a study of seventeen OECD countries between 1961 and 1972 Smith (1975) found a significant inverse relationship between the share of government final consumption expenditure in national income and gross investment ratios, and hence by implication economic growth; the work of Cameron (1978) and Mardsen (1983) has also suggested similar negative relationships. Although Gould (1983) found only a weak relationship between levels of public expenditure and economic growth, he found a significant negative relationship between increases in levels of expenditure and economic growth.

More recently Pfaller, Gough and Therborn (1989) also report evidence that the welfare state may, under certain conditions, be a drag on economic growth in OECD countries. A regression analysis of 'welfare statism' (defined in terms of the mean tax burden, including social security contributions, on GDP) and average annual real GDP growth over the period 1973–87 shows a weak negative association (−0.26). However, when two subperiods are distinguished the results show a strong negative relationship for the 1980s (−0.52); with the exception of the outlier Norway, states with the highest social expenditure ratios had the lowest growth rates in the 1980s; no systematic relationship between welfare state effort and growth was found for the 1970s.[39]

Other recent studies either find no convincing evidence of a relationship between the size of the public sector and economic growth or, in some cases, positive impacts of particular components of public sector activity. A multiple regression analysis of the relationship between general government expenditure and receipts and economic performance in OECD countries by Saunders (1985) found only weak or inconclusive evidence for a simple negative relationship between public sector size and economic performance. His findings show an inverse correlation across countries between the average economic growth and the average share of total government outlays in GDP over the periods 1960–73 and 1975–81 ($r = -0.73$ and -0.43 respectively); however the relationship is statistically significant only for the former period. Because of the large number of outliers, Saunders is sceptical of the robustness of the findings even for this period. The results are extremely sensitive to the inclusion or exclusion of certain countries, e.g., Japan or 'catch-up' growth countries such as Spain, Portugal and Turkey; for the rest of the OECD he finds no discernible relationship between government size and economic growth, which suggests the need to consider special circumstances as well as other factors.

Several recent contributions to the literature on comparative public policy have found evidence that the public sector may actually contribute to economic growth (Friedland and Sanders, 1985; Korpi, 1985; Ram, 1986). Based on a study of eighteen OECD countries between 1950 and 1982 Korpi finds no evidence for the 'self-regulating market hypothesis', i.e., that *ceteris paribus* economic efficiency and growth will decrease with increasing political intervention in market forces. For the period 1950–73, while government final consumption and civilian consumption have low and usually negative relationships to economic growth, social security transfers show a clear positive relationship; for the period 1960–73 measures of public sector size are positively related to growth and social security expenditures show a strong positive relationship. Contrary to neo-liberal expectations, public sector size in the pre-crisis period (1966–73) is also positively related to economic performance (GDP per capita and productivity growth) during the 1973–82 crisis period.

Friedland and Sanders investigated the impact of changes in four distinct types of public spending on short-term growth (one to three years) in twelve advanced market economies for the period 1962–83: transfer payments to households, direct provision of goods and services to households, subsidies and transfers to firms and military spending. Their cross-section pooled longitudinal analysis shows a strong positive relationship between transfer payments to households and economic growth but a negative relationship between government provision of goods and services and growth. While growth in transfers to firms initially stimulates growth, it is found to depress growth in the longer term. Increases in military spending are associated with higher growth but the relationship is never statistically significant. Based on a study of the relationship between government size and economic growth between 1960 and 1980 in a large sample (115) that included less developed countries, Ram (1986) finds that 'it is difficult not to conclude that government size has a positive effect on economic performance and growth'.

Castles and Dowrick (1990) analysed the impact of government spending on economic growth using cross-section data from eighteen OECD countries over the period 1960–85. This most recent analysis is representative of the increasing sophistication of this type of cross-national aggregate data study, both in the variety of variables considered and in the statistical methodology applied. They control for a number of other influences on economic growth: (a) 'catching up', i.e., the tendency for less developed countries to grow faster; (b) 'institutional sclerosis'; (c) population growth; (d) growth of employment and capital stock. The dependent variable used is the 'trend annual growth rate' rather than short-term growth. For the independent variable, government spending, a more differentiated set of measures is utilised: total expenditure is disaggregated into consumption and non-consumption expenditure or into social and other expenditure; social expenditure is further disaggregated into health, education and transfer expenditure. A constant price series for government expenditure was developed and utilised for each country where appropriate in order to control for relative prices in measuring government activities (e.g., whether government workers are paid well or poorly). Moreover, special controls were introduced to cope with the problem of outliers in sample selection (e.g., Japan) and simultaneous causation, i.e., the asserted tendency for government spending to increase with increasing per capita income (Wagner's Law). A state of the art pooled time-series analysis was used (rather than a cross-section framework), which was subdivided into four time periods (1960–68, 1969–73, 1974–79 and 1980–85).

Their findings reject 'any interpretation that argues for a statistically significant negative relationship between the level of government revenues or the components of government expenditure and medium-term economic growth'. Apparent findings to the contrary concerning the negative relationship between government consumption expenditure and total factor productivity are rejected because they fail crucial diagnostic tests. Such findings are highly unstable with respect to sample selection – i.e., the inclusion of Japan with its exceptionally high rates of economic growth and low levels of government expenditure – and they appear to reflect in part a problem of reverse causation: the percentage share of government consumption in GDP tends to fall when economic growth is rapid.

Findings in previous studies to the contrary are attributed in particular to failure adequately to control for 'catch-up' (see Baumol, 1986; Dowrick and Nguyen, 1989), which sharply reduces the estimated positive impact of social expenditure on economic growth and on total factor productivity. Conversely they question on methodological grounds the strong positive correlation between growth and social expenditure found in some previous studies (e.g., Korpi, 1985), which they attribute to the use of per capital GDP as a dependent variable without adequately controlling for population or employment growth.[40] Nevertheless, they do find a 'modest, but statistically significant, positive effect of non-consumption expenditures, and especially social transfers, on medium-term growth of productivity'. Even this mild benign effect is of major policy significance since, if corroborated, it would refute the conventional neoclassical postulate that there is an inevitable trade-off between equity and efficiency, i.e., the notion that the welfare state is from an economic point of view a 'leaky bucket' (Okun, 1975).

This brief survey serves to provide an overview of cross-national policy research on the relationship between the public sector and economic performance. We have not attempted here to examine the reasons for apparent inconsistencies in the results of different studies, which would require a more technical discussion. In general it can be said that the inconsistencies in the findings reflect differences in the definition of the public sector and growth variables, the time periods studied, the countries included in the sample, and the extent to which controls are applied for other determinants of growth (e.g., 'catch-up' effect and population growth).

Despite significant progress in our understanding of both the determinants of growth and the contribution of the public sector, there are, in our view, shortcomings in previous aggregate studies. Future cross-national research of this type requires an improved database and a more differentiated analysis based on the hypothesis that it is not the size of public services as such but their composition, institutional tradition, and effective linkage to enterprises that determines their impact on competitiveness and performance.

First, the definition of public services, the independent variable, remains too crude and needs to be further differentiated to capture distinctive national patterns. This would entail, for example, distinguishing systematically in public spending between public consumption, investment and transfers, breaking down the composition of public spending and employment into more detailed functional categories, and systematic incorporation of data on public enterprises.

Second, the dependent variable, competitiveness and economic performance, should be expanded as feasible to include additional indicators. While national competitiveness certainly entails high productivity and increasing per capita GDP (as discussed in 10.2.3 above), consideration should also be given to social and ecological indicators (e.g., unemployment, income distribution, occupational segregation, environmental quality).

Third, the relationship between public services and economic competitiveness and performance requires further elaboration. Most discussion of the role of the public sector takes place at a high level of generality, which frequently amounts to no more than a statement of ideological preferences. The comparative studies surveyed here employ sophisticated quantitative techniques to measure statistical associations; however, they usually fail to identify and investigate the mechanisms through which public sector activities impact on competitiveness and economic performance.

10.5 Conclusion

Our discussion of the relationship between public services and competitiveness began with the straightforward, if tricky, question of whether states with larger public sectors and a high level of public services are at a competitive disadvantage. We have attempted to shed light on this topic in the course of an extensive survey of issues and evidence on the relationship between the public sector and competitiveness, which cannot be easily summarised here. Our conclusion is, however, clear: there is no convincing case for such a proposition and, more importantly, there is a need to develop a more sophisticated understanding of complex policy regimes of public–private interplay.

The principal sections of this paper and considerations elsewhere[41] do not develop a single argument but rather elaborate distinct but interrelated elements of a common theme.

In a survey of recent literature on competitiveness and the role of institutions and the state, section 2 argues that the (neo-)classical paradigm of the primacy of the market is not only a poor predictor of the actual role of government but increasingly questionable on theoretical grounds. Much recent literature on international competitiveness has emphasised the role of public policy in maintaining or enhancing comparative advantage in high-wage, high value-added production of the sort that is certainly the preferred model for a European competitiveness strategy.

The next issue addressed is: What do governments do, especially in the way of public services? Our focus here (section 3) has been on the microeconomic or 'supply-side' impacts of public sector activity and not on issues of taxation, government revenues or the macroeconomic impact of government activity. Public services ('real transfers') are clearly only one mode of public activity in addition to subsidies, transfers, regulations, etc.; indeed a major policy issue over and beyond the general question of whether public intervention is called for, is the particular form (or often combination) of modalities of public sector activity and whether and under what circumstances 'public services' may exhibit a comparative advantage over other possibilities.

In general it can be said that public sector activity and public services consist primarily of the 'merit goods' of the welfare state and 'economic services' – aside from the classical public functions (defence, foreign affairs, administration of justice, etc.) and the still-important market activities of public enterprises and nationalised industries, which – for different reasons – we have treated only tangentially. The crux of the issue of the relationship of public services to competitiveness, it seems to us, concerns these areas of a public service activity. With regard to the welfare state as a negative cost factor in international competitiveness, most 'welfare' services can plausibly be regarded in a much more positive light as being indirectly productive. By contrast public economic services, broadly defined, account for a much smaller share of public activity as measured by expenditure. Although there is in the relevant policy literature a great deal of emphasis on the importance of such public sector activities for regional and national competitiveness, the vast bulk of such industrial policy expenditure in Europe goes not for modernising or 'dynamically' competitive activities but rather for defence programmes for declining industries and problem regions; it seems to be a clear case of industrial policy lagging behind the development of theory. In quantitative terms public research and development activities seem to be the strongest candidate for a major 'offensive' impact of public policy. Our review of national and sectoral level aggregate data may, however, underestimate the importance of public 'business services' in qualitative terms for particular industries or for innovative activity.

Finally, a review of recent cross-national econometric studies (section 4) concludes that there is no convincing evidence for a negative impact of the public sector on economic performance (or, for that matter, a positive impact), which suggests that the question itself may be too simplistic. There are several alternative institutional regimes for the provision of public services and a need to focus on a more complex institutional variable. While available evidence on the relative efficiency of public vs private provision of services at the micro level is inconclusive also, there is strong support for the importance of variation in institutional regimes for the efficiency of service provision.

Notes

This chapter is based on a report prepared for the Commission of the European Communities (DG V; Directorate General for Employment, Industrial Relations, and Social Affairs), 'The Contribution of Public Services to the Competitiveness and Performance of Enterprises and National Economies'.

1 See especially the work of the Growth Studies Division of the Economic and Statistics Department of the OECD, for example, Saunders and Klau (1985), and Oxley *et al.* (1990); Lybeck and Henrekson (1988) contains a representative collection of recent studies of this type.

2 For a critical overview of this literature see Saunders (1986).

3 For a recent overview see Lange and Garrett (1985).

4 See especially Soskice (1989 and 1991) for an overview of such institutional factors in competitiveness; see also Streeck, 1991; Dertouzos *et al.*, 1989; Pfaller *et al.*, 1989; Katzenstein, 1985.
5 For example, 'flexible specialisation' and 'diversified quality production' represent two recent formulations of such a mode of production.
6 Codified for example in the version of 'Wagner's Law' which regards public services as a type of luxury good, i.e., a good with a high income elasticity of demand, consumption of which increases with rising income levels. See also, for example, Bacon and Eltis's (1976) influential study of Great Britain in which this is an implicit assumption.
7 For a recent review of these issues, see Audretsch and Yamawaki, 1990.
8 This conception of comparative advantage and competitiveness is closely related to the distinction between static and dynamic efficiency and competition in the Schumpeterian tradition. Whereas static competition is based on input costs and prices, dynamic competition is driven by innovation, product quality, R&D and human capital inputs, and may require quite different supportive public policies.
9 This distinction between micro-efficiency and macro-efficiency is closely related to other concepts such as local and global maximising (Elster, 1979).
10 Some of these issues are raised in literature on European Community competition and industrial policy (see, for example, Pearce and Sutton, 1986; Hughes, 1990).
11 As noted below these data on 'general government' expenditure exclude by definition government activities that are predominantly market-oriented, i.e., public services and government enterprises that charge for their products are seriously underestimated.
12 This distinction is reflected in the preference of some critics of the welfare state for cash transfers as opposed to social services, for example, Friedman's negative income tax proposal. As noted above, data on general government expenditures do not include the activities of public enterprises.
13 See Audretsch and Yamawaki (1990) for an overview and recent contribution to this discussion. See also Eisner (1986) for an interesting discussion of the importance of distinguishing between public investment and public consumption in government budgets.
14 The exception here may be the social service activities of the welfare state.
15 Within the European Community today non-wage labour costs average about 40 per cent of total labour costs.
16 See Mosley (1991) for a more in depth discussion of the relationship between the welfare state and competitiveness in the context of the European Community.
17 This is implicit in Kamppeter's (1990) argument that competitive pressures emanating from the world market constrain only the after-tax rate of return on capital but not the distribution of the other components of national income.
18 Unless otherwise noted, all health care data cited are taken from OECD (1990a).
19 *Financial Times*, 1 September 1989.
20 Information for this stylised comparison with Canada, which is meant to be illustrative rather than exhaustive, is largely drawn from Kosterlitz (1989a and b).
21 See Klim McPherson, 'International differences in medical care practices', in OECD, 1990a, pp. 21–4. Comparative studies of medical treatment in the USA

and the UK consistently conclude that the surgical rate in the USA is almost twice that in the UK and that this is primarily a function of number of surgeons rather than of the prevalence of disease!

22 According to one expert, health insurance was a major issue in work stoppages affecting 78 per cent of all striking workers in 1989.

23 It should be noted that 'economic services' in this context includes not only public provision of services but also other types of subsidies and transfers.

24 See note 23.

25 For an overview see OECD, 1989c and 1990b. Labour market services are omitted in the discussion because they are conventionally included under social service activities.

26 Italy with its extremely inefficient public services may be a borderline case, although the competitive success of many Italian industries and the country's relatively favourable economic performance in the 1980s suggests that enterprises have on the whole been able to cope effectively with the problems of Italy's transport and communications services.

27 Or in some cases European champions: the Airbus consortium, which has established European producers in strategic competition with US firms in the civil aircraft market, represents a prominent example of European industrial policy in an area that is important not only for trade competitiveness but also for technological development. In the current controversy within GATT, the USA claims that the government-sponsored Airbus consortium has received $25.9 billion in direct subsidies; Airbus representatives counter-claim that the US aircraft industry itself has in fact received large indirect subsidies of a similar magnitude through US government support for industrial military R&D (*Financial Times*, 24 April 1991 p. 6).

28 See OECD, 1989c and OECD, 1990b. The OECD has also published a series of reports on national science and technology policy: see, for example, OECD, Reviews of National Science and Technology Policy: Switzerland (Paris: OECD, 1989c).

29 It should be noted that, based on the EC's current conception of trade distortion, 'state aids' include only assistance for specific firms or industries; by contrast general measures that are applicable economy-wide (e.g., general systems of taxation or social insurance contributions) are excluded. Aid to both private and public enterprises is included. Data on training and employment measures are, unfortunately, not included.

30 In addition to the category 'growth sectors', which accounts for only a small fraction of reported state aids.

31 Italy is omitted from the discussion due to problems in classifying a large component of Italian expenditure.

32 This distinction is of more than academic importance; it corresponds to a real difference in the organisation of public welfare activities between service-intensive and transfer-intensive welfare states (e.g., Scharpf, 1986). For example, Sweden and Holland display similar very high levels of general government expenditure as a percentage of GDP but while Sweden also ranks first in the level of public service employment, which we may take as an indicator of service-intensity, The Netherlands ranks extremely low (26.1 per cent and 8.3 per cent respectively of the working-age population in 1986). This very large discrepancy between public expenditure and public employment rates is primarily a reflection of the greater transfer-intensity of Dutch public

activities (in contrast to the service-intensity of the Swedish public sector). This difference in levels of public service employment is secondarily a consequence of the fuzziness of the boundary between the public and private sectors: in The Netherlands there is a heavy reliance on religious and other non-governmental but non-profit organisations in the provision of publicly financed health, educational and social services (Cusack, Notermans and Rein, 1989 pp. 475–80).

33 The general government, merit and economic services that we are concerned with here are in most cases non-market goods, i.e., they are provided free of charge, subsidised, etc., and hence lack a market price that can be used as a measure of value. In the national income accounts their contribution to value-added is derived from the value of their input costs, which is an obvious source of distortion.

34 See Cusack and Rein, 1987 p. 6, for a discussion of these data problems.

35 Data were compiled for sixteen countries for 1985 but for only eleven in 1980 and 1975. The resulting database distinguishes: (1) between business services and consumer services according to a variant of the 'user principle', with an intermediate category of collective services (public administration, sanitation, etc.) that are difficult to assign unambiguously, and (2) between public and private providers of services. Particular attention is given to patterns of social service employment (health, education and welfare), which was the principal focus of the project.

36 The Dutch case is deviant due to the special role of religious organisations in the provision of government financed public services.

37 See, for example, Saunders and Klau (1985) and Lybeck and Henrekson (1988).

38 There is, of course, a large body of literature on traditional macroeconomic issues such as the impact of government spending on growth and whether public spending 'crowds out' private investment, especially when it is based on deficit financing. Moreover, partial analyses of the impact of government have been a major concern of public sector economics: for example, Saunders and Klau's 1985 study for the OECD Growth Studies Division devotes considerable attention to the impact of taxation on labour supply ('poverty trap') and labour demand, on employment, and on savings and capital formation and the relationship between education and economic growth.

39 An even stronger negative coefficient (−0.63) is found if social expenditure as a percentage of GDP (in 1979) is substituted as the independent variable.

40 This procedure, they argue, leads to a systematic upward bias in the estimates: the rate of population growth is said to be negatively correlated with social expenditure, apparently because a younger population is less in need of social security support; at the same time per capita GDP tends to decline with rapid population growth. Hence 'when population growth is omitted as an explanatory variable the coefficient on social expenditures . . . rises to (apparently) very high levels of significance when the dependent variable is per capita GDP' (Korpi, 1985 p. 199).

41 See for an extended version of this chapter Mosley and Schmid, 1992.

References

Audretsch, David and Yamawaki, Hideki, 1990. 'Do services crowd out manufacturing? The case of West Germany', Berlin: WZB Discussion Paper FS IV 90.

Bacon, R. and Eltis, W., 1976. *Britain's Economic Problem: Too Few Producers*. London: Macmillan.

Bator, F. M., 1958. 'The anatomy of market failure', *Quarterly Journal of Economics*, 72: 351–71.

Baumol, W. J., 1986. 'Productivity growth, convergence, and welfare: what the long-run data show', *American Economic Review*, 76: 1072–85.

Cameron, D. R., 1978. 'The expansion of the public economy: a comparative analysis', *American Political Science Review*, 72: 1243–61.

Castles, Francis G. and Steve Dowrick, 1990. 'The impact of government spending levels on medium-term economic growth in the OECD, 1960–85', *Journal of Theoretical Politics*, 2: 173–204.

CEEP (European Centre of Public Enterprises), 1987. *Public Enterprises in the European Community*. Brussels: CEEP.

Cohen, Stephen S. and Zysman, John, 1987. *Manufacturing Matters: The Myth of the Post-Industrial Economy*. New York: Basic Books.

Commission of the European Communities, 1989. *Erster Bericht über Staatliche Beihilfen in der Europäischen Gemeinschaft* (First Report on State Aids in the European Community). Brussels: Office for Official Publications of the European Communities.

1990. *Second Survey on State Aids in the European Community in the Manufacturing and Certain Other Sectors*. Brussels: Office for Official Publications of the European Communities.

Cusack, Thomas R., Notermans, T. and Rein, M., 1989. 'Political-economic aspects of public employment', *European Journal of Political Research*, 17: 471–500.

Cusack, Thomas and Rein, Martin, 1987. 'Social policy and service employment' (manuscript) Berlin: WZB.

Dertouzos, Michael *et al.*, 1989. *Made in America: Regaining the Productive Edge*. Cambridge, MA: MIT Press.

Dowrick, Steve and Nguyen, Duc-Tho, 1989. 'OECD comparative economic growth 1950–85: catch-up and convergence', *American Economic Review*, 79: 1010–30.

Eisner, Robert, 1986. *How Real is the Federal Deficit?* New York: Free Press.

Elster, J., 1979. *Ulysses and the Sirens. Studies in Rationality and Irrationality*. London: Cambridge University Press.

Esping-Anderson, Gosta, 1990. *The Three Worlds of Welfare Capitalism*. Cambridge: Polity Press.

Friedland, Roger and Sanders, Jimy, 1985. 'The public economy and economic growth in western market economies', *American Sociological Review*, 50: 421–37.

Gould, F., 1983. 'The development of public expenditures in western industrialized countries: a comparative analysis', *Public Finance*, 38: 38–69.

Hirschman, A. O., 1982. *Private Interest and Public Action*, Princeton: Princeton University Press.

Hughes, Kirsty, 1990. 'Competition, competitiveness and the European Community – a critical analysis of "the economics of 1992"', Berlin: WZB Discussion Paper FS IV 90–7.

International Labour Office, 1990. *World Labour Report 1989*, Vol. IV. Geneva: International Labour Office.

Johnson, Chalmers, 1982. *MITI and the Japanese Miracle*. Stanford: Stanford University Press.

Johnson, Chalmers, D'Andrea Tyson, Laura and Zysman, John (eds.), 1989. *Politics and Productivity: How Japan's Development Strategy Works*. New York: Harper.

Kamppeter, W., 1990. *Kapital- und Devisenmärkte als Herausforderung der Wirtschaftspolitik*. Frankfurt: Campus.

Katzenstein, Peter, 1985. *Small States in World Markets*. Ithaca: Cornell University Press.

Korpi, W., 1985. 'Economic growth and the welfare state: leaky bucket or irrigation system', *European Sociological Review*, 1: 97–118.

Kosterlitz, J., 1989a. 'Taking care of Canada', *National Journal*: 1792–97.

1989b. 'But not for us?', *National Journal*: 1871–75.

Lange, Peter and Garrett, Geoffrey, 1985. 'The politics of growth: strategic interaction and economic performance in advanced industrial democracies', *Journal of Politics*, 47: 792–827.

Lybeck, J. A. and Henrekson, M. (eds.), 1988. *Explaining the Growth of Government*. North-Holland: Elsevier.

Mardsen, K., 1983. 'Links between taxes and economic growth', World Bank Staff Working Paper, No. 605. Washington, DC.

Mosley, H., 1991. 'The welfare state and european unity' in Zdenek, Suda (ed.), *Globalization and the Social Contract*. Pittsburgh: University of Pittsburgh Press.

Mosley, H. and Schmid, G., 1992. 'Public services and competitiveness', Berlin: WZB Discussion Paper FS I 92 7.

Musgrave, Richard A. and Musgrave, Peggy B., 1968. *Public Finance in Theory and Practice*. London: McGraw-Hill.

OECD, 1982. *Employment in the Public Sector*. Paris: OECD.

1988a. *Economic Outlook*. Paris: OECD.

1988b. *The Future of Social Protection*. Paris: OECD.

1989a. *Economic Survey Italy*. Paris: OECD.

1989b. 'Industrial subsidies in the OECD economies', Working Paper No. 74, Paris: OECD Department of Economics and Statistics.

1989c. *Industrial Policy in OECD Countries: Annual Review 1989*. Paris: OECD.

1990a. *Health Care Systems in Transition*. Paris: OECD.

1990b. *Industrial Policy in OECD Countries: Annual Review 1990*. Paris: OECD.

Okun, A., 1975. *Equality and Efficiency: The Big Tradeoff*. Washington, DC: Brookings.

Oxley, H. *et al.*, 1990. 'The public sector: issues for the 1990s', Working Paper No. 90. Paris: OECD.

Pfaller, A., Gough, I. and Therborn, G. (eds.), 1989. *Can the Welfare State Compete?* Bonn: Friedrich Ebert Stiftung.

Pearce, Joan and Sutton, John, 1986. *Protection and Industrial Policy in Europe*. London: Routledge.

Porter, Michael, 1990. *The Competitive Advantage of Nations and Firms*. New York: Free Press.

Ram, Rati, 1986. 'Government size and economic growth: a new framework and some evidence from cross-section and time-series data', *American Economic Review*, 76: 191–203.

Rose, Richard, 1985. *Public Employment in Western Nations*, Cambridge: Cambridge University Press.

Saunders, P., 1985. 'Public expenditure and economic performance in OECD countries', *Journal of Public Policy*, 5: 1–21.

1986. 'What can we learn from international comparisons of public sector size and economic performance?', *European Sociological Review*, 2: 52–60.

Saunders, Peter and Klau, Friedrich, 1985. *The Role of the Public Sector*. Paris: OECD.

Scharpf, Fritz W., 1986. 'Strukturen der post-industriellen Gesellschaft, oder: Verschwindet die Massenarbeitslosigkeit in der Dienstleistungs- und Informationsökonomie?', *Soziale Welt*, 37: 3–24.

Smith, David, 1975. 'Public consumption and economic performance', *National Westminster Bank Quarterly Review*, 17–30.

Soskice, David, 1989. 'Reinterpreting corporatism and explaining unemployment: coordinated and non-coordinated market economies' in R. Brunetta and C. Della Ringa (eds.), *Markets, Institutions and Cooperation: Labour Relations and Economic Performance*. London: Macmillan.

1991. 'Institutional infrastructure for international competitiveness: a comparative analysis of the UK and Germany' in A. B. Atkinson and R. Brunetta (eds.), *The Economics for the New Europe*. London: Macmillan.

Stiglitz, J. E., 1986. *Economics of the Public Sector*. New York: Norton.

Streeck, Wolfgang, 1991. 'On the institutional conditions of diversified quality production', in Egon Matzner and Wolfgang Streeck, *Beyond Keynesianism: The Socio-economics of Production and Full Employment*. Aldershot: Elgar.

Wolf, Charles, 1987. 'Market and non-market failure', *Journal of Public Policy*, 7: 43–70.

1988. *Markets and Governments: Choosing Between Imperfect Alternatives*. Cambridge, MA: MIT Press.

Zysman, John, 1983. *Governments, Markets and Growth*. Oxford: Martin Robertson.

11 Culture and competitiveness

SHAUN HARGREAVES-HEAP

11.1 Introduction

Most economists probably pay lip service to Weber's thesis in *Protestantism and the Spirit of Capitalism* and so acknowledge that culture plays some general role in economic performance. However, few economists take the point on board in their own work (Casson, 1991 is a recent rare exception). There may be bar-talk which allows for what has not been explained about say, poor British competitiveness to turn on the British stereotypical 'bloody-mindedness'. But culture is conspicuous through its absence when it comes to the more serious business of journal-talk. The contrast with management and business studies, where corporate cultures are increasingly included among the prime determinants of business success, could not be more marked (see, for instance, Peters and Waterman, 1982).

This chapter argues that economics needs to follow management and business studies: it needs to recover the intuitions licensed in the bar and grant culture an important role in explaining economic performance. In particular, it will be argued that culture influences performance in a way that affects both the short and long run competitiveness of an economy.

To suggest to economists that they should 'follow business and management studies' is, perhaps, not the best way to start the argument. Economists tend to jibe that management and business studies 'lack a robust theoretical backbone: they are too descriptive'. (Of course, the taunt is typically reciprocated by management and business studies: for them, economics is excessively driven by 'unrealistic' theory.) Whatever the merits of this position, it is a fact of disciplinary life. To stand the best chance of persuading economists of some argument, one needs to catch their theoretical eye. Hence, the burden of the argument, which appears in the next section, is purely theoretical. On theoretical grounds, it is suggested that economics cannot do without culture (or something like it) to fix the beliefs that agents in the economy hold and which affect competitiveness.

Even among economists, purely theoretical arguments do not cut as much ice as theoreticians might like; and so the argument is supported empirically. This is done in two ways. Firstly there are two examples in sections 3 and 4 where the purely theoretical argument from section 2 appears to have a direct bearing on the issue of competitiveness. The illustrations relate to wage bargaining and the generation of trust. They have been chosen because they both (a) require something like culture in the form of an extraneous source of belief to fix outcomes; (b) have outcomes which affect competitiveness; and (c) exhibit interestingly different outcomes across countries.

To be more specific on the connection with competitiveness. The nature of the wage bargain critically influences short-run competitiveness because economies where real wages are slow to adjust to supply shocks are liable to suffer from a lack of competitiveness which is revealed either in current account deficits or in high unemployment (which becomes necessary to avoid the current account deficits when wages are slow to adjust). Trust is crucial for the shift to manufacturing systems or 'flexible specialisation' and it is frequently argued that the long-run competitiveness of an economy will turn increasingly on how quickly and thoroughly this shift is achieved.

The evidence under (a), (b) and (c) suggests that there are interesting gaps in the conventional account of belief and behaviour in areas which affect competitiveness. The second type of evidence is given in section 5. It points to the possibility of culture filling the gap – that is, of explaining these cross-country differences in belief and hence competitiveness. This evidence is not more than a pointer (the appendix takes it somewhat further). It concerns the existence of cultural diversity in Europe together with the sketch of a cultural theory (Mary Douglas's grid–group analysis) which might be used to connect particular cultural beliefs with the gaps which need to be filled in the conventional economic account.

Thus the empirical evidence supports what is really a *prima facie* case for taking culture seriously. The case consists of a theoretical argument coupled with some evidence which, whilst far from decisive, suggests that the argument is worth pursuing. This is, perhaps, as much as can be expected at this stage, when the task is to persuade economists that talk of culture does not just belong in the bar (or in business and management studies!).

11.2 Why culture is not just an optional extra

What is meant by culture here? Culture refers to the web of shared beliefs among a group of people, an organisation or a society which are both constitutive and regulative of social life. That is to say, the shared beliefs both enable actions to be correctly interpreted and express shared views concerning the worth of actions. So, for instance, we have lots of shared beliefs, of 'rules', which enable us to interpret whether a twitch of an eyeball is a wink or a blink, and we also share beliefs about the appropriateness of winking in certain social situations. In short, culture is a shorthand for the background beliefs, ranging from the meaning of life, the universe, to something as mundane as, say, gardening, that are shared by a group of people and which pass largely unsaid and yet which bring many an action to life.

In this section, it is argued both that economics traditionally ignores culture and that it should not. The first part of this claim may seem somewhat extravagant, since mainstream economics plainly deals in beliefs and would seem to contain a theory of those beliefs. However, the reference to beliefs in economics is typically quite restricted and contains little of substance regarding those beliefs.

To be specific on the restricted nature of beliefs in economics: they are usually individually held, there is no requirement that they should be shared, and they relate only to those variables which affect an agent's calculation of what to do for the best. The last is a legacy of Hume's psychology, where 'reason is the slave of the passions'. Beliefs on this account cannot motivate. It is preferences that motivate an individual to act and beliefs only service those actions by aiding calculation with respect to how best to satisfy preferences (or more generally any set of objectives). Accordingly it is beliefs about the way the world is that matter to agents in economic theory. Such beliefs have none of the normative character which we often find with cultural belief. Indeed, insofar as individuals hold moral beliefs in economics, these beliefs are turned into a form of preference, an ethical preference about which nothing is said or demanded save the usual, that such preferences should be consistent and well ordered. The 'way the world is' is thereby maintained as the object of belief in economics.

The theories regarding these beliefs are also curiously (and temptingly, it should be said) insubstantial. These theories come in two forms. The first really does no more than to turn belief into another form of preference, a given of the situation, by endowing individuals with subjective beliefs (see Savage, 1954). Nothing is demanded of these beliefs, other than minimal forms of internal consistency like the summation of probabilities to one. People just have them.

The second approach goes further than this and demands that subjective beliefs correspond in some sense to what is objectively the case. This is the stance of the rational expectations approach and follows very naturally from the underlying picture of Humean instrumental rationality since it may be supposed that individuals prosper through acting upon objectively accurate beliefs rather than (subjectively) inaccurate ones. It is also the approach which has been traditionally embodied in game theory through the assumption of common instrumental rationality and common knowledge of this. (It is usually held, although this is becoming increasingly controversial, that these assumptions warrant the Nash equilibrium concept and the virtue of Nash is that it entails consistent beliefs, in the sense that when each player believes the other will play the Nash equilibrium strategy each will want to play the Nash strategies and so confirm those beliefs.) In both instances it is an attractive move to make because it seems only sensible that we should hold beliefs which prove accurate, but it is not without problems.

The tie to what is 'objectively' the case is relatively unproblematic when the object of belief is something in the natural world. But when it relates to the social world, the connection with what is 'objectively' the case necessarily connects rational beliefs with an equilibrium concept as this will help to tell us what actually will be the case. In game theory this has traditionally been the Nash and related perfect and sequential equilibrium concepts; and in other contexts we have the rational-expectations equilibrium concept. One line of criticism of this account of belief formation follows from this. It entails an attack on these equilibrium concepts. This is not a problem that I wish to highlight here. Instead, I shall focus on the problem which arises when there are multiple rational expectations and/or Nash equilibria. The difficulty here is how an individual comes to choose one equilibrium (that is one set of beliefs) from among the many which satisfy the condition of being beliefs which when acted upon lead to behaviours which confirm those beliefs. In these circumstances, the broadly sensible condition of 'getting it right' is not sufficient to fix which beliefs it is rational to hold.

The selection of an equilibrium and the beliefs to go with it involves an act of coordination. To see this let us suppose the multiple equilibria are distinguished alphabetically *a*, *b*, *c*, etc. Then though assumption of multiplicity, *a* will be an equilibrium provided all agents hold the beliefs which produce and are confirmed by *a*, likewise *b* will be an equilibrium provided agents hold the beliefs which produce and are confirmed by *b*, and so on. An equilibrium becomes 'the' equilibrium only when everyone recognises it as 'the' equilibrium, and this is a matter of pure coordination. So, how might this coordination be achieved? In other words, what must be added to the usual economic account of belief formation to explain belief/equilibrium selection in such cases of multiplicity?

In some circumstances, there may be explicit discussion and selection of one equilibrium – a centralised wage-bargaining system might be an example of this form of equilibrium selection. But, in many situations the coordination is achieved in a decentralised manner, as some economists have argued, through individuals conditioning their beliefs on some set of prevailing circumstances which can be observed by all. (To see this, notice that when all players share the same rule for forming (admissible) beliefs based on some aspect of their shared circumstances, then they will achieve coordination by virtue of sharing the rule and the circumstances to which it applies.) But, by definition, if beliefs are conditioned on the circumstances that define the game (or the data of the market equilibrium in the case of rational-expectations equilibria), then there is nothing in the circumstances as normally defined which will distinguish one equilibrium from another. This is the point about multiplicity: the circumstances which define the game throw up multiple equilibria. Hence the circumstances and rules for interpreting them must be unrelated to the normal definition of the game (or the market) if it is to act as method of coordination. In short, agents must condition their beliefs on information which is strictly extraneous to the game (or the data which normally constitute a market equilibrium). (Indeed, the point has been put in precisely this way by a number of economists and it has given rise, for instance, to the idea of 'sunspots' equilibria, as in Azariadis, 1981.)

The question for economics then becomes: what are the shared sources of extraneous information used by agents in the economy? And the short answer offered here is that culture as it has been defined is tailor made for the job. It satisfies the condition of being shared and extraneous to the way that economic activity (or games) are normally defined. Furthermore, as will be seen when Mary Douglas's cultural theory is discussed in section 5, it seems well placed to be selected because it has the resources for making distinctions in terms of worth which are not available to the sparse definition of beliefs in orthodox economics.

In a nutshell, then, the case for culture in economics is that it is needed to explain equilibrium selection when there are multiple equilibria. It is a way of fixing belief when the standard move employed by mainstream economics of requiring 'objectivity' is not enough. To begin to be persuasive, however, this theoretical argument needs supplementing. The problem of multiplicity must arise with a frequency which gives the matter of equilibrium selection practical significance.

Both in game theory and in the rational-expectations literature, multiple equilibria seem to be the norm rather than the exception and the normative properties of the various equilibria can be very different. In a short space, though, it is difficult to persuade the sceptical of this claim. In game theory, the various folk theorems which have been proved for repeated games and, in the rational-expectations literature, the use of overlapping-generations models, provide obvious support for the suggestion. Rather than extend this list in any comprehensive way, I shall focus instead on two areas in the economics literature where multiplicity has arisen which have a direct bearing on the question of competitiveness. One is bargaining and the other is the generation of trust in economic relationships.

11.3 Bargaining

Almost all economic change takes place in an imperfectly competitive setting and involves a bargaining question of how to distribute the gains from change. It is often argued that there is a unique solution to the bargaining game: the Nash solution (or an approximation to the Nash solution). This view is rejected here. Instead, it is argued that bargaining provides a perfect illustration of the theoretical indeterminacy sketched in the last section.

Nash first presented this solution axiomatically. That is, he set out four axioms for a solution to satisfy and then discovered that only one division of the spoils actually satisfied them. This is an impressive claim to uniqueness in a tricky area of economic life, but it is not without problem because the result is only likely to be compelling if the axioms somehow appeal to all rational agents; and this is not obviously so.

The first two axioms do not present any problem on this score. The first axiom establishes the rationality of both parties and has the effect of singling out Pareto efficient outcomes. The second axiom demands that solutions should be invariant to linear transformations of either party's pay-offs. So it should not matter to the solution whether a player measures his or her pay-offs in pounds or pence – fair enough!

The third axiom specifies 'independence of irrelevant alternatives' and this is where the problems begin. The axiom means that if x is a solution to some bargaining game then x should also be the solution to another game which shares the same conflict points as the original one and provided x is still a feasible outcome. To illustrate what this implies, let us assume there is a game where \$100 is to be divided between two players, A and B. Further suppose the solution to this game is \$50 each. The axiom entails that \$50 each should also be the solution to another game where \$100 is to be divided between the same two players subject to the constraint that player A should not get less than \$40. It is not obvious to many people that rationality demands that the proviso of the second version should be ignored.

The final axiom requires symmetry when the game is completely symmetrical as far as each player is concerned. So, if it makes no difference to the description of the game from each player's perspective when A takes over B's role and vice versa, then the pay-offs to both players should be the same. Again consider the $100 to be divided between A and B. If both players value $s in the same way, then the Nash solution with symmetry has each player getting $50. This seems fine at first, but its connection to rationality is quite tenuous on reflection. For instance, suppose each player believes that the taller person will claim $70 and the shorter person will claim $30. Acting on these beliefs, the instrumentally rational thing for the tall person is to claim $70 and for the short person to claim $30. In this way the belief will be confirmed by experience and in this regard the belief singling out height is no different to a belief in symmetry since a shared belief in symmetry will also produce actions which confirm that belief. Hence, if rationality of belief only demands that beliefs should correspond to what actually happens, then there is no reason to prefer a belief in symmetry to a belief, say, in height. Both are conventions in the sense that when acted upon they produce self-confirming actions. To prioritise symmetry must be to make a claim on some other basis than rationality in this sense.

The appeal of the axiomatic approach is often regarded as weak for these reasons and it has led some authors to adopt a different approach. They have modelled actual bargaining processes non-cooperatively and argued that the outcome of such bargaining is the Nash solution or something close to it. Taken at its face value, this would seem to provide important support for the unique Nash solution, but a close analysis reveals problems here too.

In particular, it seems that these approaches to the bargaining problem introduce something into the analysis which cannot be strictly justified in terms of rationality and that it is this 'something' which is also responsible for generating the unique result. As illustrations of the point, consider two famous attempts in this non-cooperative tradition. One, the Zeuthen–Harsanyi approach, models a process where each player issues a demand and then there is an opportunity for concession. It turns on a presumption (which cannot be connected in any obvious way to the rationality of agents) that the player with the lowest risk limit will be the first to concede – that is, the player who has lowest probability assessment of the other not conceding which will leave him or her indifferent between conceding and not conceding.

The other, the Rubinstein (1982) approach, has bargaining occurring

Table 11.1

	A concedes	A affirms
B concedes	\$40, \$40	\$40, \$60
B affirms	\$60, \$40	0, 0

over time with sequential offers from each party. It supposes that an agreement would be made some time in the future and uses backward induction to work out what the players should offer and accept at the outset. The use of backward induction is itself controversial, in the sense that not all game theorists believe it follows from the normal rationality assumption (see Binmore, 1987). In addition, the unique result does depend on offers and demands coming in sequence rather than simultaneously; and it is not clear why bargaining processes should be assumed to take this form (for further discussion, see Sugden, 1990 and Varoufakis, 1991).

The root difficulty with the bargaining game is that it seems unavoidably at some stage to involve elements of a chicken game. Go back to the division of \$100. Suppose both players issue a demand for \$60, then each faces a choice between conceding or affirming the demand with the pay-offs captured in table 11.1.

This seems to be an inescapable part of any bargaining game and there are simply two Nash equilibria in pure strategies here (and one mixed strategy equilibrium). Consequently, something more is required (other than the definition of rationality and rational belief which goes into the construction of a Nash equilibrium) if the selection of one equilibrium rather than the other is explained.

This argument may be convincing at a theoretical level, but one may still doubt that it has much practical significance. For instance, it could be the case that all economies solve the problem similarly in some manner which has escaped our theoretical ingenuity. In short, uniqueness may be there but we simply do not understand it theoretically at the moment. Alternatively, one might be inclined to think that it does not matter how the bargaining problem is solved because one solution affects economic performance much as another; and so the issue of why one solution gets chosen is neither here nor there. To head off both these thoughts, consider one area of bargaining: the wage bargain.

The first doubt is countered by an evident, superficial variety of solutions to this bargaining problem. As an illustration of one dimension of this variety, consider the degree of centralisation. This is an attribute of

Table 11.2. *The percentage change in the real wage after a 1 per cent change in unemployment*

Italy	0.7	W. Germany	2.1
Denmark	0.9	Netherlands	2.8
USA	0.9	Austria	3.7
UK	1.1	Switzerland	4.6
Belgium	1.6	Sweden	4.6
France	1.9	Norway	7.5

Source: Alogoskoufis and Manning (1988).

bargaining which differs significantly and which has recently attracted the attention of macroeconomists (see Calmfors and Driffill, 1988). (A typical ranking going from most to least centralised is: Austria, Norway, Sweden, Denmark, Finland, Germany, The Netherlands, Belgium, France, UK, Italy, Switzerland, USA.)

Does this variety of arrangement yield a variety of outcomes (in other words, is it more than superficial)? Table 11.2 reports on recent cross-country estimates of the responsiveness of real wages to a 1 per cent change in unemployment. It will be noted that there are significant differences in the degree of real wage sensitivity.

The degree of nominal wage flexibility and real wage flexibility are factors which affect the performance of the economy in response to shocks. The theory here is straightforward (see Hargreaves-Heap, 1992). In particular, real wage sensitivity affects short-run competitiveness following a supply shock and this is of direct relevance to recent performance. The supply shocks like the oil price hikes of 1973/74 and 1979/80 lowered real incomes in oil-importing countries and this generated current account deficits which disappeared more or less quickly with more or less 'help' from rising unemployment depending on the stickiness of real wages. Table 11.3 reports on this diversity by using Calmfors and Driffill's index of macro performance (this is a simple addition of the current account deficit as a percentage of GDP and the level of unemployment).

To conclude this part of the argument, there seems to be a variety of ways of bargaining over wages. The wage bargain does not admit a unique solution, just as theory suggests. Furthermore, the selection of one equilibrium, one way of resolving the bargaining problem, seems to affect economic performance in ways which influence short-run competitiveness. Thus, it seems the theoretical question of equilibrium selection is a matter of practical concern because it can affect competitiveness.

Table 11.3. *Average levels and changes in the Calmfors and Driffill index and unemployment (U) levels and changes*

	C&D level 74–85	C&D change 74/85–63/73	U 74–85	U change 74/85–63/73
Denmark	11.3	8.4	7.9	6.9
Belgium	11.0	10.0	9.3	7.1
Italy	8.6	5.1	7.9	2.8
UK	8.2	5.2	8.1	5.4
US	7.6	3.4	7.3	2.8
France	7.5	5.4	6.4	4.3
Netherlands	6.4	5.4	8.0	6.8
Norway	5.0	1.8	2.2	0.6
W. Germany	4.3	4.2	4.8	4.0
Sweden	4.1	2.3	2.4	0.4
Austria	3.6	2.3	2.5	0.8
Switzerland	−3.1	−2.7	0.5	0.3

Source: Calmfors and Driffill (1988).

11.4 Trust and competitiveness

Trust arises in almost all economic relationships and the creation of trust is one of the keys to a successful economy. Contracts which specify exactly what each agent should do in every conceivable circumstance might seem to obviate the need for trust, but it is not easy to write such fully contingent contracts when the future is uncertain and when performance cannot be publicly monitored.

These difficulties frequently surface in the relationship between employers and employees. For example, an employee has a choice between expending effort to acquire some specific human capital and not expending the effort and the employer has a choice between offering a 'low' or a 'high' wage. The acquisition of the human capital makes the worker sufficiently productive so that the employer can pay the 'high' wage and still enjoy higher profits than when paying a 'low' wage to a worker without the specific skill. This 'high' wage more than compensates the worker for the effort required, so that the 'high' wage/high effort bundle is preferred to the 'low' wage/no effort bundle. Hence there is the possibility of a mutually beneficial trade of high wage for effort in acquiring the skill. The problem is that neither party has incentive to deliver on an agreement to pay a 'high' wage for the acquisition of the skill. The employer may prefer the high wage/effort option to the low

Table 11.4

	Employer pays	
	high wage	low wage
Employee expends		
high effort	3.3	1.4
no effort	4.1	2.2

wage/no effort option but the best outcome is to pay a low wage once the worker has acquired the skill and since the skill has no value outside the firm this is the worst of all possible outcomes for the worker. Likewise the worker may prefer the high wage/effort bundle to the low wage/no effort, but the best outcome for him or her is the high wage/no effort bundle. These pay-offs are captured in table 11.4.

The interaction takes the form of a prisoners' dilemma and the Nash equilibrium is the Pareto inferior low wage/no effort pair. If only each party could trust the other to deliver on the agreement of trading high wage for high effort both could be made better off. The economics literature has suggested broadly two ways in which this trust problem might be solved when contracts cannot be used. One involves a repetition of the game and the other entails changing the motivation of preferences of agents. Repetition helps to unlock the problem because it makes both parties take account of the long-term returns from playing cooperatively. Precisely how these long-term considerations alter the playing of the game depends on whether the game is repeated finitely or infinitely/indefinitely. In the latter case, it can make sense to forgo cheating on an arrangement in the short run because this will ensure better long-run returns when playing against someone who has adopted a conditional/punishment strategy (see Axelrod, 1981). In the former, it makes sense to behave cooperatively because this fuels a reputation for cooperative behaviour which enhances the long-run prospects from playing the game (see Kreps *et al.*, 1982).

This type of solution avoids the public aspect of monitoring agreements because each player's capacity to punish the other in later plays suffices, but it does depend on each player knowing whether the other had abided by the implicit agreement ex post – otherwise the basis does not exist for a punishment strategy. A clear real-world example seems to be the career ladder found within many corporations where one level in the hierarchy oversees the one below and where movement up the hierarchy is guaranteed by satisfactory performance at the lower level.

The importance of folk theorems in this context is that they suggest that there are any number of possible conditional/punishment strategies which could be perfect equilibria in this repeated game. So the fact that a punishment strategy is sustainable does not tell us what form of punishment strategy will actually emerge, if one does at all. In other words, the corporate hierarchy may be one real-world counterpart, but it is not the only one and we shall have to look further afield if we are to understand why one form of conditional/punishment strategy is selected rather than another. (The folk theorem here seems to provide a cautionary qualification to the transaction-cost literature which often appears to operate on the premise that firms are unique vehicles for solving trust problems because they cement a long-term (i.e. repetitive) relationship between the players. The message which comes from game theory is that there is more than one way to have a long-term relationship around a particular type of transaction.)

The type of solution that works through altering preferences or motivation is more straightforward than the repeat solution. In one way or another, individuals have to take the common interest which everyone has in the Pareto superior outcome into their own individual calculations. There are a variety of ways in which this might be formally achieved. Individuals can be given a moral psychology, say like Kant's, which leads them to act differently on these preferences. Alternatively, they might respond to calculations of extended sympathy, or directly to the benefit of the group. However it is done, once group returns have been made to count in the calculus of individual decision-making, the prisoners' dilemma can be overcome.

From an explanatory point of view, both the multiplicity of solutions under the repeat strategy and the possibility of a variety of solutions under the second approach means that the economic analysis of the problem leaves us with some indeterminacy. One might expect that successful economies will solve such prisoners' dilemmas (just as one might expect that firms and workers will adopt a solution to the bargaining problem to avoid perpetual conflict), but in noting this there is no blueprint for a solution and not all solutions may be equally successful. There are any number of ways in which the problem might be solved and if we are to account for why one is selected rather than another then we will have to draw again on an understanding of the background beliefs which coordinate this decision.

As before, it is important for the persuasiveness of the argument to provide some evidence that this theoretical indeterminacy has some interesting real-world counterpart – in the sense that we can see both that there are actually a variety of responses to the problem of trust and that the choice of one rather than another impacts upon economic performance and competitiveness. This is done this time by drawing on Aoki's (1990) discussion of the advantages of the Japanese form of corporate organisation. (The variety of forms of corporate organisation in apparently the same activity can be taken as evidence that there are in practice multiple solutions to the problem of trust generation and so the argument focuses on why choice of one rather than another matters.)

The part of Aoki (1990) that is used for this purpose (and apologies to Aoki if it becomes unrecognisable in the process) is the suggestion that the switch from techniques of mass production to those which are sometimes referred to as flexible specialisation (or the move from Fordism to post-Fordism as it is known in some circles – for a recent analytic discussion, see Milgrom and Roberts, 1990) relies on new forms of specific human capital. In turn, the acquisition of these new forms of specific human capital create new problems of 'trust' which have to be solved if the new methods of production are to be embraced.

The distinctive feature of Japanese corporations as contrasted with the typical North American corporations in Aoki's argument is that problems of trust have been solved historically in different ways. To make the connection with the earlier theoretical argument on this point, one might say that while North American companies have typically relied on a conditional/punishment strategy, the Japanese companies have been able to rely more on the presence of a different motivation – one that takes into account group returns when individuals make decisions (see Morishima, 1982, on this point). The importance of this observation is that the new specific human capital skills are such that the trust problem does not lend itself as well to being solved through a conditional/punishment strategy as it does by appeal to a group motivation. Thus, the rise of Japanese corporations can be related in part to Japan's greater ability to solve the trust problems entailed in the switch to methods of flexible specialisation.

To be more specific, the crucial aspect of flexible specialisation here is the ability to respond quickly to an environment of continuous change. In this respect, the traditional hierarchic organisation, where information flows vertically and where plans are formed at the apex and instructions are codified and sent down to lower levels, is not well placed to respond to continuous change. Hierarchies are good when directed at activities which do not change very much. The apex, the planning department, can then decide what is the best way to go about things and then encode these practices in the routines which define each level of the hierarchy, and the hierarchy itself ensures performance by acting as a form of conditional/punishment strategy. In contrast continuous change requires continuous adaptation of plans and this overloads the planning department of a hierarchic organisation because no sooner has one set of practices been worked out than another becomes necessary; and it undermines the capacity of a hierarchy to overcome the trust problem because the conditions of 'performance' are always changing and become ambiguous.

In contrast, in an organisation which is geared towards continuous change, the planning department can only engage in indicative planning. Detailed application and implementation of these general goals must be left to the departments and shops. They must be free to respond to new developments as and when they arise. However, if there is to be this freedom for shops and departments then there is a gap that needs to be filled because the planning department can no longer fulfil the role of coordinating the efforts and activities of the various departments and shops. To be able to respond to a continuously changing environment may necessitate devolving decision-making, but an organisation still needs to coordinate those decisions so that different parts of the organisation are not pulling in different directions.

Aoki argues that Japanese companies solve this coordination problem, whilst preserving devolved decision-making, by encouraging continuous horizontal flows of information between departments. These flows arise through person-to-person contacts. These daily contacts enable coordination of activities and they are much more efficient as a channel of communication than the traditional codified ones of the hierarchic organisation because a complex piece of information can be conveyed relatively easily in a face-to-face encounter between people who know each other. And what is more, the participation of the ordinary worker in production planning in this way facilitates unlocking the implicit knowledge of workers which is often thought to be crucial in realising the objective of high-quality products. However, and this is the point to note, such coordination relies on very specific human capital skills.

Workers need communication skills appropriate for dealing with the other workers in that particular firm and they must have a reasonable understanding of the production process as a whole, otherwise there can be no presumption that any two units will agree to some solution to a joint problem which is helpful to the organisation as a whole. Here is the rub: how is the trust problem associated with the acquisition of these specific skills to be solved? The traditional stick and carrot of a conditional/punishment strategy cannot work as well as it does for an organisation where tasks can be readily specified because the essence of this human capital skill is that it is informal and that it evolves, so standards of performance cannot be written down and easily monitored. This does not mean that the traditional stick and carrot is not used – it is, although in an interestingly different way in Japanese companies through

Table 11.5. *Value of stock of raw materials, work in progress and finished products as a percentage of sales of car component manufacturers*

USA	UK	EC ave	W. Ger	France	Japan
21	18	14	14	11	5

Source: The *Economist*.

Table 11.6. *Percentage of car component companies claiming to use JIT*

Fra	W. Ger	Port	N. lands	Bel	UK	Ire	Spain	Italy
60	56	54	53	52	48	38	33	25

Source: Motor Industry Research Unit.

rank rather than a job hierarchy. But it does mean that insofar as the company can draw on an appeal to group interest it will be better placed to solve this trust problem than a company that relies exclusively on a conditional/punishment strategy. And the claim is that Japanese companies are in a position to do this in a way that their North American counterparts are not.

Casual empirical evidence supports the contention that Japanese companies are organised in a different manner to the traditional North American company and that they are at the forefront of the move to flexible specialisation. Indeed on the specific point above, the ability to respond to continuous change, the hallmark of Japanese companies is their much observed and venerated just-in-time (JIT) organisation of production. The flexibility of JIT enables well-documented savings in inventories and so one might expect, with all the publicity which JIT has received, that there would have been significant changes to the Japanese system. However, as the *Economist* recently remarked 'nearly all western manufacturers pay lip service to Japanese management techniques' but the practice is markedly disappointing. Table 11.5 illustrates the point for the motor industry where the 'kanban' system was first noted, while table 11.6 suggests that there is an interesting variety of adoption of JIT across European countries in the car components industry.

Tables 11.5 and 11.6 lend support to the Aoki argument because it appears that the Japanese have been able to introduce JIT in a way that many European countries have been unable to. Furthermore, there does seem to be broad support for the general proposition that Japanese companies have been better placed to make the switch to flexible special-

Table 11.7. *Industrial robots (IR) and automatic/flexible factory systems (AFFS) per million industrial employees*

	IR	AFFS
Japan	3450	5.0
Sweden	2640	7.8
Belgium	930	3.7
France	880	3.3
Germany	860	4.9
USA	670	2.2
Italy	580	2.5
UK	410	4.6

Source: *NIER Review* November 1988.

Table 11.8. *Percentage diffusion by 1981 of major new technologies*

	Germany	UK	France	Italy	Sweden	USA	Japan
Basic oxygen process	80	68	82	49	45	61	75
Continuous casting	54	32	51	51	65	21	71
Shuttleless looms	9	22	16	12	35	16	4
Tunnel kilns	90	72	90	90	95	—	—
Float glass	100	100	100	68	100	—	—

Source: Ray (1984).

isation for reasons which are specific to the needs of flexible specialisation rather than some general superiority. For instance, the NIESR has been studying the diffusion of major new technologies for the last twenty years and as table 11.7 and 11.8 suggest it is only with regard to industrial robots and automatic/flexible manufacturing systems that Japan (and Sweden) are clearly in the vanguard. The only other innovation where Japan just tops the innovation diffusion record is in continuous casting, where interestingly Aoki (1990) argues there are particular gains in the form of quality control which come with the horizontal information flows characteristic of Japanese corporations.

To summarise, there is a theoretical argument concerning the multiplicity of ways in which trust might be generated in economic relationships. The selection of one solution rather than another may be of interest because one solution may be more successful in tapping trust in certain circumstances. And indeed there seem *prima facie* grounds for taking this theoretical argument seriously because there do seem to be a variety of organisational approaches and it does seem that the Japanese corporation has tapped into a form which is well adapted to embrace the move to flexible specialisation. The final part of this argument comes by making the connection between the move to flexible specialisation and long-run competitiveness. This connection is not without controversy, but this is not the place to address it. (The connection arises loosely in the work of those who argue that long-run competitiveness in world markets comes from shifting into medium and high tech activities because these are relatively high growth and high productivity areas of manufacturing, and it is at its most explicit in the work of the 'Regulation' and 'Social Structure of Accumulation' schools – see for instance Lipietz, 1987 and Bowles, Gordon and Wciskopf, 1986.)

11.5 Is it culture which explains the difference?

Suppose, then, there is an interesting question concerning equilibrium selection which traditional economic analysis does not answer. Culture, as I have defined it, is an obvious candidate to fill part of the answer, and indeed the economics literature makes use of the idea when it refers to the use of shared extraneous information, but is it really fit for the part?

The case for culture partially depends on whether there is actually the diversity of cultural belief across countries to connect with the variety of solutions. This is the easy part of the case because there have been several European and worldwide surveys of cultural beliefs (see for instance Hofstede, 1984; Harding, Phillips and Fogarty, 1986; Inglehart, 1990) and they demonstrate diversity of beliefs. Table 11.9 provides an illustration.

The more difficult part turns on whether such cultural differences can be systematically related to equilibrium selection. It is best to acknowledge from the outset that this part of the case is 'not proven'. There is also a deeper (but, as we shall see, potentially related) issue concerning the status of culture in such an explanation. What is the explanatory status of culture here? Do we just have these beliefs? Are they a given of our situation, much as we might take preferences as a given in consumer theory? What if anything causes them to change? – this last question is, of course, particularly important for policy.

There are many theories of culture which might supply answers to these questions, but Mary Douglas's (1978; 1986) cultural theory seems promising. Essentially, she argues that an individual's social interactions can be decomposed along two dimensions: group and grid. The group

Table 11.9. *Percentage of respondents placing this quality in top five qualities to be encouraged in children*

	Belg	Den	Sp	Fra	GB	Neth	Eire	Ita	W.Ger
Hard work	33	2	41	36	26	13	25	13	22
Thrift	36	15	11	32	9	17	15	19	31
Tolerance	45	58	44	59	62	57	56	43	42
Independence	20	55	24	16	23	28	29	22	46
Leadership	6	2	8	2	4	3	7	3	31
Politeness	48	50	20	51	27	42	23	36	29
Obedience	28	14	30	18	37	23	33	27	15

Source: Harding, Phillips and Fogarty (1986).

dimension refers to the extent to which an individual has group affiliations that overlap significantly to produce a clear boundary between insiders and outsiders. At the low end of the axis the individual has so many affiliations, she or he shifts from one group to another with little shared membership, so that it makes little sense to think of the individual belonging to a group within society. Upon following the pattern of social interactions we find only an ever expanding network rather than a closure to form a group. The contrast at the other end of this dimension is the case where an individual's social relations circuit through the same group. Different activities overlap with the same people: for instance, when some of the people at work are also those who are met while ten-pin bowling, while drinking at the pub, at the children's school and so on. Here there is a clear boundary between those who are inside and those who are outside the group.

The grid dimension focuses on the rules which govern individuals in their personal interactions. At the strong end, there are very visible roles which provide a script for individual interaction. They might be the roles of caste or class, for instance, which prescribe how people of different or of the same rank should behave towards each other. With movements towards the weak end of the axis, these public signals of rank and status fade away and more ambiguity enters into relationships. Individuals no longer have the guidance of a script, individuals are valued as individuals and relate to each other as such. The constraints are correspondingly weaker, coming only in the form of generalising everyone's uniqueness into respect for the individual.

The two dimensions yield four ideal types of social interactions, as in figure 11.2.

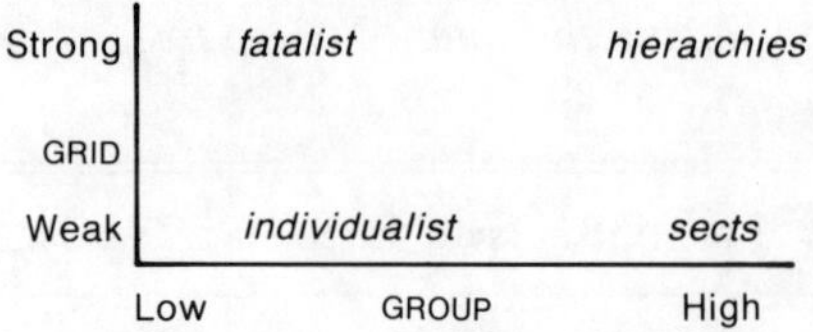

Figure 11.1

In this way, Mary Douglas fractures the familiar markets vs hierarchies (or individuals vs bureaucracies) opposition across two dimensions to produce a four-way split of institutions or social organisations/practices. She goes on to provide a taxonomy of the beliefs associated with each ideal type. This is not the place to provide an exhaustive discussion. A sketch of the beliefs is given in the appendix, together with an attempt by Grendstad (1990) to fit European culture into this framework.

In part, Mary Douglas treats these associations as empirical descriptions and in part they are more speculative and follow from the role played by beliefs in providing an internally coherent account of why this method of social organisation/interaction is to be preferred to the others. This is what makes Mary Douglas's framework potentially of great interest to economists because she ties beliefs directly into the selection of particular forms of social organisation (i.e., particular ways of bargaining or generating trust). In effect, she gives culture the independence to select one way of organising social life from another, while at the same time acknowledging that there are limits to the range of possible beliefs set by the material conditions of the group. It is exactly as if the material conditions throw up the multiple equilibria and it is culture which then selects one from among the many. This is worth exploring in slightly more detail.

How is Mary Douglas's grid–group framework going to help us to understand equilibrium selection? She is offering a taxonomy of possible background beliefs and she is relating these beliefs to the attributes of the relevant social practices of the individuals involved in an economic relationship. Thus she is offering us a theory of what determines background shared beliefs in a manner which is at least in principle amenable to empirical testing (i.e., we should be able to plot the beliefs of individuals and the type of social interactions among those individuals and see whether they correlate with attributes of economic performance). As a tentative move towards this end, the appendix provides a rough speculative mapping between Grendstad's plot of European cultures and the performance indicators discussed in sections 3 and 4. It appears in the appendix because it is extremely tentative and should only be taken as a pointer that the cultural theory might be useful in this task.

The theory also contains certain implications. Suppose there is a set of people engaged in some economic activity. Mary Douglas suggests that we should expect the social practices of this group to generate beliefs of one kind or another depending on the characteristic forms of social interaction they engage in, and that these beliefs will lead the group to select solutions to new economic problems which conform with those beliefs. Since the beliefs typically make the existing practices of the group seem intelligible and correct, it is likely that the solution which is selected will reproduce the characteristics of the pre-existing practices. In this way, Mary Douglas is providing a gloss on how institutions/social practices reproduce themselves through the connection between institution and beliefs of the people who reproduce its practices. This is an important gloss and a powerful reminder that it is never easy to change social practices because what is often at stake is a whole web of beliefs which touch on the cosmic as well as the more mundane. In other words, what starts out as a point about culture can easily be turned with the aid of Mary Douglas's analysis into a point about institutions, and in particular a point about institutional inertia (i.e., the earlier point about culture can be recast as one about the need for a theory of institutions if there is to be an account of equilibrium selection in economics; and given a theoretical expectation of institutional inertia a large part of the explanation of why institutions are the way they are must be historical. Thus the message changes again, this time into one about the need for history in economics).

On the one hand this may seem to weaken the role played by culture *per se*. After all, culture is now fused with social practices/institutional arrangements and does not seem to stand on its own as a determining factor in equilibrium selection. On the other hand, whilst this weakening seems inevitable, it sets a useful agenda for understanding how cultural and institutional change come about: we need to understand better how beliefs and institutions which are normally fused together can nevertheless come apart on occasion. While this is for the future, it is possible to see some lines of potential enquiry.

One is a development on the theme found in Mary Douglas's work. She detects a tendency of culture to go beyond what can be said and this means there are always anomalies thrown up or weaknesses revealed in particular ways of organising social interaction. This is really the other side of the coin to the fixing of arrangements which is performed by the shared beliefs. The beliefs have to single out the way of arranging social life which they support, but in reality there are rarely unambiguously better ways of organising social life. This is the message of economics with its multiple equilibria. The very act of selecting entails claims which cannot be warranted and this always builds a weakness into the system of beliefs.

The tension between institutional arrangements and beliefs can also come from another quarter. It is rare for any group of people in economically complex societies to be engaged in social practices which exhibit a uniform set of characteristics. For instance one need only contrast the apparent lack of grid in social interactions among shoppers in a US supermarket with the high grid found in some interactions within a US corporation. In turn most individuals are likely to be able to draw on a variety of competing webs of belief and so the response to new situations which require new practices are never foreshadowed in existing practices. The plurality of institutions and beliefs means that there are a variety of options which can sit more or less comfortably with existing practices and beliefs.

Finally it is worth noting that although equilibrium selection involves solving a coordination game, this need not mean that one equilibrium/ institutional arrangement is much like another. One may perform better than another in many respects and when such superior performance arises it is likely through demonstration effects to act as source for changing beliefs. Of course, it is in the nature of a solution to a coordination game that such demonstration effects are not always sufficient since it requires coordination to change the equilibrium (and there are the problems of institutional inertia to be overcome).

These points can be assembled to see what might be at stake in this argument for the conduct of policy. A society might get stuck with a largely inferior solution to a coordination game. The fact that it is inferior is not sufficient to guarantee a change since coordination is required to change the equilibrium. On this ground, the situation seems ripe for some form of government/collective action. However, little is known about such actions at the moment, save that, given the inbuilt bias towards institutional inertia, the only successful actions will be those that are sensitive to where the weak links are in the web of beliefs which support the current (and inferior) institutional arrangements.

11.6 Conclusion

The main argument is that economics needs a theory of culture if it is to explain equilibrium selection. Such an explanation is necessary because equilibrium selection affects economic performance in ways which impact on economic competitiveness; and two concrete illustrations of this connection in the area of wage bargaining and trust generation have been given. Most recently (and tentatively because there is much work to be done here), it has been suggested that Mary Douglas's theory of culture will be helpful in this regard. In saying this the case for culture *per se* may be weakened by giving it an equal billing with institutions. Nevertheless, the point remains that a theory of culture-cum-institutions is needed to supplement the normal economic discussion of these matters. Furthermore while Mary Douglas's theory carries with it the expectation of a bias towards the status quo (whatever it should happen to be) it also sets several research agendas in this area. For instance, there is the need to look at social practices along two dimensions rather than the normal single one, and the need to look at how constellations of institutions and beliefs create weaknesses and strengths which are the catalyst for change.

Appendix: A summary of the belief taxonomy in Mary Douglas's cultural theory[1]

One traditional way of categorising beliefs in anthropology is around the views of nature and the relationship between nature and society. This practice is followed below, and to illustrate how these broad differences translate into some more mundane differences, some specific ideas on time, education, punishment and justice are also reported (Douglas, 1978, can be consulted for further details).

Hierarchies

These are organisations where a strong boundary is drawn between outsiders and insiders, and where the individual has rights and obligations to the insiders who form the group. These are formalised in a series of clear roles, which avoid conflict through scripting social interaction within the group and which provide for levies on the individual to ensure the existence of the group.

Nature is locally stable and benign, but if it is disturbed too much then it will become unstable.

Society and nature exhibit an isomorphic structure. There is a natural order as there is a social order: nature is good and provides moral justification for social behaviour which follows the map given by nature.

Time and death are part of the closed cycle of life which the group encompasses and transcends by its persistence. Time is regulated by the routines of the group just as time is ordered by the laws of nature. History is an important record and monument to the group. Traditions are almost a part of nature and just as nature will continue so will social institutions, there is no reason to fear tomorrow, tomorrow will come as it has done since time immemorial.

Education is important because children require direction. There may be a natural order as there is a social order, but just as a species is accommodated within that order painfully, so the same applies to children and the social order, thus

Punishment is often exemplary and appeals to deterrence. The only unforgivable deviation is disloyalty which is revealed in the failure to observe the internal rules.

Justice, inequality poses no problem because it is found in nature.

Individualism

Individuals are freewheeling, all classifications are provisional and all obligations are ambiguous, and at best implicit. It is a competitive environment where rank and group count for nothing. Instead, there is value in numbers, in being able to persuade others to join you or in springing surprises on others by innovating.

Nature is regarded as benign and stable over all disturbances.

Society by contrast is experienced as anonymous, merciless, and it is an unremitting source of worry. Nature is thus idealised as good and simple, but a wistful sense of alienation never wins against the excitement and rewards of competition. Society is therefore separate from nature, it has its own rules and creates its own resources: it has culture with a capital C!

Time is used flexibly, there are no routines and this always makes the future uncertain. To focus on tomorrow and the short term is about all that you can do in the cut-throat competitive world where you make your own rules and they get remade overnight. History provides a stockpile for culture with a capital C.

Education appeals to the natural sense of goodness supplied by nature, and thus there are voluntaristic conceptions of education as a form of self realisation and self expression with beliefs that individuals should be allowed to move at their own pace.

Punishment is based on desert; there is no need for exemplary displays. The great fear is that people who lose under the competitive market will seek succour in hierarchies.

Justice, low grid ethics of individual equality are daily confronted by the gross inequality generated in competition. This can only be explained by reference to innate differences in aptitude.

Sects

The group is as crucial to sects as it is to hierarchies, only here there is no internal differentiation. Low grid leads to strong commitment to internal equality among group members, this creates leadership problems and a tendency to fracture.

Nature is regarded as unstable, it contains both wolves and lambs and one group can easily unbalance the other.

Society is like nature, and the task of the group is to 'fight the good fight' and unmask all the wolves who wander in sheep's clothing. The boundary between insiders and outsiders is an attempt to hold the line.

Time is more pressing for sects than hierarchies because history like nature is full of convulsions. Sects are concerned with the long run. But it cannot look after itself, the long term must be fought for.

Education and punishment follow closely that of hierarchies, except that disloyalty is not revealed in the failure to observe internal rules: it is contamination from relations with those outside the group which reveals disloyalty.

Justice: there is strong commitment to mechanisms which guarantee equality within the group.

Fatalist

Low group and high grid are isolated and fatalistic. Social interactions are individually highly structured and yet there is no over-arching group commitment which gives order and meaning to this structure. People who operate only in organisations like this feel the powerlessness that comes from being outsiders who have little control over individual actions. Nature like society is largely unintelligible. It could do anything. There are few justificatory theories. People here experience the world as power relation and they are on the wrong side of that relation.

Figure 11A.1 presents a summary of Grendstad's (1990) attempt to relate the information provided by the study of European values to Mary Douglas's grid–group framework. Here he locates the values of each country in the grid–group space.

It is tempting to use this and see whether these positions bear any relation to the aspects of economic performance discussed in the main text; and if they do, then to see whether the relation makes sense from the perspective of Douglas's theory. The temptation should probably be avoided. Nevertheless, it is difficult to resist making some comparisons, just to see whether there is any sign of Douglas's theory fitting the picture. So here is a preliminary and very quick attempt – and it comes with all the appropriate warnings to 'take this with a large pinch of salt'.

It is first worth reflecting on how Douglas's cultural theory might be related to economic performance with respect to wage sensitivity and

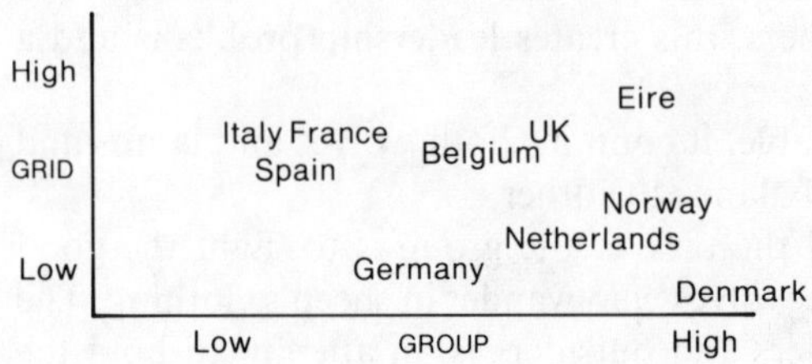

Figure 11A.1 Source: Grendstad (1990).

flexible specialisation. Aoki's analysis of the Japanese corporation suggests that it embodies a combination of low grid and high group – the low grid is necessary because there has to be autonomy for individual decision-making, but high group is necessary to preserve the informal guidance for these decisions in group interests. Likewise, low grid and high group appear the right combinations for real wage sensitivity because individuals need both to feel that they have discretion to change the wage and to take account of group interests when they set the wage if wages are to respond to shocks and prevent the occurrence of significant unemployment. If low grid and high group deliver 'good' performance in these two respects, then we can plot iso-performance lines in the grid–group space. They will have positive slopes since increasing 'group' raises performance and increasing 'grid' lowers performance; and it follows that the level of performance will fall with upward vertical movement.

Hence, in this preliminary fashion, Douglas's theory predicts that there will be these positively sloped iso-performance lines for economies located in the grid–group space. The question then becomes: is there any evidence from the data presented on performance that performance does lie on such iso-performance lines? Table 11A.1 summarises qualitatively the evidence from sections 11.3 and 11.4.

Figure 11A.2 reproduces figure 11A.1 with the addition of some tentative iso-performance lines drawn from the earlier reflections. These should not be compared with the qualitative assessment of performance in table 11A.1.

Plainly, not much should be made of this exercise and that is why it has been confined to the appendix. But the signs are moderately encouraging. Apart from the UK which does not do as well as one might expect and Denmark which does badly when it ought to do very well, the predictions seem roughly to fit the facts!

Table 11A.1. *Level of performance with respect to real wage flexibility and JIT/Flexible specialisation*

Level	Real wage flexibility	Flexible specialisation
poor	Italy Denmark UK Belgium France	Spain Italy UK France
intermediate	W. Germany Netherlands	Belgium Netherlands
good	Norway Sweden	W. Germany Sweden

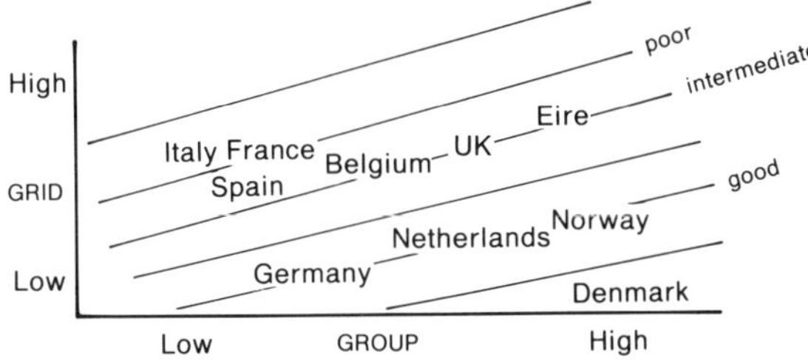

Figure 11A.2

Notes

I wish to thank Susan Clitheroe for valuable research assistance.

1 This draws on Hargreaves-Heap and Ross, 1991.

References

Alogoskoufis, G. and Manning, A., 1988. 'On the persistence of unemployment', *Economic Policy*, 7, 427–69.

Aoki, M., 1990. 'Towards an economic model of the Japanese firm', *Journal of Economic Literature*, 28, 1–27.

Axelrod, R., 1981. 'The emergence of cooperation among egoists', *American Political Science Review*, 75, 306–18.

Azariadis, C., 1981. 'Self fulfilling prophecies', *Journal of Economic Theory*, 25, 380–96.

Binmore, K., 1987. 'Modeling rational players: part I', *Economics and Philosophy*, 3, 179–214.

Bowles, S., Gordon, D. and Weiskopf, T., 1986. 'Power and profits: the social structure of accumulation and the profitability of the postwar US economy', *Review of Radical Political Economics*, 18, 132–67.

Calmfors, L. and Driffill, J., 1988. 'Bargaining structure, corporatism and macroeconomic performance', *Economic Policy*, 6, 14–61.

Casson, M., 1991. *The Economics of Business Culture*, Oxford: Clarendon.

Douglas, M., 1978. *Cultural Bias*, London: Royal Anthropological Society.

1986. *How Institutions Think*, Syracuse: Syracuse University Press.

Grendstad, G., 1990. 'Europe by cultures', unpublished graduate thesis, University of Bergen.

Harding, S., Phillips, D. and Fogarty, M., 1986. *Contrasting Values in Western Europe*, London: Macmillan.

Hargreaves-Heap, S., 1992. *The New Keynesian Macroeconomics: Time, Belief and Social Interdependence*, Aldershot: Edward Elgar.

Hargreaves-Heap, S. and Ross, A., 1991. *Understanding the Enterprise Culture*, Edinburgh: Edinburgh University Press.

Hofstede, G., 1984. *Cultures Consequences*, London: Sage.

Inglehart, R., 1990. *Culture Shift*, Oxford: Princeton University Press.

Kreps, D., Milgrom, P., Roberts, J. and Wilson, R., 1982. 'Rational cooperation in the finitely repeated prisoners' dilemma', *Journal of Economic Theory*, 27, 245–52.

Lipietz, A., 1987. *Mirages and Miracles: The Crises of Global Fordism*, London: Verso.

Milgrom, P. and Roberts, J., 1990. 'The economics of modern manufacturing: technology, strategy and organisation', *American Economic Review*, 80, 511–28.

Morishima, M., 1982. *Why Has Japan 'Succeeded'?* Cambridge: Cambridge University Press.

Peters, T. and Waterman, R., 1982. *In Search of Excellence*, London: Routledge and Kegan Paul.

Ray, G., 1984. *The Diffusion of Mature Technologies*, Cambridge: Cambridge University Press.

Rubinstein, A., 1982. 'A perfect equilibrium in a bargaining model', *Econometrica*, 50, 97–109.

Savage, L., 1954. *The Foundations of Statistics*, New York: Wiley.

Sugden, R., 1990. 'Convention, creativity and conflict', in Y. Varoufakis and D. Young (eds.), *Conflict in Economics*, Hemel Hempstead: Harvester Wheatsheaf.

Varoufakis, Y., 1991. *Rational Conflict*, Oxford: Basil Blackwell.

12 Industrial policy and international competitiveness: the case of Eastern Europe

DAVID AUDRETSCH

12.1 Introduction

That the notion of industrial policy as a mechanism for promoting international competitiveness has enjoyed considerable attention in both the popular press and academic circles is hardly surprising. Along with the increased globalisation of markets has come an increased consciousness about the manner in which market structure and firm conduct is inextricably linked with performance, not only in domestic markets, but also internationally (Caves, 1989; Hughes, 1986 and 1991a).

While the relationship between various instruments of industrial policy and the subsequent impact on international competitiveness has been the focus of research for the most developed nations, such as the United States (Tyson and Zysman, 1983; Baldwin, 1988), the Federal Republic of Germany (Stille, 1990), and Japan (Audretsch, 1988), as well as for Europe as a whole (Geroski, 1990; Neumann, 1990), the case of Eastern Europe remains largely unexplored. In fact, because of the extent of planning and control that was implemented throughout the Eastern European countries, they provide an important example for evaluating the success of certain types of industrial policies. Thus, the purpose of this chapter is to describe the manner in which industrial policies influenced the industrial structure in Eastern Europe during the 1980s and to examine the impact these policies had on the area's subsequent competitiveness in international markets. Based on the economic results from four decades of Eastern European industrial policy, several broad suggestions for the appropriate stance of industrial policy in the newly reformed economies are provided.

The manner in which industrial policy affects international competitiveness and why this is applicable to the countries of Eastern Europe is explained in section 2. In section 3 the policies shaping the industrial landscape of Eastern Europe are described and their ultimate impact on industrial structure is documented. The underlying factors triggering the economic crisis that left no Eastern European nation unscathed at the end of the 1980s is presented in the fourth section. In section 5 the appropriate role of industrial policy in facilitating the transition from a centrally planned economy to a more market oriented economy is explained. Finally, a summary and conclusions are presented. In particular, it is emphasised that the case of Eastern Europe provides one of the most striking examples where a consistent and far-reaching set of industrial policies were applied over a long period of time. These policies were effective, in that they resulted in the desired impact on the industrial structure. The subsequent trade performance, however, is predictable from the goals of industrial policy and the manner in which the industrial structure was shaped. Thus, to at least some extent, the failure of the economies of Eastern Europe represents a failure of the industrial policies that were implemented.

12.2 Industrial policy and trade performance

An actual definition of industrial policy may be as difficult to formulate as it is prevalent in practice. As one United States Supreme Court Justice expressed when trying to find a definition of pornography, 'You know it when you see it, but you can't define it.' Johnson has provided one of the most widely accepted descriptions of industrial policy:

> Industrial policy means the initiation and coordination of governmental activities to leverage upward the productivity and competitiveness of the whole economy and of particular industries in it. Above all, positive industrial policy means the infusion of goal-oriented strategic thinking into public economic policy ... In more abstract terms, industrial policy is the logical outgrowth of the changing concept of comparative advantage (Johnson, 1984, p. 8).

Based on these criteria, the Eastern European countries certainly applied a set of powerful and even consistent industrial policies during the past four decades. These policies were above all 'goal-oriented and strategic'. They were certainly 'coordinated governmental activities'. And they were implemented to 'leverage upward the productivity'.

That is, the countries of Eastern Europe undertook a set of industrial policies that had a profound and devastating impact on the industrial structure of each country. As is documented in the next section, these policies generally consisted of a degree of economic centralisation unprecedented by anything experienced by the West, along with a virtual elimination of market competition. That these policies were effective becomes clear when the resulting industrial structure is examined. Similarly, the rigid system of planning imposed a wider-ranging set of regulations of enterprise conduct in the Eastern European countries beyond anything imaginable in the West.

As the mainstream doctrine in industrial economics suggests (Scherer and Ross, 1990), the structure of markets along with the conduct of enterprises will have an impact on the resulting economic performance. I argue in my 1989a study that policies shaping the industrial structure – policies which are commonly referred to as industrial policies – will therefore have a subsequent impact on the performance of the economy. It has often been claimed that the United States has no industrial policy (Wildavasky, 1984). However, others, including Owen (1986), point out that policies such as anti-trust have a distinct impact on market structure and therefore fall under the rubric of industrial policy. For example, there has been a recent attempt by the American anti-trust agencies to take a more active role in shaping industry structures, so that mergers that are more likely to bring efficiency gains and less likely to cause social losses due to collusion are permitted, while those of an opposite nature are not allowed.

The impact of policies shaping market structure does not remain limited to the sphere of domestic economic performance. Rather, through the linkage of international markets, industrial policies play a significant role in determining a nation's competitive advantage. That is, as Hughes (1991a; 1991b; 1991c) shows, elements of domestic market structure influence the nation's competitiveness in international markets. Thus, industrial policies affecting domestic market structure will ultimately impact international competitiveness. This is consistent with the findings of Audretsch (1988 and 1989b) and Audretsch and Yamawaki (1988), who have shown that specific industrial policies did, in fact, serve to promote the international competitiveness of targeted manufacturing industries in Japan during the 1950s and 1960s.

As will be documented in the following section, a remarkably consistent set of industrial policies was implemented throughout Eastern Europe during the past four decades, in that these policies had a devastating influence on the industrial structure and conduct of enterprises. This leads to the prediction that both the domestic economic performance as well as the international competitiveness of Eastern Europe is attributable to a considerable extent to these industrial policies.

12.3 Industrial policy in Eastern Europe

During the previous four decades there were three distinguishing features of industrial policy in Eastern Europe – state ownership of economic

Table 12.1. *Size of the state sector, comparison between Eastern and Western countries (by percentage)*

Country	Share of Output	Share of Employment
Eastern Europe		
Czechoslovakia (1984)	97.0	–
East Germany (1982)	96.5	94.2
Soviet Union (1985)	96.0	–
Poland (1985)	81.7	71.5
Hungary (1984)	65.2	69.9
Western countries		
France (1982)	16.5	14.6
Austria (1979)	14.5	13.0
Italy (1982)	14.0	15.0
Turkey (1985)	11.2	20.0
Sweden	–	10.6
Finland	–	10.0
United Kingdom (1988)	11.1	8.2
West Germany (1982)	16.7	7.8
Portugal (1976)	9.7	–
Denmark (1974)	6.3	–
Greece (1979)	6.1	–
Norway (1979)	–	6.0
Spain (1979)	4.1	8.0
Netherlands (1973)	3.6	8.0
United States (1983)	1.3	1.8

Source: Milanovic, cited in Lipton and Sachs (1990b).

assets, the centralisation of those assets, and a system of planning used to allocate their use. As Román (1989) observes, the political power based on a monolithic one-party system rapidly appropriated the means of production on a vast scale throughout the Eastern European countries. This resulted in the bulk of economic assets being controlled by the governments. As table 12.1 shows, the share of economic activity, measured either by output or employment, emanating from the state sector was substantially greater in the Eastern European nations than in Western countries. In Eastern Europe the amount of national output accounted for by state-owned enterprises ranged from 97 per cent in Czechoslovakia (1986) to about 65 per cent in Hungary (1984). By contrast, even in France, which has the greatest share of assets controlled by the state of any Western nation, only 16.5 per cent of national output emanated from state-owned enterprises.

In Hungary, which had the smallest state-sector presence of any of the major Eastern European nations, the role of the state changed little over the previous three decades. In 1960 the goverment accounted for 67.4 per cent of national income, and by 1970 the state-owned enterprises claimed over 70 per cent of national income (Román, 1990a).

In Poland, the largest of the Eastern European nations, there were 3,177 state-owned industrial enterprises as of 1988 (Johnson and Loveman, 1992). As was typical among all the Eastern European countries, these state-owned firms were under the formal control of a ministry of the government. The functions of the enterprise were guided by the central plan of the state (Kornai, 1990a).

As Kornai (1986 and 1990) emphasises, embedded in the socialist model was a deep underlying adherence to the economies reaped from large-scale production. According to this view, large units of production were the most efficient means of transforming inputs into outputs, and any deviation from mass production was regarded as a socially wasteful use of resources (Piore and Sabel, 1984). In fact this fundamental belief in the pervasiveness of scale economies dates back at least to Karl Marx, who prophesied that the corporate form of organisation would lead to a 'constantly diminishing number of the magnates of capital, who ursurp and monopolize all advantages of transformation'. The limit was a state in which 'the entire social capital would be united, either in the hands of one single capitalist, or in those of one single corporation' (Marx, 1912 p. 836).

The obsession with scale economies was also taken up by Lenin (1916), who based his 'socialist growth theories' on the efficiencies to be gained by unprecedented scale of production units. Such thinking did not particularly diverge from the common doctrine in the West, where the importance of size and economies of scale was emphasised. The 1950s and 1960s saw the zenith of mass production in the United States. This was the world of countervailing power, so aptly described by Galbraith (1967), where virtually every major institution in society acted to reinforce the stability needed to promote mass production (Audretsch, 1989a). In fact, the unprecedented growth witnessed during this period in the West has been attributed less to the outcome of technology than to the result of prevailing social and political forces working to provide the market stability required for successful mass production (Piore and Sabel, 1984). Thus, the emphasis on large units of production and scale economies did not seem to be particularly at odds with the contemporary Western economic doctrine of production during the 1950s and 1960s.

As a result of the obsession with large-scale production, economic assets became increasingly concentrated throughout Eastern European countries. According to Román (1990a p. 1), 'Centrally planned economies prefer large organizations due both to economic and political considerations. They overestimate the significance of the economies of scale, in particular the size of the enterprises, neglecting both the emerging diseconomies and the potential of small business.'

Accompanying this adherence to the importance of large-scale production was a commitment to avoiding the waste of economic resources devoted to competition. According to Jones and Meurs (1990 pp. 4–5), 'Competition has been seen as engendering needless duplication of productive capacities and wasting resources.' Since market competition was undesirable, the existence of giant monopolies was perfectly acceptable. Not only did they exploit the potential offered by scale economies, but they facilitated the exercise of power and control for both economic and political decisions.

Thus the centralisation of economic assets provided three mutually compatible functions. First, it enabled the unprecedented exhaustion of scale economies. Second, it avoided wasteful duplication that would otherwise occur through the process of competition. Third, it facilitated the command and control of economic processes and agents. According to Murrell

> Centrally planned economies have a hierarchical organization that is based on a philosophy that decisions emanate from the central authorities. Consequently, there is a large degree of centralization of decisions . . . From this fact flow many consequences. For example, the decision-making overload at the center, with the consequent need to reduce the amount of information processing, probably accounts for some lack of variety in consumer goods. Moreover, once one combines centralization with the absence of capitalism, profit-oriented price competition will have little role in the economy (Murrell, 1990 p. 56)

Inherent in the centralised economies of Eastern Europe was a ponderous bureaucracy charged with decision-making and implementation of economic plans. As Balcerowicz (1989) emphasises, the bureaucracies generally influenced two key decision-variables of the state-owned enterprises – wages and investment. Lipton and Sachs (1990a) argue that employee compensation tended to be 'excessive' because otherwise the income stream would be funnelled into the treasury of the central government. Similarly, due to the incentives facing managers which based compensation upon the enterprise's size, there was a clear tendency to over-invest in capital projects. The size of capital investments was generally decided through a trilateral process involving the enterprise, the appropriate government ministry and the central planning commission. Investment plans which made it through this maze of bureaucracy were financed through a specific investment fund allocated in the government budget, and in certain instances, by loans from the central bank. Lipton and Sachs (1990a p. 81) observe that 'None of these funding sources requires an adequate assessment of investment prospects.'

According to Amann and Cooper (1982 pp. 11–19), the structure of Eastern European bureaucracies resulted in the following tendencies: (1) the introduction of new technologies tended to be impeded because of the approval and assistance required from the most important economic and social institutions, which are generally preoccupied with the immediacy of routine decisions; (2) due to a lack of direct contact between purchasers and suppliers, the diffusion of technological information tended to be retarded; (3) the decision to invest in cost-cutting process innovations would invariably be sacrificed to attain and exceed the gross output targets erected by the central planning authority; and (4) even if an enterprise developed and introduced a new product, the lack of price flexibility dampened the rewards accruing to such innovative activity.

The result of this bureaucratic system of decision-making was a set of incentives facing enterprises that not only did not encourage innovation, but openly discouraged it. As early as 1941, Georgi Malenkov reported to the 18th Congress of the Communist Party that 'highly valuable inventions and product improvements often lie around for years in the scientific research institutes and enterprises, and are not introduced into products' (Berliner, 1987 p. 72). More recently, Bannasch (1990 p. 310) observed 'when compared to western economies, the adaption of new technologies [in the East] lags substantially behind the west'.

The consequences of Eastern European industrial policies has been a dramatic centralisation of economic assets on a scale unmatched by anything imaginable in the West. Table 12.2 shows the firm-size distribution of Czechoslovakian manufacturing firms between 1956 and 1988, based on the measure of employment. In 1988 only 1.4 per cent of manufacturing workers were in enterprises with fewer than 500 employees. The employment share of small firms has decreased steadily since 1956, when 13 per cent of employees were in firms with fewer than 500 employees. By contrast, the share of employment accounted for by gigantic enterprises having more than 2,500 workers rose from less than one-third in 1956 to well over half by 1988. The firm-size distribution in Czechoslovakia provides a marked contrast to that in the developed Western nations. For example, the share of manufacturing employment accounted for by firms with fewer than 500 employees was 39.9 per cent in the United Kingdom (1986), 57.9 per cent in the Federal Republic of Germany (1987), 35.2 per cent in the United States (1986), and 71.8 per cent in Portugal (1986) (Acs and Audretsch, 1993). However, the astonishingly high concentration of economic assets exhibited by Czechoslovakia in table 12.2 is typical of Eastern European countries. Just over

Table 12.2. *Firm-size distribution (employment) of Czechoslovakian manufacturing firms, 1956–1988 (percentage share in parentheses)*[a]

	Employment size class			
Year	Fewer than 500	500–2500	more than 2500	Total
1956	193.2	826.0	466.6	1515.8
	(13.6)	(55.6)	(31.4)	
1960	154.7	745.4	857.9	1758.0
	(8.8)	(42.4)	(48.8)	
1970	37.0	729.0	995.0	1761.0
	(2.1)	(41.4)	(56.5)	
1988	26.0	751.0	1052.0	1837.0
	(1.4)	(42.8)	(55.8)	

Note: [a] Employment is listed in terms of thousands of workers. The figures do not sum perfectly due to measurement errors at the original data source.
Source: *Statistical Yearly*, Prague, various years.

1 per cent of manufacturing employment in East Germany (1986) was in firms with fewer than 500 employees (Bannasch, 1992), while in Poland (1985) the small-firm share of employment was somewhat higher at 10 per cent (Johnson and Loveman, 1993).

Not only is the bulk of manufacturing employment in gigantic enterprises in Eastern Europe, but the firm-size distribution is highly skewed towards large firms. Table 12.3 shows the size distribution of Bulgarian firms between 1965 and 1987. In contrast to table 12.2, which measures the firm-size distribution on the basis of employment, table 12.3 examines the firm-size distribution on the basis of the number of enterprises. That is, in 1987 only 1.92 per cent of the enterprises in Bulgarian manufacturing had fewer than 100 employees. Not only was this a more than 50 per cent decrease since 1965, but it provided a marked contrast to the firm-size distribution in Western nations. For example, in the United States nearly 95 per cent of all manufacturing firms have fewer than 100 employees (Acs and Audretsch, 1990, ch. 4). In fact, well over 90 per cent of enterprises have fewer than 100 employees in most Western nations, such as (the Federal Republic of) Germany (Schwalbach, 1989) and the United Kingdom (A. Hughes, 1993).

The exact effect of the prevalent industrial policy designed to concentrate economic assets can be seen more clearly in table 12.4, which tracks the shift of the size distribution of establishments, or plants, in East German manufacturing between 1971 and 1987. There are two important points in table 12.4 which should be emphasised. First, the number of

Table 12.3. *Size distribution of Bulgarian firms (percentage enterprise share in parentheses)*

Number of employees	1965	1970	1975	1980	1985	1987
Fewer than 100	73	59	46	21	25	41
	(5.04)	(3.30)	(2.27)	(1.10)	(1.26)	(1.92)
100–399	379	322	264	123	103	98
	(26.16)	(18.02)	(13.03)	(6.45)	(5.17)	(4.58)
400–4999	857	1131	1273	1111	1084	1116
	(59.14)	(63.29)	(62.83)	(58.26)	(54.42)	(52.15)
5000–19999	110	218	355	467	516	567
	(7.59)	(12.20)	(17.52)	(24.49)	(25.90)	(26.50)
20000 +	30	57	88	185	264	318
	(2.07)	(3.19)	(4.34)	(9.70)	(13.25)	(14.86)
Total	1449	1787	2026	1907	1992	2140

Source: *Statistical Yearbook of Bulgaria*, various years.

Table 12.4. *Number of establishments in East-German manufacturing by size class, 1971–1987*

Number of workers and employees	1971	1978	1987
Fewer than 25	3864	716	131
25–50	2559	1084	186
51–100	1812	1130	343
101–200	1147	946	519
201–500	845	1074	861
501–1000	405	517	558
1001–2500	406	480	540
2501–5000	133	178	215
5001–10000	62	69	75
10001–20000	15	16	21
20000 +	5	3	–
Total	11253	6183	3449

Source: *Statistisches Jahrbuch der DDR*, 1988.

manufacturing plants in East Germany fell from over 11,000 in 1971 to less than 3,450 in 1987. Second, the number of small plants fell even more drastically. For example, there were nearly 3,900 manufacturing establishments with fewer than 25 employees in 1971. By 1987 there were just over 131 such plants. In contrast, the number of large manufacturing plants rose considerably over this period. The shift in the establishment size distribution in East Germany provides a striking contrast to the experience in West Germany. In 1987 about a quarter of all West German manufacturing plants had fewer than 25 employees (Fritsch, 1992). In East Germany, however, only about 3 per cent of the manufacturing establishments employed fewer than 25 workers.

In fact, table 12.4 does not reveal the true concentration of economic assets in East Germany. The establishments were linked to parent firms through what was known as the system of combines. A combine is the equivalent of a giant conglomerate in the West, and it typically consists of hundreds of individual plants. In essence, one giant firm, the combine, was responsible for virtually all the plants within each major industrial sector. As table 12.4 indicates, smaller manufacturing plants and firms were gradually closed or merged and their workers were shifted to or placed under the control of a combine. The relationship between each individual establishment and its parent combine is somewhat different than that between a plant and the parent firm in a Western enterprise. The East German combines generally had rigid control of the individual establishments, whereby most of the important decisions were centralised and made at the combine level and not at the establishment level.[1]

As of 1989 there were 224 combines in existence, of which 180 were in manufacturing. County authorities controlled 95 of the combines and 126 were controlled by government officials in East Berlin (Audretsch, 1990). The distribution of enterprises in Poland in 1990 is shown in table 12.5. The largest 100 Polish enterprises accounted for 39 per cent of total sales, 43 per cent of net income, and 18 per cent of all employment. The largest 500 enterprises accounted for about two-thirds of all sales, 68 per cent of net income, and 40 per cent of employment. Thus, just as the bulk of economic activity emanated from 224 combines in East Germany, the largest 500 enterprises accounted for the bulk of economic activity in Poland. Johnson and Loveman (1992) report that the average state enterprise in Poland had 1,132 employees. The mean number of employees per plant was 378. By contrast, the mean plant size in Western nations is well under 100 employees per establishment (Acs and Audretsch, 1993).

In order to facilitate the centralisation of economic assets, all the Eastern European countries virtually choked off any meaningful entry into the manufacturing industries (Balcerowicz, 1989). As Murrell (1990 p. 66) observes, ‘Like Sherlock Holmes’ dog that didn’t bark, the importance of entry to the centrally planned economies might have been somewhat overlooked because of entry’s most significant feature – its absence. Lack of entry of new firms could result from the fact that hierarchies like a stable structure.’ And, as Kornai (1980) and Granick (1987) emphasise, the refusal to let state-owned enterprises fail along with the guaranteed

Table 12.5. *Size distribution of Polish firms, 1990 (percentage share in parentheses)*

Number of enterprises	Sales[a]	Net income[b]	Employment[c]
Top 100	18.1 (39)	2.9 (43)	711 (18)
Top 200	23.1 (49)	3.6 (53)	1036 (26)
Top 300	26.5 (57)	4.0 (59)	1261 (31)
Top 400	29.1 (62)	4.4 (65)	1461 (36)
Top 500	30.9 (66)	4.6 (68)	1612 (40)
Total	46.8	6.8	4051

Notes: [a] Sales are measured in terms of billions of US dollars; [b] net income is measured in terms of billions of US dollars; [c] employment is measured in terms of thousands of workers.
Source: *Informacja Statystyczna*, 1990.

protection of job rights undoubtedly served to diminish the establishment of new enterprises. Thus, a host of studies ranging from Bulgaria (Puchev, 1990; Jones and Meurs, 1990), to Czechoslovakia (McDermott and Mejstrik, 1992; 1993), Hungary (Román, 1989; 1990a), to Yugoslavia (Estrin and Petrin, 1991), and East Germany (Bannasch, 1990; 1993) have all identified a conscious policy to restrict entry into Eastern European nations contributing to the bloated concentration of economic assets across the Eastern European industrial landscape. According to Lipton and Sachs

> The socialist economies also lack adequate procedures for the entry and exit of enterprises. Enterprises are typically founded by ministries or local authorities, which at the same time arrange for the funding to begin operations. Absent such sponsorship, there is little chance that state enterprise activity can spring up to meet even the most obvious economic needs ... bankruptcy and liquidation of state enterprise activity has been virtually unknown. In fact, the absence of markets and meaningful relative prices in the economy means that it is difficult, if not impossible, to distinguish between enterprises that should and should not survive (Lipton and Sachs, 1990a pp 84–5).

Industrial policies throughout Eastern Europe generally served to funnel resources away from services, light industries and consumer goods and into heavy industry and capital goods. As Lipton and Sachs (1990a) observe, these policies reflected two factors. The first was what they term as the 'obsessive growth orientation of the Stalinist model' (Lipton and Sachs, 1990a p. 82). The second was the structure of trade imposed by the dominant political and military force in the area, the Soviet Union, whereby the satellite countries of Eastern Europe were required to develop sufficient manufacturing capacity to process raw materials shipped from the Soviet Union and then subsequently export the semi-processed or processed products back to the Soviet Union (Grachev *et al.*, forthcoming).

As a result of these industrial policies targeting heavy manufacturing industries, both output and employment tended to be much more concentrated in the industrial sector than is the case in the West. For example, in Poland, manufacturing accounted for 41.7 per cent of gross domestic product in 1987.[2] By comparison, the share of gross domestic product emanating from the manufacturing sector in the same year was 30.6 per cent in Portugal, 29.1 per cent in Spain, and 25.1 per cent in Greece. Similarly, the 1987 share of employment in the Polish manufacturing sector was 28.5 per cent. In Portugal the manufacturing employment share was 26.5 per cent, in Spain it was 24.2 per cent, and in Greece it was 21.5 per cent (Lipton and Sachs, 1990a). That the share of output accounted for Polish manufacturing is so much greater than the share of employment, in comparison with its Western counterparts, reflects the strikingly low productivity of labour in that sector in Poland. That Polish productivity was relatively low compared with Western nations such as Greece, Spain, and Portugal, suggests how poor Polish industrial performance was compared with the Western powerhouses of, say, West Germany, Japan, or the United States.

12.4 The crisis

When Soviet Premier Nikita Khrushchev banged his shoe on the negotiating table at the United Nations in 1961 and challenged President John F. Kennedy, 'We will bury you', the West was alarmed. At the heart of Khrushchev's challenge was not necessarily a military threat but rather an economic threat. After all, not only had the Soviets beaten the Americans in the space race with the launching of Sputnik-I in 1957, but, perhaps even more disconcerting, was the growth in Soviet productivity which considerably exceeded that in the West.

In the early 1960s, there was little doubt among politicians, intellectuals or economists about the credibility of the economic threat from the East. After all, the nations of Eastern Europe had a 'luxury' inherent in their systems of centralised planning – the concentration of economic assets – that exceeded anything imaginable in the West, which had the 'burden' of a commitment to democracy and therefore political and economic decentralisation. That is, the Soviet Union, as well as all the Eastern European countries, was free to concentrate economic assets and exploit scale economies in a manner that could never be acceptable in the West, at least under the prevailing commitments to democracy and decentralisation. Not only would the massing of economic assets lead to unprecedented productivity growth in the East, but perhaps what was of paramount concern was the assumed leaps and bounds in technological progress that would result from resources devoted to research and development on an unprecedented scale. In the 1950s and 1960s the conventional wisdom left no doubt that the giant corporation was best suited as the engine of innovation. According to John Kenneth Galbraith (1956 p. 86), 'There is no more pleasant fiction than that technical change is the product of the matchless ingenuity of the small man forced by competition to employ his wits to better his neighbor. Unhappily, it is a fiction.' This view mirrored Schumpeter's (1950 p. 106), who admonished, 'What we have got to accept is that the large-scale establishment has come to be the most powerful engine of progress.'

Thus, thc Wcst was indccd alarmcd into thinking that it may, in fact, bc buried by the East – productivity gains and a surge of invention and innovation emanating from overpowering, efficient, Eastern European enterprises would simply overwhelm the outdated and out-scaled firms in the West, burdened with antiquated constraints, such as the anti-trust laws.[3]

In fact, as has been made all too clear by events throughout Eastern Europe in 1989, the West was not buried by an avalanche of productivity growth and technological change from the East. What happened? What went wrong?

A paradox seems to be that the systems of centralised planning in Eastern Europe that placed such a high premium on economic growth, resulted in exactly the opposite – stagnation – both in terms of production and technological change. The failure of Eastern Europe can be inferred from the macroeconomic statistics on expansion of national output, changes in productivity, and changes in real income and consumption. According to Lipton and Sachs

> The intense desire [of Eastern Europe] to rejoin the economies of Western Europe reflects both an attraction to the obvious achievements of Western Europe and a revulsion against the failures under communism. The low per capital incomes in Eastern Europe do not fully explain the pervasive sense of frustration in the region. It is one thing to be poor, but it is quite another to have become impoverished needlessly as a result of the failure of the communist system. It is the sense of unnecessary decay, as much as the deprivation itself, that motivates the impulse of change (Lipton and Sachs, 1990a p. 76).

Similar sentiment was recently expressed to the 27th Party Congress in Moscow by Mikhail Gorbachev that 'many scientific discoveries and important inventions lie around for years, and sometimes decades, without being introduced into practical applications' (Berliner, 1987 p. 72). At least part of the cause of this technological sluggishness can be attributed to a system of bureaucratic centralised decision-making, where the disincentives to innovate may be even greater than the incentives. For example, Yuri Andropov complained that, 'The business leader who has introduced in the enterprise a new technology not infrequently is a loser, while those who avoid which is new lose nothing' (Hewett, 1988 p. 216).

A growing body of empirical research has identified the sluggish rate of technological change in Eastern Europe (Hanson, 1981; Berliner, 1976; Amann and Cooper, 1982). For example, Popper (1988) found that the diffusion of numerically controlled machine tools in Hungary lags considerably behind that in the West (Carlsson, 1989). Similarly, Leary and Thornton (1989) found that not only is the diffusion rate of innovation slower in the Soviet steel industry than in the steel industry in Western countries, but that the capacity utilisation ceilings tend to be much lower.

Even in the German Democratic Republic, which was the showcase of centralised planning among the Eastern European nations, productivity lagged far behind that of the West. Table 12.6 compares the productivity differentials between East Germany and West Germany shortly before the Wall fell in November 1989. For example, East German productivity in the power and coal-mining sector was 48 per cent of that in West Germany, although the differential varied considerably across sectors. The extent of the differential was influenced to a considerable extent by the industrial policies described in the previous section which funnelled resources into the heavy manufacturing sectors and away from light industries and high-value consumer products. Thus, in the basic and luxury food sector, East German productivity was only 43 per cent of that in the West. By contrast, in the steel, plastic, and glass industries, the productivity of East Germany did not lag far behind productivity in the Federal Republic of Germany.

The low levels and growth rates of productivity resulted in concomitant low wage rates and employee compensation. For example, in 1989 the average hourly factory wage was \$5.40 in East Germany, compared with \$21.00 in West Germany, \$17.50 in Japan, and \$16.40 in the United States (Audretsch and Wayland, 1992). In addition, the mean working week of factory workers in East Germany was 15.78 per cent longer than in West Germany, ten per cent longer than in the United States, and 4.76 per cent longer than in Japan (Audretsch and Wayland, 1992).

A comparison of the household goods found in West German and East German households in 1989 is shown in table 12.7. For example, about two-thirds of West German households had a car while only about half the households in East Germany had one. Similarly, about fifty per cent

Table 12.6. *Productivity differentials between East and West Germany*

Industrial domains and branches	East German productivity (West Germany = 100)
Power and mining industry	48
Rubber, plastic and chemical products	50
Natural gas, oil and coal	26
Inorganic and organic basic chemistry	46
Pharmaceuticals	68
Special chemical and technical products	59
Weaving mills and synthetics	20
Plastic	72
Rubber and asbestos	48
Potassium and rock salt	50
Metal production and processing	47
Steel	62
Non-ferrous metals	21
Stone and clay	41
Water provision	70
Steel, machine and transportation equipment	56
Heavy machinery and facility construction	64
Machine tool and processing equipment	60
General and agricultural machinery	48
Transportation equipment	37
Electrical engineering, precision mechanics and optics	52
Measuring, rating and regulating technology	46
Electrical engineering and electronics	54
Data processing and office machinery	28
Precision mechanics and optics	52
Textiles	56
Production of other non-durable goods	57
Woodworking	58
Synthetics and paper	62
Polygraph	56
Musical instruments, toys and sporting goods	31
Apparel	44
Leather, shoes and furs	69
Glass and fine ceramics	88
Basic and luxury food production	43
Fish	44
Meat	60
Milk and eggs	58
Processed foods and baked goods	50
Vegetable oil and fat	30
Sugar and starch	25
Sweets, coffee, tea and cocoa	58
Fruit and vegetable processing	11
Spices and other small food items	29
Beverages (including alcohol)	53
Tobacco products	20
Total industry	52

Source: Document 11/11 – calculations and estimations from the German Institute for Economic Research (West Berlin).

Table 12.7. *Possession of household equipment in West and East Germany (percentage of households)*

	West Germany	East Germany
Car	67.8	52.0
Motorcycle	7.2	18.4
Freezer	70.4	42.7
Washing machine	85.7	99.0
(of which automatic)	(76.0)	(10.0)

more households had a colour television in West Germany than in East Germany. Perhaps most strikingly, only one in six households in East Germany was equipped with a telephone, while this was nearly universal in the Federal Republic; and, fewer than three-quarters of all households in East Germany had a toilet.

Table 12.7 does not explicitly account for quality differences, of course. For example, cars in West Germany tend to be Volkswagens, Mercedes, and BMWs; those in East Germany were typically Trabants.

Although the deterioration of the macroeconomic performances of the Eastern European economies has received widespread attention, the structure of international trade resulting from the set of industrial policies described in the previous section has been paid only scant attention. One good way to characterise the international trade structure of Eastern Europe is through the indexes of revealed comparative advantage constructed by Murrell (1990) using the standard United Nations trade data for 182 three-digit SITC (Standard International Trade Classification) commodity groups. Following the method introduced by Balassa (1967) and Bowen (1983), the indexes of what Balassa termed the 'revealed comparative advantages' are calculated by

$$X_{ij} = \frac{X_{ij} \Big/ \sum_{n=1}^{N} X_{nj}}{\sum_{t=1}^{T} X_{it} \Big/ \sum_{n=1}^{N} \sum_{t=1}^{T} X_{nt}} \tag{12.1}$$

$$m_{ij} = \frac{M_{ij} \Big/ \sum_{n=1}^{N} M_{nj}}{\sum_{t=1}^{T} M_{it} \Big/ \sum_{n=1}^{N} \sum_{t=1}^{T} M_{nt}} \tag{12.2}$$

and $$w_{ij} = x_{ij}/m_{ij} \tag{12.3}$$

where X refers to exports, M refers to imports, i refers to a specific commodity, N is the number of goods produced, T is the number of countries, and j refers to a particular country. Thus, x_{ij} measures the share of exports of commodity i from country j relative to the share of world exports of good i. That is, this measure indicates the extent to which country j succeeds in exporting product i relative to the export success of all other countries in the world.

The revealed indexes of comparative advantage are compared for 'Western' countries,[4] the 'poor Western' countries, which include Austria, Greece, Ireland, Italy, Portugal, Spain, and Turkey, and the Eastern European countries.[5]

The commodity groups can be classified according to fundamental economic characteristics. What is particularly useful here is to compare the indexes of revealed comparative advantage across these three groups of countries for what is commonly known as 'Ricardo goods', 'product-cycle goods', 'R&D-intensive goods', 'high-advertising goods' and 'high-concentration goods'.[6]

Commodities which are classified as being Ricardo goods are generally high in natural resource content and serve as key inputs into producing processed and semi-processed goods. Ricardo goods include food, wood, fibres, minerals, paper, non-ferrous metals, oils, ores and raw fuels.[7] Product-cycle goods include commodities that are high technology where information serves as a crucial input. Chemicals, medicinals, plastics, dyes, fertilisers, explosives, machinery, aircraft, instruments, clocks and munitions are all classified as being product-cycle goods.[8]

Commodities classified as being R&D intensive include all industries where US R&D expenditure amounts to at least 5 per cent of value-of-shipments. Pharmaceuticals, office machinery, aircraft and telecommunications are all R&D intensive goods.[9] High-advertising goods refer to consumer goods that are highly advertised in Western economies. Commodities for which advertising expenditure is at least 5 per cent of value-of-shipments are classified as being high-advertising. Wines, beers, beverages, cereals, drugs, soaps, perfumes and watches are all considered to be high-advertising goods.[10] Finally, high-concentration industries include the tobacco, petroleum products, edible oils, tubes, office machines, telecommunications and domestic electrical equipment, motor vehicles, railway vehicles and aircraft sectors.[11]

The computed indexes of revealed comparative advantage for these five product-characteristic groups are compared among Western, poor Western, and Eastern European countries in table 12.8. There are five important points to be emphasised from table 12.8. First, in 1975 the

Table 12.8. *Revealed comparative advantages: comparison between Western and Eastern Europe*

	Ricardo goods		Product-cycle goods		R&D-intensive		High-advertising		High-concentration	
	1975	1983	1975	1983	1975	1983	1975	1983	1975	1983
West										
X	0.70	0.75	1.21	1.21	1.20	1.20	1.19	1.21	1.15	1.11
M	1.06	1.03	0.91	0.94	1.03	1.03	1.04	1.02	1.00	1.04
X/M	0.66	0.72	1.33	1.39	1.16	1.16	1.15	1.19	1.15	1.07
Poor West										
X	1.90	1.77	0.30	0.44	0.52	0.63	0.41	0.43	0.39	0.56
M	0.87	0.79	1.28	1.31	1.14	1.08	1.12	1.05	1.03	0.96
X/M	2.19	2.25	0.24	0.34	0.45	0.58	0.36	0.41	0.38	0.52
Eastern Europe										
X	1.35	0.83	0.61	0.44	0.21	0.16	0.45	0.31	0.91	1.15
M	0.92	1.26	1.24	1.06	0.44	0.36	0.55	0.68	0.73	0.59
X/M	1.46	0.66	0.49	0.42	0.47	0.27	0.82	0.45	1.24	1.96

Source: Compiled from various tables in Murrell (1990).

Western countries exhibited a revealed comparative disadvantage for Ricardo goods, while the comparative advantage was held by both the poor Western nations and Eastern Europe. This situation had changed somewhat, however, by 1983. The Eastern European countries exhibited a trade structure more closely resembling that of the West than that of the poor Western nations. Like the West, Eastern Europe also had a comparative disadvantage in Ricardo goods. This shift in the trade structure of Eastern Europe may indicate its inability to compete against those developing countries which are rich in natural resources and have access to relatively low-cost labour.

Second, as would be expected, the Western countries tend to have a comparative advantage in product-cycle goods, while the poor Western nations along with the Eastern European countries exhibit a clear comparative disadvantage. These relationships have remained remarkably constant over time. Third, the countries of Eastern Europe have clearly not had a comparative advantage in R&D-intensive commodities. In this respect, they again resemble the poor Western nations, whereas the West has overall exhibited a substantial comparative advantage in high-R&D products.

Fourth, the West tends to have a comparative advantage in commodities which are advertising-intensive. Both the poor Western nations and the countries of Eastern Europe have a comparative disadvantage in markets where advertising plays an important role. Finally, both Eastern European countries and Western nations tend to have a comparative advantage in highly concentrated industries. By contrast, the poor Western nations are at a comparative disadvantage in markets which are highly concentrated.

Thus, in terms of the structure of international trade, Eastern Europe resembles the West in Ricardo goods and in highly concentrated markets. Neither the countries in Eastern Europe nor those in the West tend to hold a comparative advantage in such markets. However, the international trade structure of Eastern Europe resembles the poor Western nations for product-cycle goods, R&D-intensive industries and high-advertising industries. Only the more advanced Western countries possess a comparative advantage for these commodities. What emerges then is that Eastern Europe is at a comparative disadvantage not only for high-technological and information-intensive industries, but also for industries which contain a high component of raw materials and unprocessed goods. That is, the Eastern European nations have been squeezed out of export markets at both the high-value and low-value ends. Only for goods which tend to be produced in highly concentrated markets do the Eastern European nations exhibit a semblance of competitiveness in international markets. This reflects two related phenomena. First, according to the law of comparative advantage, every country must have a comparative advantage in something; and second, the industrial policies of the previous four decades have devoted themselves to amassing economic assets which, as described in the previous section, resulted in a degree of competition unmatched by any Western country. Thus, in industries where market concentration is a fundamental economic attribute, the Eastern European economies have been able to glean the comparative advantage, at least vis-à-vis their counterparts in the poor Western countries, and presumably in the developing nations.

However, as the empirical evidence suggests, the industrial policies of concentrating economic assets, centralising decision-making, and choking off entry has not proved to promote international competitiveness in high-technology and information-intensive markets. In such markets industrial structures promoting the entry of new firms and the exit of unsuccessful firms, or a generally turbulent industrial environment, have proven to be much more conducive to innovative behaviour (Acs and Audretsch, 1990; Scherer, 1991). Thus, it is not surprising that Eastern Europe, which through its industrial policies devoted itself towards achieving and preserving industrial stability, fared quite poorly in terms of international trade in high-technological and information-intensive markets.

12.5 The great transformation

When the Berlin Wall fell on 9 November 1989, a fundamental and inevitable economic, political, and social revolution began. The Wall had been built to serve four functions: (1) to insulate Eastern Europe from lower-priced and more desirable Western goods and services; (2) to impede any erosion of the investment in human capital by Eastern European nations through the emigration of educated and trained workers to the West; (3) to prevent subsidised low-priced 'mass-consumption' staple goods, such as bread, from being shipped to the West; and (4) to choke off alternative opportunities for workers, producers and consumers. Without the Wall, Eastern Europe's forty-year experiment with a planned centralised economy would never have been possible. As long as the Wall remained in place and the economy was insulated from foreign competition, the system remained viable. The standard of living behind the Wall, however, continued to slip behind that of the West, and at an alarming and ever-increasing rate.

The opening of the Berlin Wall left entire economic structures, agents, and institutions exposed. Not only were Western consumer goods and assets available with hard currency at sometimes incredibly attractive prices, but huge numbers of workers, particularly the most educated and skilled, began flocking westward in search of higher wages. The Eastern European societies that had striven so hard to sustain stability were suddenly confronted with an unprecedented degree of instability.[12]

What should be the role of industrial policy in the new Eastern Europe? A first answer is to discontinue those industrial policies that created the unfortunate economic disarray in Eastern Europe in the first place – the state ownership of the means of production, the centralisation of economic assets, the absence of market competition, the virtual prohibition of the entry of new firms, the refusal to allow firms to fail, the elimination of important competition and the channelling of resources away from consumer goods and services and into heavy manufacturing industries.

The prospects of undertaking a policy of privatisation or, at least in some instances, reprivatisation, are as daunting as they are essential. Economically and socially, no country anywhere in the world has achieved viability where the state owns around 90 per cent of property and assets – as was the case in Eastern Europe. Thus, it remains virtually uncontested that these government-held assets must be put into the hands of private enterprises. However, even the unanimity about the policy objective does not render it easy or in any sense automatic. Lipton and Sachs (1990b p. 293) warn that, 'There are enormous challenges in transferring state-owned property to private hands in a manner that is rapid, equitable, and fiscally sound.' The two primary goals of the privatisation of assets throughout Eastern European nations is to provide a sector of private enterprises that are technically and managerially efficient, even by Western standards, and to create a functioning and viable capital market. Without the development of such a capital market the greatly hoped for emergence of private enterprise will be aborted.

The fundamental difficulty confronting the policy of privatisation is its scope and scale. According to Lipton and Sachs

> In Eastern Europe, privatisation is a very difficult task, involving nothing less than the complete redefinition of property rights for literally thousands of enterprises. Privatisation means creating anew the basic institutions of a market financial system, including corporate governance of managers, equity ownership, stock exchanges, and a variety of financial intermediaries, such as pension funds, and investment trusts ... The economic challenge, then, is to combine the redefinition of property rights with the creation of vital financial market institutions. The political challenge is also awesome: to design a mechanism for creating private property rights that can win broad, lasting social approval (and prevent special interests from paralyzing the process through a fight for the spoils) (Lipton and Sachs, 1990b p. 294).

A second policy which must be emphasised throughout the Eastern European nations is a reduction of the gross centralisation of economic assets. As was emphasised in section 3 of this chapter, the degree of centralisation in Eastern Europe was beyond anything imaginable in a Western context. It is unthinkable that a Western country would allow and even encourage a single monopoly to exist in virtually every major industry of the economy. Thus, Román emphasises,

> In the seventies and eighties when we have spoken about structural adjustment (and we did it recurrently), as a rule we emphasized the urgent need to change the pattern of production by branches and products. Now in the framework of the on-going systemic changes another kind of structural adjustment comes into the fore in the Eastern European economies: the radical modification of the size-pattern of enterprises (Román, 1990a p. 3).

However, McDermott and Mejstrik (1992a) warn that privatisation alone will not alleviate the problem posed by the centralisation of assets. They describe the existence of a 'coalition structure', whereby a system of informal and formal contacts and a network of administrators is able to retain monopolistic control of industries, even once the enterprises have been privatised. According to Mlcoch

> The enterprise in a non-parametrical environment is a coalition of internal and external participants. The internal participants include the 'control group' – the power center of the enterprise, the worker aristocracy, and the administrative apparatus. The main goal of this group is not to improve efficiency and innovation, but rather to establish close links with all members of the external hierarchal superiors, i.e., planning commission, industry ministers, and regional Party bosses, as well as with key suppliers and customers. These links help to insure the fulfillment of personal interests of the 'control group' – their material and political welfare (Mlcoch, 1990 p. 15).

That is, the privatisation and even break-up of an existing state-owned enterprise would result in a number of individual plants all belonging to and being administered by the same coalition structure.

As was described in section 3, the two central features inherited in the industrial structure – a high degree of centralisation and generally outdated technology – beg a question fundamental to my ambivalence with respect to the privatisation debate: how valuable are all these outdated and technologically backward assets to be privatised anyway? Before the Berlin Wall fell, Eastern European countries were assured of export markets – more often than not with their own Eastern European neighbours. In fact, as was documented in the previous section, under the protection of the Iron Curtain, the Eastern European nations had established a systematic comparative advantage in mass-produced standardised goods where innovation and product differentiation do not play an important role. But now that the Berlin Wall is only a memory, and the Eastern European nations are free to trade with whom they want, the export markets in Eastern Europe for their Eastern European neighbours are rapidly disappearing. Former trading partners in the East are instead turning increasingly to the West for imports of intermediate production goods and high-value consumer goods (Audretsch, 1992).

The fundamental problem throughout Eastern Europe is that firms and plants are structured around a capital stock and technology designed for centralisation and stability. Will shifting ownership from the state into private hands somehow transform the value of these assets? My reading of the situation is no – in internationally linked markets the problem confronting the Eastern European nations is that their assets simply are not worth very much. They were not worth enough under Communist systems to maintain the viability of those systems, and now that they are exposed to internationally linked markets they are worth even less.

The policy prescription of Mr Sachs notwithstanding, the solution to the Eastern European transformation problem needs something more than enlightened macroeconomic policy and the privatisation of state-held assets. That is, in terms of that simplest of all economic models, yes, resources must certainly be redeployed in such a manner as to attain the production possibility frontier – but, more importantly, the frontier itself must be pushed out. New productive assets must be created. But from where? I doubt that the source will be the existing plants and firms, even if they are rapidly and equitably privatised. Why not? For the same reason that the US Steel Corporation – a privately held company – was not able to restructure itself successfully and remain in the steel business. The American steel industry did, in fact, finally manage to become restructured. But this was largely accomplished through the creation of new firms and plants – the so-called mini-mills – and not through a revamping by the incumbent corporations. A drive alongside the Saar river in west Germany, which is littered with the corpses of abandoned steel plants, indicates that the United States has no monopoly on the problem posed by the need to restructure entrenched corporations. Is it realistic to expect Eastern European firms to accomplish what their Western counterparts could not?

The privatisation debate in Eastern Europe is somewhat misguided: while the privatisation of state-owned assets is surely a step in the right direction, the success or failure of the transformation process currently taking place in Eastern Europe hinges on the creation of new productive assets which can best be generated by the entry and start-up of new firms.

This points to the importance of a third area for industrial policy – to serve as a catalyst for the start-up and entry of new firms. As Johnson and Loveman (1993) argue,

> The absence of a significant small business sector in Poland raises severe problems. As the large state-owned firms begin to contract and, eventually, go bankrupt, and as privatization and reorganization of these firms take place, the economy must rely on smaller businesses to provide employment and to sustain the economy . . . But it is precisely these small businesses that have not existed to any significant degree in Poland for decades.

So, from where is this new entrepreneurial wave expected to emerge? On the one hand, the existing administrative and legal barriers to entry must simply be removed. On the other hand, the institutional infrastructure has to be developed in order to generate a viable and vital entrepreneurial sector. Legislation facilitating new-firm start-ups appears to be gaining momentum throughout Eastern Europe. In January 1989 Czechoslovakia enacted several statutes legalising private retail shops. In anticipation of the full legalisation of the private sector, the Association of Private Entrepreneurs was founded in February 1990. By the end of the year, the Association had around 220,000 members, of whom one-quarter were in the restaurant and food sector, one-fifth were in transportation and shipping, nearly one-third were in construction and repair services and one-fifth were in diversified activities, such as crafts (McDermott and Mejstrik, 1992; 1993). In fact, in April 1990, the Czechoslovakian parliament enacted a new law legalising certain private enterprises. In particular, this statute removed restrictions on the number of workers an enterprise could hire as well as the amount of property that could be purchased. However, enterprises with more than 25 employees and a yearly income in excess of 500,000 Kcs are required to register with the government as a large firm and are subject to the same regulations as a state-owned enterprise. In particular, large firms are subject to a double rate of taxation, extensive wage and price controls, and internal administrative procedures dictated by the state (McDermott and Mejstrik, 1993).

In Poland, as well, there are signs of a surge in new-firm start-ups. By the end of 1990 more than 360,000 new private enterprises had been established (Johnson and Loveman, 1993). Still, in Poland, as throughout Eastern Europe, certain key reforms are needed to stimulate entrepreneurship: (1) the absence of tax or other financial advantages for engaging in a joint venture. At the same time no minimum capital requirements should be placed on joint ventures (for example, this is currently $50,000 in Poland); (2) the excess wage tax should be eliminated. This tax is presently applied to new private enterprises as a means of mitigating inflation. However, it provides a clear incentive for workers not to invest in human capital and for employers not to expand their workforce; and (3) the present tax structures need to be redesigned. In order to encourage investment, tax credits should be granted. At the same time, the current practice of double, and in some cases triple taxation of dividends needs to be eliminated.

In addition, McDermott and Mejstrik (1993) report that a number of daunting barriers to new-firm start-ups are likely to remain entrenched in the near future. For example, although the central bank has been formally separated from administrative control of the commercial banking sector, the so-called 'commercial' banks arc, in fact, still fully owned by the government. Similarly, under the current policies of the Ministry of Finance, regulations on credit have actually been tightened, so that potential entrepreneurs are likely to experience a credit squeeze. And, in practice the 'commercial' banks give a preference to making loans to the large state-owned establishments.

Industrial policies towards foreign trade in Eastern European countries also need to be reformed and reoriented. During the previous four decades trade policy served largely to insulate the domestic economies from international competition. For example, even under the contemporary policy in Czechoslovakia a private firm is allowed to import a foreign-produced good only after substantiating that the imported product is needed to improve the value of the domestic good by at least 30 per cent. In addition, 30 per cent of all 'hard' currency earnings made from exports must be relinquished to the state bank in exchange for domestic 'soft' currency. Industrial policy in Eastern Europe needs to use foreign competition as a mechanism for injecting competition into the domestic economies.

Finally, the conscious channelling of resources into the production of heavy manufacturing industries should be ended. While, at least in the near future, heavy industries may, in fact, lie within the domain of Eastern European comparative advantage, largely as a result of a set of industrial policies creating an industrial structure that is relatively efficient at production in such markets, the long-run policy must be a more balanced approach.

The policies identified above are essentially negative in nature, in the sense that they generally require ending some specific pro-active industrial policy currently being implemented. However, there are several major areas where a pro-active industrial policy is required in order to enhance the international competitiveness of Eastern European countries. The first is to direct massive investments into improving the industrial infrastructure. For forty years Eastern European industry focused narrowly on increasing short-run productivity, neglecting to a large extent the maintenance of the infrastructure. For example, in East Germany, 60 per cent of all city streets and nearly half of all highways are classified in the highest damage category. Similarly, East German railways are reported as being 'run-down, unreliable, and insufficiently expanded' (Audretsch and Wayland, 1992). Telephone connections throughout Eastern Europe are poor and highly unreliable. Problems such as these pose an increasing obstacle to gaining competitiveness in international industrial markets. Studies have generally shown (Audretsch and Yamawaki, 1990) that services, including the infrastructure, are a vital input into the manufacturing of goods. To the extent to which Western countries have a superior infrastructure, production costs are that much lower, and productivity that much higher. This leads to the prediction that the Eastern European countries will tend to have the competitive advantage only in industrialised goods whose production damages the environment. While the West generally imposes severe cost-elevating pollution-abating restrictions on such goods, the countries of Eastern Europe can enjoy a cost advantage and ultimately a competitive advantage in the international market by accepting a higher level of environmental damage. This is clearly not a desirable alternative.

Another area where a pro-active industrial policy can make an important contribution is in the development of human capital. This is important because, compared with other countries at a similar stage of industrial development, the Eastern European countries tend to have a relatively skilled and educated labour force. Johnson and Loveman (1993) argue that a significant reason for the relative success of small West German firms in global markets is the long tradition of vocational training. This training system has served to provide a relatively large supply of skilled labour, which has provided small firms with the ability to manufacture high quality, customised goods. In fact, an apprentice system was also implemented in East Germany, which has, as a result, built up a pool of highly qualified skilled workers.

12.6 Conclusion

This paper makes it clear that a consistent and powerful set of industrial policies were implemented throughout Eastern Europe during the previous four decades. Because these policies were so effective, they drastically altered the industrial landscape across Eastern Europe. As a result, the nations of Eastern Europe ended up with a concentration of economic power that is unmatched by anything imaginable in the West. Similarly, the stability of the industrial structure in the East defies the Western experience. Not only was a virtual prohibition placed on the entry of new firms, but enterprises were not allowed to fail. This provides a striking contrast to the turbulent nature of Western markets.

As would be predicted, under the regime of centralised planning, the Eastern European nations had the competitive advantage in industries which are highly concentrated in Western nations. In these industries, which by their nature apparently require a concentrated industrial structure, the Eastern European nations were able to 'out-concentrate' the West. However, in industries in which technology and information play an important role – industries which have proven to be particularly turbulent in the West (Acs and Audretsch, 1990) – the competitive position of the Eastern European nations has continued to deteriorate over time.

It is clearly beyond the scope of this chapter to provide a detailed blueprint of specific industrial policies which need to be pursued to revitalise Eastern Europe. However, the findings here do suggest that the unprecedented degree of industrial centralisation needs to be abandoned. Rather, more emphasis needs to be placed on developing a dynamic entrepreneurial sector that at least begins to approach the dimensions of the firm-size distributions typically found throughout the developed nations of the West. Manfred Neumann's (1990 p. 564) advice for the West – 'From the point of view of the evolutionary approach, industrial policy should aim at keeping the process of discovery going' – is certainly no less true for the East.

Notes

I would like to thank Kirsty Hughes for her thoughtful suggestions and the participants at the Workshop on European Competitiveness, held at the Wissenschaftszentrum Berlin für Sozialforschung, for their comments. All errors and omissions remain my responsibility.

1 'Norbert Walter zur deutschen Konjunktur', *Wirtschaftswoche*, June 22, 1990, 29.

2 Steinitz (1989) similarly shows that the growth in major economic sectors in the German Democratic Republic between 1950 and 1987 was highly skewed in the heavy manufacturing sector.

3 For example, Galbraith (1967 pp. 187, 197) charged that because anti-trust law 'exempts those who possess the market power and concentrates on those who would try to possess it', its enforcement 'defends and gives legitimacy to a charade'. More recently, Lester Thurow (1980 pp. 145–6) argues that the anti-trust laws prohibit American firms from realising scale economies that its international competitors enjoy:

> The time has come to recognize that the antitrust approach has been a failure ... The attraction of the competitive ideal has faded ... If they do anything they only serve to hinder US competitors who might live by a code that their foreign competitors can ignore ... If we are to establish a competitive economy

within a framework of international trade and international competition, it is time to recognize that the techniques of the nineteenth century are not applicable.

4 These actually include the OECD countries and therefore several non-Western nations.

5 The nine countries included are Bulgaria, Czechoslovakia, East Germany, Hungary, Poland, Romania, the USSR, Yugoslavia, and Albania.

6 For a more detailed description of these different classifications, see Audretsch (1987).

7 Ricardo goods include SITC groups 011–13, 022–5, 041–8, 051–5, 061, 071–072, 074, 075, 121, 242, 243, 251, 261–3, 271, 274, 281, 283, 285, 321, 331, 341, 411, 421, 422, 431, 667, 681–7, 689.

8 Product cycle commodities include SITC product groups 512–15, 521, 581, 532, 561, 571, 711, 712, 714, 715, 717, 718, 722, 723, 726, 729, 734, 861, 862, 864, 951.

9 R&D-intensive commodities include SITC product groups 714, 724, 734, and 861.

10 Commodities classified as high-advertising include SITC commodity groups 111, 112, 048, 553, 554, and 864.

11 Commodities classified as high-concentration include SITC commodity groups 122, 332, 431, 678, 714, 723–25, 731, 732, and 734.

12 For example, one Eastern European reports, 'Sometimes there is a feeling of helplessness ... There is no money left for a number of scientific institutions, and educational, cultural, or sports facilities. There are fundamental changes in our daily life, even in our family relationships. Women fear cuts in their independence ... Today everything in our lives is insecure' (Grünert, 1990 p. 10).

References

Acs, Zoltan J. and Audretsch, David B., 1990. *Innovation and Small Firms*, Cambridge, MA: MIT Press.

1993. *Small Firms and Entrepreneurship: An East–West Perspective*, Cambridge: Cambridge University Press.

Amann, Ronald and Cooper, Julian, 1982. *Industrial Innovation in the Soviet Union*, New Haven, CT: Yale University Press.

Audretsch, David B., 1987. 'An empirical test of the industry life cycle', *Weltwirtschaftliches Archiv*, 123, 297–308.

1988. 'An evaluation of Japanese R&D and industrial policies', *Aussenwirtschaft*, 43 (1/2), 231–58.

1989a. *The Market and the State: Government Policies towards Business in Europe, Japan and the US*, New York: New York University Press.

1989b. 'Joint R&D and industrial policy in Japan', in Albert N. Link and Gregory Tassey (eds.), *Cooperative Research and Development: The Industry–University–Government Relationship*, Boston: Kluwer, pp. 103–26.

1990. 'Investment opportunities in a unified Germany,' *Global Economic Policy*, 2 (2), 14–24.

1992. 'Industrial restructuring and policy issues in Czechoslovakia', Discussion Paper FS IV 92–4, Wissenschaftszentrum Berlin.

Audretsch, David B. and Wayland, Heather, 1992. 'The economics of German unification', in Josef Brada and Michael P. Claudon (eds.), *German Reunification and the Privatization of Czechoslovakia, Hungary, and Poland*, New York: New York University Press.

Audretsch, David B. and Yamawaki, Hideki, 1988. 'R&D rivalry, industrial policy and US–Japanese trade', *Review of Economics and Statistics*, 70 (3), 438–47.

1990. 'Do services crowd out manufacturing?', report, presented to the Directorate General II of the Commission of the European Community, 1990.

Balassa, Bela, 1967. *Trade Liberalization among Industrial Countries: Objectives and Alternatives*, New York: McGraw-Hill.

Balcerowicz, Leszek, 1989. 'Polish economic reform, 1981–1988: an overview', *Economic Reforms in the European Centrally Planned Economies*, New York: United Nations and the Economic Commission for Europe.

Baldwin, Richard E., 1988. 'Evaluating strategic trade policies', *Aussenwirtschaft* 43 (1/2), 207–30.

Bannasch, Hans-Gerd, 1990. 'Small firms in East Germany', *Small Business Economics*, 2 (4), 307–12.

1993. 'The evolution of small firms in East Germany', in Zoltan J. Acs and David B. Audretsch (eds.), *Small Firms and Entrepreneurship: An East–West Perspective*, Cambridge: Cambridge University Press.

Berliner, Jospeh S., 1976. *Innovation Decision in Soviet Industry*, Cambridge, MA: MIT Press.

1987. 'Organizational restructuring of the Soviet economy', in US Congress, Joint Economic Committee (eds.), *Gorbachev's Economic Plans*, Vol. I, Washington, DC: US Government Printing Office.

Bowen, Harry P., 1983. 'On the theoretical interpretation of indices of trade intensity and revealed comparative advantage', *Weltwirtschaftliches Archiv*, 119, 464–72.

Carlsson, Bo, 1989. 'Small-scale industry at a crossroads: U.S. machine tools in global perspectives', *Small Business Economics*, 1 (4), 245–62.

Caves, Richard E., 1989. 'Exchange-rate movements and foreign direct investment in the United States', in David B. Audretsch and Michael P. Claudon (eds.), *The Internationalization of U.S. Markets*, New York: New York University Press, pp. 199–228.

Estrin, S. and Petrin, T., 1991. 'Entry and exit in Yugoslavian manufacturing', in Paul Geroski and Joachim Schwalbach (eds.), *Entry and Market Contestability: An International Comparison*, Oxford: Basil Blackwell.

Fritsch, Michael, 1992. 'The role of small firms in West Germany', in Zoltan J. Acs and David B. Audretsch (eds.), *Small Firms and Entrepreneurship: An East–West Perspective*, Cambridge: Cambridge University Press.

Galbraith, John K., 1956. *American Capitalism: The Concept of Countervailing Power*, revised edn, Boston: Houghton Mifflin.

1967. *The New Industrial State*, revised edn, Boston: Houghton Mifflin.

Geroski, Paul A., 1990. 'European industrial policy and industrial policy in Europe', in Keith Cowling and Horst Tomann (eds.), *Industrial Policy after 1992: An Anglo-German Perspective*, London: Anglo-German Foundation, pp. 265–76.

Grachev, Machael V., Ageev, Alexander A., Chuenko, Alexander M., and Kousin, Dimistri V. (forthcoming) 'Entrepreneurship and small business in the Soviet economy', *Small Business Economics*.

Granick, David, 1987. *Job Rights in the Soviet Union: Their Consequences*, Cambridge: Cambridge University Press.

Grünert, Holle, 1990. 'Searching for one's way in a new Germany', *Geonomics*, 2 (6), 9–10.

Hanson, Phillip, 1981. *Trade and Technology in Soviet–Western Relations*, New York: Columbia Univesity Press.

Hewett, Ed, 1988. *Reforming the Soviet Economy*, Washington: Brookings Institute.

Hughes, Alan, 1993. 'Industrial concentration and the small business sector in the UK: the 1980s in historical perspective', in Zoltan J. Acs and David B. Audretsch (eds.), *Small Firms and Entrepreneurship: An East-West Perspective*, Cambridge: Cambridge University Press.

Hughes, Kirsty, 1986. *Exports and Technology*, Cambridge: Cambridge University Press.

1991a. 'Comparative trade performance in the 1980s – an analysis of the largest six industrial economies', Discussion Paper FS IV 91–3, Wissenschaftszentrum Berlin.

1991b. 'Intra-industry trade in the 1980s: a panel study', Discussion Paper FS IV 91–8, Wissenschaftszentrum Berlin.

1991c. 'Trade performance in the main EC economies relative to the USA and Japan in the 1991-sensitive sectors', Discussion Paper FS IV 91–4, Wissenschaftszentrum Berlin.

Johnson, Chalmers, 1984. 'The idea of industrial policy', in C. Johnson (ed.), *The Industrial Policy Debate*, San Francisco: Institute for Contemporary Studies.

Johnson, Simon and Loveman, Gary, 1993. 'The implications of the Polish economic reform for small business: evidence from Gdansk', in Zoltan J. Acs and David B. Audretsch (eds.), *Small Firms and Entrepreneurship: An East–West Perspective*, Cambridge: Cambridge University Press.

Jones, Derek C. and Meurs, Mieke, 1990. 'On entry in socialist economies: evidence from Bulgaria', Working Paper 90/1, Department of Economics, Hamilton College.

Kornai, János, 1980. *Economics of Shortage*, Amsterdam: North-Holland.

1986. 'The Hungarian reform process: visions, hopes, and reality', *Journal of Economic Literature*, 24, 1687–737.

1990a. *The Road to a Free Economy, Shifting from a Socialist System: The Example of Hungary*, New York: Norton.

1990b. *Vision and Reality, Market and State*, London: Harvester and Wheatsheaf.

Leary, Neil and Thornton, Judith, 1989. 'Are socialist industries insulated against innovation? A case study of technological change in steelmaking', *Comparative Economic Studies* 31 (1), 42–65.

Lenin, Vladimir, 1916. *Imperialism as the Latest Phase of Capitalism.*

Lipton, David and Sachs, Jeffrey, 1990a. 'Creating a market in Eastern Europe: the case of Poland', *Brookings Papers on Economic Activity*, 75–133.

1990b. 'Privatization in Eastern Europe: the case of Poland', *Brookings Papers on Economic Activity*, 293–333.

Marx, Karl, 1912. *Capital*, translated by Ernest Untermann, Vol. I, Chicago: Kerr.

McDermott, Gerald A. and Mejstrik, Michael, 1992. 'The role of small firms in the industrial development and transformation of Czechoslovakia', *Small Business Economics* 4 (2).

1993. 'The role of small firms in Czechoslovak manufacturing', in Zoltan J. Acs and David B. Audretsch (eds.), *Small Firms and Entrepreneurship: An East–West Perspective*, Cambridge: Cambridge University Press.

Mlcoch, Lubomir, 1990. 'The behaviour of Czechoslovak enterprises', Research Paper No. 348, Institute of Economics, Prague.

Murrell, Peter, 1990. *The Nature of Socialist Economies: Lessons from Eastern Europe Foreign Trade*, Princeton: Princeton University Press.

Neumann, Manfred, 1990. 'Industrial policy and competition policy', *European Economic Review*, 34, 2 (3), 562–7.

Owen, Brus M., 1986. 'The evolution of Clayton Section 7 enforcement and the beginnings of US industrial policy', *Antitrust Bulletin*, 31.

Piore, Michael J. and Sabel, Charles F., 1984. *The Second Industrial Divide: Possibilities for Prosperity*, New York: Basic Books.

Popper, Steven W., 1988. 'The diffusion of numerically controlled machine tools in Hungary', in Josef Brada and Istvan Dobozi (eds.), *The Hungarian Economy in the 1980s*, Greenwich, CT: JAI Press, pp. 162–86.

Puchev, Plamen, 1990. 'A note on government policy and the new "entrepreneurship" in Bulgaria', *Small Business Economics*, 2 (1), 73–6.

Román, Zoltan, 1989. 'The size of the small-firm sector in Hungary', *Small Business Economics*, 1 (4), 303–8.

1990a. 'Strengthening small and medium-sized enterprises in the Eastern European economies', paper presented at the UNDP/UNIDO workshop, Trieste, November 27–30.

1990b. 'Four decades of public enterprise in Hungary', in John Heath (ed.), *Public Enterprise at the Crossroads*, London: Routledge, pp. 108–20.

Scherer, F. M., 1991. 'Changing perspectives on the firms size problem', in Zoltan J. Acs and David B. Audretsch (eds.), *Innovation and Technological Change: An International Comparison*, Ann Arbor: University of Michigan Press, pp. 24–38.

Scherer, F. M. and Ross, David, 1990. *Industrial Market Structure and Economic Performance* (3rd edn), Boston: Houghton Mifflin.

Schumpeter, Joseph A., 1950. *Capitalism, Socialism and Democracy*, 3rd edn, New York: Harper and Row.

Schwalbach, Joachim, 1989. 'Small business in German manufacturing', *Small Business Economics*, 1 (2), 129–36.

Steinitz, K., 1989. 'Innovationsprobleme und Strukturwandel in der DDR', *Politik und Zeitgeschichte*, March.

Stille, Frank, 1990. 'Industrial policy in West Germany: the 1980s', in Keith Cowling and Horst Tomann (eds.), *Industrial Policy After 1992: An Anglo-German Perspective*, London: Anglo-German Foundation, pp. 86–104.

Thurow, Lester, 1980. *The Zero Sum Society*, New York: Basic Books.

Tyson, J. and Zysman, J., 1983. 'American industry in international competition', in J. Zysman and L. Tyson (eds.), *American Industry in International Competition: Government Policies and Corporate Strategies*, Ithaca: Cornell University Press.

Wildavasky, A., 1984. 'Squaring the political circle', in C. Johnson (ed.), *The Industrial Policy Debate*, San Francisco: Institute for Contemporary Studies.

Index